MEDICAL FAMILY THERAPY

THE AUTHORS

Susan H. McDaniel, Ph.D.
Associate Professor of Psychiatry and Family Medicine
University of Rochester School of Medicine and Highland Hospital

Jeri Hepworth, Ph.D.
Associate Professor and Director of Behavioral Sciences,
Department of Family Medicine
University of Connecticut School of Medicine

William J. Doherty, Ph.D.
Professor, Department of Family Social Science
University of Minnesota

MEDICAL FAMILY THERAPY

*A Biopsychosocial Approach to
Families with Health Problems*

SUSAN H. McDANIEL

JERI HEPWORTH

WILLIAM J. DOHERTY

BasicBooks
A Division of HarperCollins*Publishers*

An excerpt appearing on p. 231 from the poem "Encounter with Evolution" by Nancy Ann Dahl is reprinted with the kind permission of the author.

The unpublished poem "Second Thoughts," on p. 131, is reprinted with the kind permission of the author.

The cases reprinted on pp. 120 –121 are used by permission of the *Journal of Marital and Family Therapy*.

LIBRARY OF CONGRESS CATALOGING-IN-PUBLICATION DATA

McDaniel, Susan H.
   Medical family therapy: a biopsychosocial approach to families with health problems/
      Susan H. McDaniel, Jeri Hepworth, William J. Doherty
      p.   cm.
   Includes bibliographical references and index.
   ISBN 0-465-04437-9
   1. Family psychotherapy.   2. Family medicine.   3. Sick—Family relationships.   4. Sick
   children—Family relationships.
   I. Hepworth, Jeri, 1952–   . II. Doherty, William J. (William Joseph), 1945–   . III. Title.
   [DNLM: 1. Chronic Disease—psychology.   2. Family.   3. Family Therapy.   4. Stress,
   Psychological—therapy.   WM   430.5.F2   M4775m]
   RC488.5.M393   1992
   616.89'156—dc20
   DNLM/DLC
   for Library of Congress   92-11151
                                                                                                CIP

Designed by Ellen Levine

94 95 96 CC/HC 9 8 7 6 5 4 3 2

This book is lovingly dedicated to our families,
close and extended, and especially
from Susan to Grover and Anna McDaniel, Ann McDaniel,
and Mary and Gary Johnson;
from Jeri to Robert, Jon, and Katie Ryder;
from Bill to Leah, Eric, and Elizabeth Doherty.

Contents

Foreword

IN RECENT YEARS family therapy practitioners have been working more and more often in physical health care environments. They have done so in response to rapid and pervasive change in these environments. This process has been less than graceful at times: there has often been confusion as to the proper role for the family therapist in such settings. Yet the logic of the movement of family therapists as psychosocial providers into the world of physical medicine has been so strong that it has steadily gained ground.

Within biomedicine itself there have been persistent and visionary advocates for change in the direction of simplifying and humanizing the practice of medicine. The changes needed are to increase the relative importance of primary care medicine and to strengthen and redefine the place of psychosocial providers in the health care system. The development of a new collaborative field which the authors of this book have aptly called "medical family therapy" will be noted in the future as a marker of important progress on these issues; this volume provides a solid foundation for the next stages of work in this field.

Medical family therapists are not the only psychosocial providers in the health care setting: psychologists, social workers, psychiatrists, and nurses, as well as physicians themselves, provide psychosocial care. However, the contribution of family therapists is distinctive and significant for two reasons: they have expertise in understanding and working with *families*, and their work is informed by a *systems orientation*. Both are critically important in the present health care scene.

We have made a number of false starts in this field: the competent and experienced family therapist is not *de facto* a competent *medical* family therapist. A different knowledge base is needed to work as a psychosocial provider in physical health care settings. The authors of this book are well aware of this, and show that different skills are needed to be effective in these complex environments.

During the late nineteenth century, the practice of medicine became, increasingly, scientific medicine; the hegemony of physicians, hospitals, and medical schools over this developing field was established. At that time the practicing physician had a limited armamentarium. He was a prognosticator, reliever of pain, healer, and comforter of the soul of the patient and of the family. In most instances he—the physician then was almost always a male—knew the medical and social history of his patients but had few tools other than simple medicines and some surgery for treatment.

Looking back over more than forty years, since I was trained as a young physician, means to contemplate an array of technical advances that are almost beyond description. Antibiotics, cancer therapy, organ transplants, molecular medicine—each of these advances has produced a dense thicket of new medical capabilities that in turn generates a host of novel human problems with consequences for the family.

These transformations of the physician and the institutions of medicine have been ably depicted by Paul Starr,[1] among others. Although these spectacular advances generated a new scientific persona for physicians, the price was for them to be steadily less capable than their predecessors in the role of healer. They also were less knowledgeable about the real lives of their patients. Meanwhile, the treatment-related burdens on families increased. The advances of biomedicine created chronicity where it had not existed before. Early on, sick

1. Paul Starr, *The Social Transformation of American Medicine*. New York: Basic Books, 1982.

people mostly got well by themselves, or died. In conquering acute illnesses, biomedicine has produced a multitude of treatment-related chronic illnesses.

A few examples illustrate the point. Starting from the beginning of life, even before the moment of conception, men and women can encounter a host of bioengineered family stressors—artificial insemination, the arduous and usually unrewarding road of in vitro fertilization, the various possibilities of surrogate pregnancy. These are always family dilemmas, in addition to being ethical, religious, and legal questions (see chapter 6).

These days very low weight premature infants are being kept alive by pediatric intensive care units. The success of the ICU environment depends on advanced technology and on an expensive and highly trained staff. Such efforts require large financial resources and create a high-risk environment for the infants and their families. The dangers of intracranial hemorrhage as well as other complications are ever present; they are inversely proportional to the birth weight and directly proportional to the scientific "derring-do" that is involved in the care of the infant.

What are families to do? What can they do? They usually have little choice. The low birth weight premature infant triggers a sequence of focused medical attention whether the family wants it or not. Often the outcome is excellent but rarely is that known at the outset. A partially successful result may be a family disaster, with a brain-damaged child who must be sustained for a long time by a family depleted of its economic and emotional resources. Families need choices, guidance, and support at these times. They need informed advocates who can accumulate and present them with relevant experience so that they can make appropriate choices. The medical family therapist can fill this role (see chapter 8 for issues concerning illness in children).

Family is connected with the important life-style illnesses. Smoking, alcohol, and other addictions are implicated in a large proportion of the cases that the physician deals with. The eating disorders, anorexia, bulimia, and obesity, should be mentioned here as well. It is an oversimplification to regard any of these as monolithic entities with one cause and one correct mode of treatment. All are better understood as resulting from a complex interplay of genetic, developmental, psychological, and cultural factors. I believe it is fair to say that family work—family therapy in many instances—must be a significant part of any treatment approach to these syndromes (see chapter 5).

Today the clinical mix of cases being treated involves more chronic cases, more complex treatment problems, and in terms of the thesis being advanced here, cases where there is more clear impact on—and response to—the psychological and social aspects of the patient's life (see chapters 8 and 9).

Severe and chronic physical illness acts like a magnifying glass for families. Everything is exaggerated, is seen in bold relief, in high intensity, so that those issues that families are dealing with in the normal developmental process can become part of an amplifying distortion—in a word, become pathological.

Biomedical treatment procedures have become ever more complex and stressful for patients and their families. Complex cancer protocols are a case in point. Many of us have lived with a friend or relative, a client or patient, through the protracted business of chemotherapy, surgery, and radiation. The illness and its treatment affect families in ways that might not be readily apparent, requiring major role realignments or activating old family patterns of response to loss, grief, illness, and caretaking.

I worked extensively with a family that was dealing with a son who had Hodgkin's disease, a cancer of the lymphatic system. There have been wonderful advances in the treatment of this disease, and survival rates continue to climb, but the procedures are often painful and difficult to endure. There may be a lot of chemotherapy; the spleen may have to be removed, and so on. The mother was a family therapist just reentering the work world. In the face of this illness she and her husband had to make difficult decisions about her career; the patient was their fourteen-year-old son. The patient had to deal with his illness and also with being an adolescent. He had to take his chemotherapy through a tube which ran into his body and had to remember to care for and clean that tube—not easy for anyone, let alone an adolescent just learning to live with a new body.

Prior to the illness the mother had been returning to the work world, taking on the challenges that involves; now she found herself having to be the parent of last resort, as women commonly are. The father traveled to another city for an arduous job but needed to do this to generate the income to support the whole process. Not surprisingly there were major stresses on the marital relationship. There were other children in the family, now semi-orphaned. And on and on—what has been described as "a cataract of consequences."

AIDS is certainly the exemplar of all of these trends. AIDS is a pistol aimed point blank at the functional heart of the family: love, trust, sexuality. Families of origin and present-day intimates are stressed and tested in every way imaginable. AIDS also stresses our health care delivery system along every dimension: it is the scientific puzzle par excellence; it poses almost incalculable financing problems; excellent psychosocial services must be provided to highly vulnerable, under-resourced patients and their intimate networks; and health care workers are at risk for contagion and at even greater risk for emotional depletion. The medical family therapist is a necessary member of the team caring for these patients (see chapter 10).

The geriatric population increasingly demands our attention; pro-portionally the most rapidly growing age group in the United States today consists of persons over 100 years old. To be a *healthy* aged person means to need care. How can people live their last years with dignity and self-respect? Because of the advances in scientific medicine, the family has evolved, in many instances, into a four- to five-generation entity, but without the social support structures of the families of an earlier time. Many of us are caretakers both of our parents and of our adult children, and then we ourselves go on ultimately to needing sophisticated medical and nursing care. Bioscience can often sustain physical life beyond a point where most of us would care to be alive. So we make some kind of "living will" and leave the hard decisions about "Do Not Resuscitate" to whom? To our families.

Negotiating this developmental stage is a wrenching process for many families: old wounds open; rivalries, conflicts, and jealousies long dormant break out. Sibling groups struggling with economic and emo-tional pressures may neglect their strengths and lock in to highly dysfunctional patterns of withdrawal or sacrifice, blame and scapegoat-ing in an attempt to deal with these pressures. Medical family therapists have a significant contribution to make to primary care, nursing home, and geriatric teams working with these families.

Philip Roth's book *Patrimony* addresses just these issues as it tells us about his relation to his widowed father in the latter years of the father's life. Feisty, contentious, and life-affirming Mr. Roth, senior, has a benign brain tumor that slowly but inexorably is disabling him and crowding out his normal functional capabilities. The tumor is operable, up to a point: the operation would be in two stages, would take many hours, be debilitating, and be palliative at best. Philip and his brother ask, "What shall we do?" and wonder how to involve their father in this decision. In describing how this decision gets made and what it involves, Roth tells us the story of our lives.

Our national health care system is manifestly dysfunctional, with ever-increasing costs and gaping holes in the care provided to sectors of our population. Any new service must demonstrate its social utility against this background. One promising direction is to reduce dependence on specialists and subspecialists and to put more health care in the hands of a generalist—the family or primary care physician. This fosters a natural alliance between family therapy and family practice and energizes the further development of the profession of medical family therapist.

To contribute to more humane, clinically effective, and *cost effective* patterns of care will require reconceptualization and design changes in the delivery system. When the interface between the family/patient system and the provider system breaks down, the provider system's capabilities are not properly utilized. This misutilization includes non-compliance or nonadherence (the patient does not follow the agreed on treatment plan), failure to thrive (the patient seems to follow an appropriate treatment plan but it does not produce the desired result), over-utilization (when the patient complains that the problem is not attended to and seeks or is referred to a costly series of diagnostic procedures and subspecialty referrals), and non- or underutilization (in which conditions that are known to be ameliorable are not presented for treatment, for example, hypertension).

In these situations the locus of some problems is heavily skewed towards family, for example, the somatizing family; some problems appear to be located in the differing realities of the provider and family/patient systems; and in some instances the provider system is organized in a way that does not adequately communicate its intentions or its rules. These sociopathological syndromes can be dealt with using the same analytic tools that we would bring to other systems problems. The locus of breakdown needs to be defined, and intervention strategies must be developed, put into place, and evaluated. The medical family therapist, using an eco-systemic paradigm as a basic working tool, has a contribution to make in collaboration with others toward improving this situation.

As this field has developed we have needed to find a term to describe ourselves. I think there is an excellent chance that "medical family therapist" might do it. The authors of this volume have given us a fine name by which to call ourselves; and much more than that, they have conceptualized the boundaries of this challenging new role for family therapists and laid the technical foundation for the work that will be done in the years to come.

Donald A. Bloch, M.D.
March 23, 1992

Preface

IN THIS BOOK we propose a new paradigm for the biopsychosocial treatment of patients and their families who are dealing with health issues. Our commitment to the practice we now call "medical family therapy" dates back to the late 1970s and early 1980s. During that period, we all worked to apply the systems concepts developed in family therapy to the world of modern medical care. In addition to being involved in family therapy training, each of us was teaching through the 1980s at a medical school in a department of family medicine. Much of our attention focused on expanding the view of the family physicians we taught and helping them to incorporate the needs and concerns of families and other relevant systems (such as other medical specialists or social agencies) into their thinking and patient care. In this book we turn our attention to our fellow therapists by offering a new model for working with the impact of health problems on patients and families. This is the first book for therapists that describes a family systems approach to a broad range of medical issues that occur at the interface between biology and family dynamics.

This book extends our prior work into the arena of family therapy. William Doherty's collaboration with family physician Macaran Baird resulted in the landmark 1983 book, *Family Therapy and Family Medicine.* Susan McDaniel, family physician Thomas Campbell, and family therapist David Seaburn worked especially to develop the pragmatics of family-oriented medical care. This resulted in a 1990 book for medical providers, entitled *Family-Oriented Primary Care.* Jeri Hepworth has developed important ideas about collaboration between physicians and therapists, which have been published in journal form. She also started a family therapy internship in her family medicine department. This experience, and those shared by Susan and Bill in their training capacities, led to our desire to develop our ideas about family systems, medical illness, and the medical system specifically for other therapists.

Our experiences as both medical educators and family therapy trainers have allowed us to identify the unique opportunities for family systems—oriented therapists to assist families with health problems. The audience for this book consists of family therapists, psychologists, behavioral medicine specialists, medical and psychiatric social workers, psychiatric nurses, and psychiatrists. Although primary care physicians and nurses may benefit, the strategies and techniques are intended primarily for therapists who are fully trained in family systems therapy.

Some colleagues and trainees have reacted to our interest in this area with caution and not a little skepticism. When one of us accepted a job in family medicine, more than one therapist colleague said, "Why in the world would you want to go and hang out with all those doctors?" When it comes to trying to collaborate with a physician on a case, the common complaint by therapists is that these doctors can never be reached and seem uninterested in coordinated treatment plans. The fascinating experience for each of us is that physicians make the same complaints about working with therapists! Some of these physicians do question whether psychotherapy does anyone any good, but most all of them complain that therapists are unresponsive to referrals. ("We never hear one word from them after we send a patient.") Hearing these two sides of the story is something like hearing from one spouse, and then another, in a marital dispute.

What is not disputed is the need for patients and families to receive better and more comprehensive medical care. Soaring costs and the advent of new technologies for diagnosis and treatment have resulted in fragmented, specialized, and impersonal care in too many circumstances. Patients and families often feel lost in the maze of the medical system at a time when they feel the most vulnerable. Consumer groups have become increasingly vocal in their complaints. In response, the primary care disciplines of pediatrics, internal medicine, and especially family medicine have begun to develop a biopsychosocial approach to the common medical concerns of their patients. While these medical groups have groped their way towards a biopsychosocial framework, many therapists have lagged behind, staying focused on issues narrowly considered "psychosocial." This book is designed to help therapists advance with this broader movement in health care.

As we discuss in the early chapters of the book, family therapists have a tremendous opportunity to play a significant role in the changing world of health care delivery. When patients and their families face problems like chronic illness, infertility, or cancer, collaboration between family therapists and medical providers can result in more personal, more effective, and more comprehensive care. We hope this book will open dialogue and focus more attention on how therapists can productively participate in and influence the health care system. We want to encourage more research on the interaction between emotional and interpersonal process and biomedical events. And, finally, we seek to stimulate more innovation and clinical study of how people respond to illness and how they might use it, as family therapist Donald Williamson suggests, as a "call to consciousness" (1991, p. 229).

A word about the term "medical family therapy." We use the word "medical" to convey a focus on health problems such as chronic illness, disability, and health behaviors. We use "family therapy" to emphasize the family systems framework that informs our model. This label is consistent with other disciplines such as "medical anthropology" or "medical social work." However convenient and descriptive, the label is not without ambiguity. We do not wish to convey that medical family therapy is ordinarily practiced by physicians or that it necessarily involves prescribing medications. Nor do we wish in any way to exclude our family nursing colleagues who do not identify with the word "medical." ("Health care family therapy" seems cumbersome and ambiguous.) So, we conclude that "medical family therapy" is the best term to define what it is we do.

This book represents a genuinely collaborative project. We jointly planned and brainstormed about the contents of each chapter, debated ideas, and took individual responsibility for first drafts of different chapters. We reviewed, revised, and enlarged on each others' chapters, which often resulted in another round of excitement and debate that allowed us to define our joint vision. As an aside, this level of collaboration would have been impossible for three people living in New York, Minnesota, and Connecticut before the advent of electronic mail. We "spoke" to each other on an average of once a day, and often more, during the project. This communication allowed us to attend to the details of writing as well as the development of ideas in a way that was practical, effective, efficient, and, we might add, fun.

Many people have contributed directly and indirectly to this book. We would like to thank the Chairs of our departments for encouraging this work, and our colleagues for providing us with supportive and stimulating atmospheres. We especially would like to thank the physicians and the therapists who reviewed different chapters in progress. As always, our medical colleagues kept us honest about the medical details of our work. All the readers helped us to further define and refine what are still emerging thoughts about this area. Our reviewers were Thomas Campbell, Kathy Cole-Kelly, Robert Cushman, Perry Dickinson, Steven Eisinger, Barbara Gawinski, Katherine Krause, Grover McDaniel, William Miller, Jo Ellen Patterson, Donald Ransom, Robert Ryder, David Seaburn, David Siegel, Earl Siegel, and Beatrice Wood. Thanks to all of them. And thanks to the students to whom we have presented these ideas. They helped immeasurably in forcing us to clarify our thinking.

Many people helped in the administrative tasks involved in putting this book together. Thanks to Teal King, a reference librarian at St. Francis Hospital and Medical Center, who helped Jeri research special topics. Thanks to Sally Rousseau, research assistant at Family Medicine in Rochester, who went the extra mile as usual and helped with computer searches and drawing figures and tables. Thanks to Susan's ever-cheerful and always competent secretary, Jeanne Klee, who helped in many of the final details of pulling this volume together. Thanks also to our editor, Jo Ann Miller, and her assistant editor, Stephen Francoeur, who encouraged us from beginning to end and who give the best feedback in the business.

Thanks to our families who understand our enthusiasm for this work and cheer us along from the sidelines. We want to extend particular thanks to the medical providers with whom we have shared joys, tears, and challenges, and the patients and families who allowed us into their lives during painful times. It was these two groups, the medical providers and the families, who taught us what we now know about medical family therapy.

CHAPTER 1

Family Therapy and Medical Illness

ONCE UPON A TIME, when the problems people brought to a therapist's office could be neatly divided into psychosocial and physical domains, many therapists persuaded themselves that they dealt only with the psychosocial part of life. These therapists did not pursue an understanding of the place of medical illness in the patient's personal and family life because physical health problems were the province of other professionals. Patients* with medical problems may have received compassion and support from these therapists but not comprehensive therapy. And few therapists actively collaborated with physicians and other health professionals in the treatment of patients. It is as if patients and families checked their bodies at the door of the therapist's office.

The days of innocence are over. We now know that human life is a seamless cloth spun from biological, psychological, social, and cultural threads; that patients and families come with bodies as well as minds, feelings, interaction patterns, and belief systems; that there are no biological problems without psychosocial implications, and no psychosocial

---

*Although many therapists use the term *client*, we have adopted the term *patient* because of its universal use in medical settings.

problems without biological implications. Like it or not, therapists are dealing with biological problems, and physicians are dealing with psychosocial problems. The only choice is whether to do integrated treatment well or do it poorly.

These statements may appear obvious to some and controversial to others. But few would argue with the notion that most therapists are ill prepared to address the role played by medical illness and disability in patients' lives. Which of us learned in graduate school about the impact of juvenile-onset diabetes on a child and a family, or about the anguish involved in infertility and its aftermath? And which of us in graduate school was introduced to the culture of the medical field and learned ways to interact with physicians for the benefit of patients? With experience, some of it personal, we pick up knowledge about these issues, but most of us lack a systematic way of assessing and working with the medical issues and medical providers that are major parts of the lives of many of our clients.

This book aims to fill this knowledge gap for therapists. We introduce the term *medical family therapy* to refer to biopsychosocial treatment of individuals and families who are dealing with medical problems. As we conceptualize it, medical family therapy works from a biopsychosocial systems model and actively encourages collaboration between therapists and other health professionals. The term *biopsychosocial*, which is discussed extensively in chapter 2, communicates the idea that all problems are at once biological, psychological, and social. We add the term *systems* to emphasize our family systems approach to working with medical problems and their contexts. Family systems theory provides a sophisticated way to analyze and work with circular interaction processes, triangles, boundaries, and beliefs in the complex system involving a patient, a family, medical providers, therapists, and a variety of other groups that impinge on health care treatment. The systems approach we advocate cannot be reduced to simply adding a family therapy component to traditional health care delivery; rather, it offers a new way to understand the relationships among all the parties involved in treatment (Baird and Doherty, 1990).

In this introductory chapter, we review family therapy's on and off again relationship with biology, its place in the overall professional treatment picture, and the challenges and opportunities that medical family therapy offers to the field of family therapy, and we offer two goals for medical family therapy. We begin with a case illustration.*

Martha, age thirty-two, and Richard, age thirty-four, are two remarkably attractive and friendly people who married three years ago when both were apparently in good health. Shortly after their marriage, Martha began to experience fatigue, joint soreness, and a number of other disturbing symptoms. She embarked on a long diagnostic process that eventually led to the diagnosis of systemic lupus erythematosus, an autoimmune disease that typically strikes young adult women. Martha decided to quit her writing job in favor of freelance writing at home, where she could better adapt her work schedule to her physical condition.

Although she did her best to maintain a constructive attitude, at times she was depressed, especially when she and her husband had trouble conceiving and were told by their physician that the chances of miscarriage were significant if she did become pregnant. Richard took a consistently upbeat attitude, telling her that he could support her financially and that they should forget about having their own child and adopt. Martha felt hurt by Richard's brusqueness in dealing with her fragile feelings about her body and her prospects for motherhood. And she was bothered by his family's overly optimistic approach to her, in which they told her how well she looked and encouraged her not to have negative thoughts. A friend referred the couple to a therapist known to have an interest in working with families dealing with medical problems.

Much of the treatment of this couple was standard marital therapy—clarifying family-of-origin boundaries, facilitating clearer communication and better problem solving, and identifying and changing the "cheer up" and "you don't understand me" interaction pattern. In addition, the medical family therapist knew enough about lupus to help the patient, and especially the husband, appreciate the challenges of living with the disease's unpredictable flare ups and remissions. The therapist sought permission to talk with Martha's

*This illustration, like the others in this book, is based on an actual case, with some facts disguised for reasons of confidentiality.

physician about her fertility status and probability of miscarriage. The therapist also helped the couple to distinguish between the lupus, which they could not eliminate but could learn to better cope with, and their desire to have a child, which they could do something about by adopting or continuing to try to achieve conception. The couple ultimately decided not to risk a pregnancy and miscarriage, shared the grief that accompanied their decision, and began the adoption process with joyful anticipation. They also opened their affective communication channels so that each could express a full range of feelings about the illness without fear of rejection from the other.

A Unique Role for Medical Family Therapy

Therapists from a behavioral medicine tradition have been dealing with medical problems for many years, and consultation-liaison psychiatrists have also worked at the interface between medical problems and psychosocial problems. Some primary care physicians work with psychosocial as well as medical aspects of their patients' problem (Doherty and Baird, 1983). What, then, is unique about medical family therapy?

Medical family therapy is distinguished by its conscious attention to medical illness and its role in the personal life of the patient and the interpersonal life of the family. It combines biopsychosocial and family systems perspectives and uses them to work simultaneously with patients, families, health care professionals, and community groups and agencies. Its family systems perspective distinguishes medical family therapy from behavioral medicine and consultation-liaison psychiatry— fields that traditionally focus on individual patients and do not offer extensive family therapy training. In behavioral medicine and consultation-liaison psychiatry, families generally are seen not as complex systems but as background factors influencing an individual patient's well-being. However, medical family therapists can learn much from the long experience of these professionals in dealing with medical issues.

Unlike primary care physicians and nurses who do psychosocial

4

counseling, medical family therapists are trained to work with difficult cases in an intense and sometimes prolonged manner. Few primary care physicians or nurses have the training or the time to help Martha and Richard, in the case just cited, work through their multifaceted problems in a series of hour-long sessions. Although many primary care physicians and nurses do important psychosocial work with patients and families, their activities do not substitute for the activity of a medical family therapist. Indeed, we believe that the ideal collaborative team for delivering biopsychosocial care consists of psychosocially sophisticated primary care physicians and nurses and medical family therapists.

In the current health care system, then, few professionals deliver care as we envision it in medical family therapy. Individual-oriented therapists, even the few who are trained in a biopsychosocial model, tend to neglect members of the patient's family, who often are suffering as much as the patient. The family, if it is involved at all, is likely to be viewed as an adjunctive aid in treating the patient, not as a group of people who need help in their own right. This practice unfortunately replicates how families are treated throughout the health care system: they are either marginalized or treated as tools of health professionals to help patients (Doherty and Campbell, 1988). Medical family therapy provides an antidote to treatment that disqualifies families.

Family Therapy's Relationship with Biology

Although family therapists do not neglect families, they historically have neglected the biological side of life and have not collaborated well with medical providers. Important exceptions to this trend, however, have appeared in the history of family therapy. Early pioneers such as John Weakland, Lyman Wynne, Carl Whitaker, Murray Bowen, Salvador Minuchin, and Edgar Auerswald foresaw the benefits of using family therapy to address problems of both mental and physical health. Carl Whitaker and Thomas Malone's *The Roots of Psychotherapy* (1953) included a chapter titled "The Biological Basis of Psychotherapy" that argued that "the science of psychotherapy must be developed within the framework of the biological sciences" (p. 17). Edgar Auerswald (1968) used an ecological model for providing coordinated physical and mental health care for inner-city families. Murray Bowen (1976) described his early theoretical interest in connections between human behavior and accepted science. His theory purposely included terms and concepts derived from biological and natural science, such as *symbiosis* and *differentiation*. Foreshadowing resistance to this approach, Bowen said that when reading extensively in biology, he was cautioned by a psychoanalyst friend to give up "holistic" thinking before he got "too far out" (p. 58).

Several later contributions in family therapy integrated biological and social conceptualizations of health and illness. Salvador Minuchin and colleagues (1975, 1978) have been recognized for their research interest in family interaction and physical illnesses such as diabetes and asthma. Their "psychosomatic families" model was a major breakthrough in the application of family systems theory to medical problems. Lyman Wynne is respected for integrating biological and social perspectives about schizophrenia. With colleagues Rue Cromwell and Steven Matthysse, Wynne edited *The Nature of Schizophrenia* (1978), a compilation of papers focusing on neurological, biochemical, family, and communication theories and treatments.

This initial interest in a biopsychosocial perspective on family treatment, however, was not shared by most family therapists. John Weakland (1977) expressed concern about family therapy's neglect of "family somatics." He described how a wider application of the interactional viewpoint could prove fruitful in research and clinical work but also observed the field's reluctance to return to the "old imposition of the medical model on 'mental illness' " (p. 270). Weakland prophetically concluded his article with a question about whether family therapy should be involved in family somatics: "Should we, perhaps, just mind our own business and not get involved? The choice is up to us" (p. 272).

Although medical family therapy clearly traces its intellectual heritage to the pioneers of mainstream family therapy, a larger debt is owed to family therapists working in medical settings during the 1970s and 1980s. The new specialty of family medicine, created in 1970 out of the older general practice model, attracted a significant number of family therapists, including the three authors of this book, to the medical schools to train medical students and residents. These therapists, already trained in systems assessment and intervention, evolved toward a biopsychosocial/systems orientation through their everyday clinical work in these settings and their reading in literatures outside family therapy. At the same time, family nurses and psychiatric nurses began using family systems theory to understand their work with patients and families (Gilliss, Highley, Roberts, and Martinson, 1989; Wright and Leahey, 1987). In the 1980s, experiments in collaborative health care involved family therapists and physicians and nurses working in biopsychosocial teams (Glenn, 1987). In 1984, the new journal *Family Systems Medicine* was launched by Donald Bloch, Donald Ransom, and Michael Glenn. A spate of books appeared in the 1980s, mostly on the application of family systems ideas to primary medical care. By the early 1990s, when this book was being written, medical family therapy had clearly captured the imagination of practitioners in the field of family therapy.

The Challenge for Family Therapy Training

Medical family therapy is more than the simple extension of family systems concepts to new problems and new settings. The therapist must be prepared for the delicate task of entering a system with its own culture (Wynne, McDaniel, and Weber, 1986). Yet family therapy training programs generally do not prepare trainees to negotiate systems that differ from the context of training or, at best, the mental health delivery system. Don Bloch (personal communication, 1990) wryly suggested that family therapists often believe that, armed with systems theory, they can parachute into any setting and quickly understand— and change—the terrain. Unfortunately, untrained parachutists often break legs, harm the environment, or meet with more serious consequences. The following story illustrates this point:

> A family therapy trainee read about psychosomatic families in an early graduate course and tried to apply what she learned to her sister's history of asthma and questionable history of depression. The trainee remembered how frightening the asthma attacks had been to her family and how concerned and solicitous of her sister her parents had been, which led her to believe that her family had caused or certainly maintained her sister's illness. By the time the trainee presented her genogram to one of us, she believed that her

7

family had been enmeshed in and responsible for her sister's difficulties and described them with some shame. This woman was not a naive, literal thinker, and the writings about psychosomatic families do not intentionally blame families for the patient's illnesses. Yet it is a common misconception among family therapists that if families and illness are related, then families in some way must be responsible for creating the illness or for prolonging it by not implementing appropriate treatment.

Medical family therapy challenges therapists to think in complex ways about health and illness and to understand medical cultures and health care providers, so that collaborative, effective care can ensue. Chapter 2 lays out some of the new knowledge needed by family therapists who are bold enough to parachute into the medical world.

NEW POSSIBILITIES FOR COLLABORATION

We believe that medical family therapy can help patients, families, other providers, and the health care system. But family therapists who develop competence in medical family therapy and who work collaboratively with physicians and other health professionals also gain many benefits.

First, medical family therapy provides therapists with skills to treat a wide variety of problems and thus increases the potential scope of a clinical practice. Donald Ransom (1983a) suggested that collaboration with health providers allows family therapists to see "families with fewer problems and less entrenched problem-solving styles than those who wind up in tertiary care family therapy centers" (p. 95).

By injecting new ideas and approaches, medical family therapy brings an intellectual excitement that enhances the work that therapists do with families. We can share a rich literature on biopsychosocial health care and interact with a new group of medical and nursing colleagues. Expanding our perspectives usually leads to new visions and possibilities.

Finally, medical family therapy also paves the way for family therapists to affect the changing health care system. As respected colleagues in health care, we can influence the health care delivery process in our communities. Hospitals and tertiary care facilities are sure to value for economic and advertising reasons our ability to address families and their needs in a medical setting. Family therapists have served on hospital committees and have been invited to speak to groups as diverse as hospital administrators, rehabilitative specialists, and surgeons: these are opportunities to show how a family systems perspective can be included in economic and clinical decisions.

GOALS OF MEDICAL FAMILY THERAPY: AGENCY AND COMMUNION

Much of the work of any therapist is helping patients achieve their particular goals for therapy. In medical family therapy, these patient goals take the form of being able to cope with a chronic illness or disability, feeling less conflicted about handling a medical regimen, communicating better with physicians, accepting a medical problem that cannot be cured, or making lifestyle changes. Underlying these particular objectives, however, are two general goals that we propose for medical family therapy: promoting agency and communion.

Richard Totman (1979) uses the term *agency* to describe active involvement in and commitment to one's own care. Agency refers to a sense of making personal choices in dealing with illness and the health care system, both of which often contribute to a patient's feelings of passivity and lack of control. Sometimes promoting agency involves helping patient and family set limits on the amount of control an illness or disability has over their lives, as in deciding to proceed with holiday celebrations despite the patient's partial incapacitation. Other times promoting agency involves helping the family to negotiate for more information or better care arrangements with health professionals, hospitals, or insurance providers. Within the family itself, the therapist can promote the agency of the patient in relation to other family members. This can take the form of setting boundaries on family members' helpfulness or teaching a family member to ask assertively for help, as when the caregiver of an Alzheimer's disease patient is coached on how to insist on family assistance.

Communion refers to emotional bonds that often are frayed by

9

illness, disability, and contact with the health care system. It is the sense of being cared for, loved, and supported by a community of family members, friends, and professionals. Serious illness or disability is an existential crisis that can isolate people from those who care for them, but the quality of the patient's social relationships appears to be the most powerful psychosocial factor in health and illness. One of the chief reasons for emphasizing medical *family* therapy is that serious illnesses and disabilities provide opportunities for resolving old conflicts and for forging new levels of healthy family bonding.

During the acute phase of a life-threatening illness, family members may be emotionally available to each other in unaccustomed ways, but during the chronic phase many families find that their sense of common purpose and common feeling deteriorates. One of the medical family therapist's most important tasks is to help family members join together to cope with an illness and to do so within the context of allowing the patient maximum feasible autonomy and agency. Similarly, families who deal with catastrophic medical stressors, such as a child with a fatal form of degenerative muscular dystrophy, often benefit from support groups of other families experiencing their problem. The sense of communion that these groups provide cannot be matched by any other relationship. Sadly, however, parents generally are not given assistance in dealing with their own extended families, many of whom misunderstand their behavior and turn away emotionally from families with disabled or seriously ill members. Medical family therapists are ideally positioned to help build interpersonal communion among these families.

These primary goals of agency and communion reflect our own commitment as therapists to promoting self-determination in patients and their families. Because the health care system often erodes patients' sense of control over their bodies and behavior, medical family therapists must hold patient autonomy as a high priority, even if the patient decides not to cooperate with treatment. Balancing this commitment to personal choice with the relational nature of human life and human illness is the challenge: we do not live for ourselves alone, and personal agency is only one note on the musical chord that also contains communion with others. Medical family therapists—as they deal with individual patients, family members, and health care professionals—are well situated to advocate for this kind of balanced and integrated health care.

Conclusion

Medical family therapy represents a maturing of the professional discipline of family therapy. Family therapy can be more than treatment of behavioral problems and communication disorders. As this new discipline integrates family therapy ideas with those of medicine, family therapy is being challenged to better define its terminology and concepts, to specify data and assumptions, and to collaborate with related disciplines (Ransom, 1983a). Infusing pertinent biological concepts into family therapy can return the field to the dreams of its pioneers. Family therapists can participate in and help define biopsychosocial models of health and health care delivery systems. Such an approach might help to salvage a crumbling health care system and provide better care for patients and families.

CHAPTER 2

Foundations of Medical Family Therapy

FAMILIES DEALING WITH CHRONIC ILLNESS or disability find that interactions with health care professionals, HMOs, insurance providers, and government agencies are among the most stressful aspects of their situation. To help them, medical family therapists need a working knowledge of these health care and community systems. During the 1980s the field of family therapy began studying families' relationships with larger systems, as seen in the work of Lyman Wynne, Susan McDaniel, and Timothy Weber (1986) and Evan Imber-Black (1988a). The central notion for medical family therapy that emerged from that period is that the unit of assessment and treatment must include the family, the therapist, and the relevant health care system. Three models can be used to examine this complex treatment system.

The model proposed by David Reiss and Atara Kaplan de-Nour (1989) links medical staff, family, and patient within a social system that proceeds through three identifiable phases, each with its own developmental tasks: the central task of the acute phase is "assessment and support"; the central task of the chronic phase, "vigilance versus burnout; maintenance of morale, development, and rehabilitation"; and of the terminal phase, "comfort and composure." Reiss and Kaplan de-Nour describe how roles and interactions among patients, medical staff, and families change during these phases and suggest that the caregiving system's success in coping with later stages depends on success in earlier phases.

William Doherty and Macaran Baird (1983) maintained that the fundamental unit of health is the triangle of clinician, patient, and family. In John Rolland's (1987) view, the illness and its psychosocial characteristics become an additional part of the treatment systems and expand the therapeutic triangle into a therapeutic quadrangle of health care team, patient, family, and illness. By acknowledging the medical family therapist to be a distinct member of the health care team, a pentagon is created, with the therapist attending to issues involving illness, patient, family, and other members of the health care team.

A third useful conceptual approach to systems dynamics in health care is Edgar Auerswald's ecological systems approach (1968). Unlike the interdisciplinary approach, in which each provider maintains the conceptual vantage point of his or her own discipline, the ecological approach uses multiple perspectives to create entirely new approaches. Auerswald cautions that interdisciplinary discussions can lead to much "head-banging" and that by using an ecological approach providers shift their perspectives from a single discipline to the interfaces between the interdisciplinary systems and the communications between systems. In medical family therapy, the ecological approach to management of diabetes would address how the patient, the family, and the health care provider respond to the illness and treatment and how the interactions between the family and health care team affect treatment and responses.

The Biopsychosocial Model: Beyond the Biomedical Model

Modern medical training has emphasized the biomedical model, which attributes pathology to biological and molecular processes. Consumers desire this biomedical expertise but often complain that competent biomedical practitioners tend to ignore the person who has the disease. Internist George Engel noted that medical care and training reflect a cultural context and that the "biomedical model is now the dominant folk model of disease in the Western world" (Engel, 1977, p. 130). This biomedical model, which accounts for disease by its biochemical factors without considering social or psychological dimensions, separates mind from body. It was this separation of the biological elements of disease from the psychosocial contexts in which they occur that led Engel to propose the biopsychosocial model for organizing medical care. Based on general systems theory principles attributed to Von Bertalanffy, the biopsychosocial model acknowledges the hierarchical, interdependent relationships of biological, psychological, individual, family, and community systems (see figure 2.1). The model reminds providers that they affect multiple levels of systems simultaneously. Heart bypass surgery, for example, requires attention primarily at the organ system level, but most agree that the surgery also affects the cells, the patient, and the social system of the patient.

Engel's systems-oriented work was revolutionary for mainstream medicine but was published in a nonmedical journal, *Science*, the most prestigious journal in American science. Engel used terminology familiar to family therapists to describe isomorphisms across the levels and urged a systemic understanding of the relationship between biological and social spheres. The biopsychosocial model was presented as a framework for understanding how psychophysiologic responses to life interact with somatic factors, how a patient's understanding affects communication of symptoms and use of treatment strategies, and how communication and treatment are affected by relationships between the patient and health care providers.

Biopsychosocial theory, however, is often far apart from practice. Although most recent medical school students are exposed to the biopsychosocial model in their preclinical years, clinical training generally focuses on the biomedical aspects of disease. Psychosocial considerations are addressed only "when there is time"; when the psychosocial situation is a blatant and major part of the illness, as when depression predates a new cancer diagnosis; or when the psychosocial situation distracts from treatment.

As was discussed in chapter 1, family therapists have not practiced within a biopsychosocial model but have tended to operate solely within their field of comfort—the family system—and to pay only minor attention to the individual biological or physical dimensions. By neglecting the other levels of organization, they are at risk for "psychosocial fixation" (McDaniel, Campbell, and Seaburn, 1989).

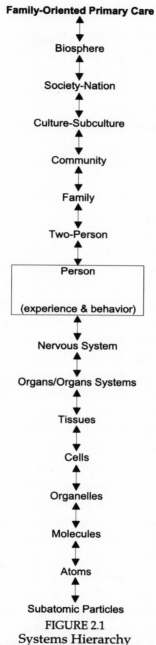

Family-Oriented Primary Care

Biosphere

Society-Nation

Culture-Subculture

Community

Family

Two-Person

Person

(experience & behavior)

Nervous System

Organs/Organs Systems

Tissues

Cells

Organelles

Molecules

Atoms

Subatomic Particles

FIGURE 2.1

Systems Hierarchy

Source: G. L. Engel (1980), The clinical application of the biopsychosocial model. *American Journal of Psychiatry, 137,* 535–544. Copyright May 1980. The American Psychiatric Association. Reprinted by permission.

We do not recommend that physicians become family therapists or that family therapists become experts on biology. Culturally we believe that biomedical treatment of disease provides the greatest success, so health care consumers expect a nephrologist, for example, to specialize in kidneys. Consumers also want family therapists who specialize in encouraging change at the interactional level. It is consistent with the biopsychosocial model to address a particular level of the system at one time but to consider other levels of the system as well. A person has the illness, and that person is embedded within a network of people who also are affected by the illness. Their families interact with larger societal organizations to assist and cope with illness in one of their members.

In Carl Whitaker and Thomas Malone's (1953) early writings, a biopsychosocial model, although not termed such, provided the theoretical basis for the science of psychotherapy. "Any change in a part of the organism, regardless of whether the change comes in the province of the physiological, genetic, chemical, or psychological, results in changes which affect every other aspect of the total organism. The dynamic continuity between these different levels of integration means that any change in a lower level will result in corresponding changes in higher levels, and vice versa" (p. 18). Yet no single provider can have expertise at all organismic levels.

William Doherty, Macaran Baird, and Lorne Becker (1987) reviewed the ways in which the discipline of family medicine has accepted the biopsychosocial model. They suggested that family medicine is following the "split biopsychosocial model"—a transitional phase in which psychosocial issues are recognized as important but are not integrated into clinical care, and assessment and treatment of medical and psychosocial issues are separated and not coordinated or integrated. The split biopsychosocial model also describes the viewpoints of most family therapists, who consider biological and psychosocial domains as separate and distinct, with each involving different professionals. Despite the difficulties raised by attempting to move beyond clinical dualisms and having medical providers, therapists, and families work together collaboratively, the paradigm of integrated biopsychosocial treatment builds on the dreams of early family therapists to offer creative opportunities for medical family therapists.

The Contexts of Medical Care

During the past twenty years, increasing numbers of family therapists have been working in medical and private practice settings with medical colleagues. Some medical family therapists also are physicians, nurses, pastoral counselors, or medical social workers, with traditional ties to medical settings. Increasingly, people primarily trained as family therapists and psychologists are working effectively in hospital and outpatient settings in family medicine, pediatrics, internal medicine, oncology, and subspecialty areas such as transplant and dialysis units. The roles played by therapists in these contexts depend on the particular characteristics of the medical settings.

THE THREE LEVELS OF CARE: PRIMARY, SECONDARY, AND TERTIARY

Medical settings and specialties are grouped into three levels—primary, secondary, and tertiary. Primary care specialties generally provide the first link for patients and families to health care settings. Families go to a family physician, internist, pediatrician, or nurse practitioner for routine health maintenance and for initial evaluation of symptoms. Primary care specialists are trained to treat 80 to 90 percent of all medical problems (Carmichael and Carmichael, 1981; Geyman, 1981). The primary care setting includes the medical office, the community health center, and the walk-in health care facility. Many family therapists have become integral parts of family medicine training programs and private practices. Much of the literature on collaboration between family therapists and physicians reflects the experiences of these family therapists in primary care settings.

When medical problems require specialized care, such as complicated heart disease or complex fractures, patients work with cardiologists or orthopedic surgeons, the secondary care providers. Families may go directly to the specialists or be referred to them by the primary care provider. Chiropractors and acupuncturists, often considered nontraditional providers, are secondary care providers when patients are referred for specific treatments. Secondary care settings include specialty offices and hospitals.

Family therapists in private practice who receive referrals from physicians may be considered secondary care providers. We recently met an obstetrician who pays a full-time salary to a family therapist in his office. The therapist meets with all expectant couples to provide education and support, provides therapy if necessary, and leads groups for pregnancy loss, adjusting to parenthood, sibling issues, and so on. The services are so appreciated by families in the area that the obstetrician believes that the office makes money with this arrangement.

Tertiary care settings provide treatment in highly specific areas, such as pediatric cancer or kidney disease. Tertiary care settings include university teaching hospitals with units designed for care of a particular disease. Family therapists in tertiary care settings become experts in helping families cope with these diseases. They may work in kidney units in which they assist families with coping with dialysis or with deciding whether to have a transplant or have a family member become a donor. These therapists become knowledgeable about medical aspects of the disease, potential problems and coping strategies, and common individual and family responses to the disease.

Most of the examples cited throughout this book highlight family therapists in primary care settings, although examples of work in secondary and tertiary care settings also are described. Primary care settings currently provide the most common context for medical family therapy. However, more and more secondary and tertiary care settings are becoming interested in family therapists who provide medical family therapy.

THE EXAMPLE OF FAMILY MEDICINE

Primary care specialties have been enthusiastic about the biopsychosocial model of health care, and many residency and advanced training programs within primary care specialties are pushing toward an integration of biology and medicine within personal and social contexts. The specialty of family medicine was founded on exactly this premise in an attempt to encompass the biopsychosocial model in theory and practice.

Family medicine arose as a reform movement to counter specialization and fragmentation of patient care (Cogswell, 1981) and in 1968 was recognized as the twentieth medical specialty by the Council on Medical

Education of the American Medical Association. According to the American Academy of Family Physicians (1989), a family physician is trained "to provide continuing comprehensive health maintenance and medical care to the entire family regardless of sex, age, or type of problem, be it biological, behavioral, or social."

To distinguish itself from the old general practice model (which required one year of internship before physicians could practice), the American Board of Family Practice requires three years of training in internal medicine, pediatrics, surgery, emergency care, obstetrics, behavioral science, and numerous subspecialties. John Geyman (1981) noted that "particular attention is directed to the integration of behavioral science with clinical medicine" (p. 109). Accredited residency programs require at least one faculty member to coordinate the teaching and integration of behavioral science. Donald Ransom (1981), a pioneer "behavioral scientist" teacher in family medicine, provided an excellent historical discussion of the roles for such faculty members and described how family theory became popular for guiding behavioral science teaching. Not all residency programs emphasize family systems to the same degree; in some a behaviorally oriented psychologist may direct a program in which residents are exposed primarily to behavioral medicine techniques, such as hypnosis and desensitization, with only superficial exposure to family perspectives. It is increasingly common, however, for programs to be directed by psychiatrists, psychologists, social workers, family therapists, or family physicians with training and interest in family therapy. Thus most family physicians who completed their training during the 1980s have at least minimal competence in family assessment, convening family meetings, and referring families for family therapy.

A Brief History of Family Therapy in Medicine

The recent enthusiasm for the role of family dynamics and family treatment in medicine, which started in the late 1970s and began to flourish in the 1980s, historically can be considered a third wave of interest in the topic. In this century, the first wave of interest in family care occurred in the 1920s through 1940s, and the second wave in the 1950s through 1970s, the early period of family therapy.

Donald Ransom (1981, 1983b) described the early period, beginning with the 1926 Peckham experiment, a research-oriented family club and health clinic in London, and the Pioneer Health Centre, a larger structure and community system organized in 1935 to study the reciprocal interactions of physical and social health of the family unit. Services such as health examinations, health information, and group discussions were supplemented with recreational, gymnasium, and social opportunities. Alternative birthing arrangements, in which mothers and babies could return home after forty-eight hours, and a parent-preschool educational nursery planned by Maria Montessori demonstrated the Centre's commitment to family care and education. A number of significant family systems principles were observed during this project, including the ways in which individual and family development and adaptation to crisis resulted in predictable changes in family structure and adaptation.

In the United States, in 1937, the Macy Project began its study of the family in sickness and health care. This cooperative project of the departments of public health, medicine, and psychiatry at Cornell Medical College and social work and nursing at New York Hospital studied a group of fifteen families for two years. The project report, *Patients Have Families*, was written by Henry Richardson in 1945. Although the book is now out of print, its vivid formulations of the reciprocal influences of families and health are memorable. Ransom (1984) presents a widely quoted passage from Richardson's book: "The idea of disease as an entity which is limited to one person and can be transmitted to another, fades into the background and disease becomes an integral part of the continuous process of living. The family is the unit of illness, because it is the unit of living" (p. 110).

Ransom's (1984) attempt to have *Patients Have Families* reissued led to discussions with Margaret Mead, the member of the original study group responsible for research design and later organization of the family case studies. Surprised by Richardson's (1945) sophisticated description of family processes, Ransom learned that the book drew extensively on the ideas of Mead and Gregory Bateson, who were married at the time. Ransom (1981) notes that Richardson and his team were thirty years ahead of their time. Had World War II not interrupted the project and then been followed by twenty years of emphasis on biomedical technology, the field of family systems medicine might have developed more rapidly.

The third and most prolific wave of development in family therapy occurred in the late 1970s and the 1980s. Within the discipline of family medicine, family physicians like David Schmidt (1978), Jack Medalie (1978), and Lynn Carmichael (1976) have tried to integrate a family systems context into practical care. The most extensive example of this work is F. J. A. Huygen's (1982) English translation of his 1978 volume *Family Medicine: The Medical Life History of Families*. Huygen, a general practitioner from the Netherlands, kept detailed family case histories over decades and documented his patient's relationships between life events, social and developmental stresses, and physical symptoms and use of medical systems. Through his understanding of family dynamics and the role of family therapists, Huygen made distinctions between family therapy and family medicine that are useful for clinical care.

Interest in the role of family theory and therapy in family medicine grew during the 1980s. In 1981, the Society of Teachers in Family Medicine sponsored a conference on "The Family in Family Medicine," which grew to become an annual meeting of clinicians and researchers. An informal newsletter, *Working Together*, was edited for a couple of years in the early 1980s by Michael Glenn, a physician who promoted collaboration between physicians and family therapists. In 1982, the Ackerman Institute sponsored an important conference on "Therapy of Families with Physical Illness." Following the conference, Don Bloch (1983), with Don Ransom, Michael Glenn, and Barry Dym, began publication of *Family Systems Medicine*, a journal at the "confluence of family therapy, systems theory and modern medicine." This journal has published much of the literature on collaboration that is described in chapter 3, as well as interesting research on families and health.

A number of texts for family physicians have emphasized how families can be used in medical care. In *Family Therapy and Family Medicine* (1983), Doherty and Baird, a family therapist and a family physician, identified how family therapy concepts could be used by family physicians to care for common family problems. Janet Christie-Seely (1984), a family physician, edited an extensive text, *Working with the Family in Primary Care*, that includes family theory and clinical applications for the primary care physician. Other texts such as Henao and Grose (1985), Crouch and Roberts (1987), and Sawa (1985) present conceptualizations, techniques, and examples that integrate family systems concepts into medical care. Susan McDaniel, Thomas Campbell, and David Seaburn's (1990) book is a practical, skill-based manual for primary care professionals. The volume and sophistication of these writings fed enthusiasm for this field.

An ongoing debate in the field of family systems medicine examines the appropriate roles of the physician and the family therapist doing counseling or therapy. William Doherty and Macaran Baird (1983) provided a clear distinction between family therapy and primary care family counseling for primary care physicians. Their book documents how primary care physicians inevitably become part of a triangle with the family, whether or not they choose to meet with family groups. Thus physicians are encouraged to think and practice in terms of families by including families in routine health care decisions and management plans. In Janet Christie-Seely's text (1984), she and Yves Talbot contrasted "working with families," in which there is no contract for emotional change, to family therapy, in which families request change. If change does occur in the medical setting, the impetus for change should come from within the family.

Doherty and Baird's recommended skills for primary care physicians were further clarified in their edited casebook, *Family-Centered Medical Care* (1987). The book demonstrated the growth of interest in family systems medicine, for its cases were submitted by many physicians and therapists who were in collaborative and solo practices. Doherty and Baird organized the clinical cases within a framework of levels describing physician involvement with families (see table 2.1). These levels have become a useful means for distinguishing skills for general family physicians and family therapists. The levels represent different degrees of interest and training in family skills and allow physicians to choose how to interact with families and obtain pertinent skills.

- *Level 1: Minimal emphasis on the family.* At this baseline level families are considered as necessary only for medical or legal reasons. No special communication skills are deemed necessary for the caregiver.
- *Level 2: Ongoing medical information and advice.* At this level participants understand the triangular nature of patient-family-provider relations and exercise skills in communicating with

families, primarily about medical issues. Affective communication is not a deliberate focus of the family conference.

- *Level 3: Feelings and support.* This level requires participants to have knowledge of normal family development and responses to stress. As at level 2, the physician meets with families, provides information and medical advice, but also responds to emotional needs of family members. Support, encouragement of alternative responses, and facilitating referrals to therapists when necessary are skills required in level 3 involvement, but no intervention occurs.

- *Level 4: Systematic assessment and planned intervention.* This requires participants to have training and supervision in family assessment and intervention skills. The physician engages members in a counseling session, avoids coalitions, reframes difficulties, and encourages mutually advantageous problem solving. These brief, limited interventions focus on family patterns directly related to the medical problem. Working in this level, the physician monitors progress and refers the family to a family therapist if problems are not amenable to primary care treatment. McDaniel, Campbell, and Seaburn's volume, *Family-Oriented Primary Care: A Manual for Medical Providers* (1990), articulates the specific skills and concepts needed to practice medicine at levels 1 through 4.

- *Level 5: Family therapy.* Providing therapy requires extensive training and supervision beyond primary care residency training. Involvement with families at this level requires the ability to handle intense emotional responses elicited by the work. Just as some primary care physicians choose to obtain special expertise, perhaps through fellowship training in cardiology or infectious disease, others will obtain advance training in family therapy, perhaps by attending a postdegree program. Most family medicine residency training programs promote the distinctions between therapy and counseling in curricula. A small number of family physicians do proceed with advanced family therapy training. In recent years, Macaran Baird (personal communication, 1990), a family physician and family therapist, has abandoned trying to combine the roles of family therapist and family physician with the same families, but other family physician—

TABLE 2.1
Levels of Physician Involvement with Families

Level One: Minimal Emphasis on Family	Level Two: Ongoing Medical Information and Advice	Level Three: Feelings and Support
This baseline level of involvement consists of dealing with families only as necessary for practical and medical-legal reasons, but not viewing communicating with families as integral to the physician's role or as involving skills for the physician to develop. This level presumably characterizes most medical school training in which biomedical issues are the sole conscious focus of patient care.	*Knowledge base:* Primarily medical, plus awareness of the triangular dimension of the physician-patient relationship.	*Knowledge base:* Normal family development and reactions to stress.
	Personal development: Openness to engage patients and families in a collaborative way.	*Personal development:* Awareness of one's own feelings in relationship to the patient and family.
	Skills: 1. Regularly and clearly communicating medical findings and treatment options to family members. 2. Asking family members questions that elicit relevant diagnostic and treatment information. 3. Attentively listening to family members' questions and concerns. 4. Advising families about how to handle the medical and rehabilitation needs of the patient. 5. For large or demanding families, knowing how to channel communication through one or two key members. 6. Identifying gross family dysfunction that interferes with medical treatment, and referring the family to a therapist.	*Skills:* 1. Asking questions that elicit family members' expressions of concerns and feelings related to the patient's condition and its effect on the family. 2. Empathically listening to family members' concerns and feelings, and nomalizing them where appropriate. 3. Forming a preliminary assessment of the family's level of functioning as it relates to the patient's problems. 4. Encouraging family members in their efforts to cope as a family with their situation. 5. Tailoring medical advice to the unique needs, concerns, and feelings of the family. 6. Identifying family dysfunction and fitting a referral recommendation to the unique situation of the family.

Source: W. J. Doherty and M. A. Baird, eds. (1987), *Family-centered medical care: A clinical casebook* (New York: Guilford). Reprinted by permission.

TABLE 2.1 *(continued)*

Level Four: Systematic Assessment and Planned Intervention	Level Five: Family Therapy
Knowledge base: Family systems	*Knowledge base:* Family systems and patterns whereby dysfunctional families interact with professionals and other health care systems.
Personal development: Awareness of one's own participation in systems, including the theraputic triangle, the medical system, one's own family system, and larger community systems.	*Personal development:* Ability to handle intense emotions in families and self and to maintain one's balance in the face of strong pressure from family members or other professionals.

Skills:
1. Engaging family members, including reluctant ones, in a planned family conference or a series of conferences.
2. Structuring a conference with even a poorly communicating family in such a way that all members have a chance to express themselves.
3. Systematically assessing the family's level of functioning.
4. Supporting individual members while avoiding coalitions.
5. Reframing the family's definition of their problem in a way that makes problem solving more achievable.
6. Helping the family members view their difficulty as one that requires new forms of collaborative effort.
7. Helping family members generate alternative, mutually acceptable ways to cope with their difficulty.
8. Helping the family balance their coping efforts by calibrating their various roles in a way that allows support without sacrificing anyone's autonomy.
9. Identifying family dysfunction that lies beyond primary care treatment and orchestrating a referral by educating the family and the therapist about what to expect from one another.

Skills:
The following is not an exhaustive list of family therapy skills but rather a list of several key skills that distinguish level five involvement from primary care involvement with families.
1. Interviewing families or family members who are quite difficult to engage.
2. Efficiently generating and testing hypotheses about the family's difficulties and interaction patterns.
3. Escalating conflict in the family in order to break a family impasse.
4. Temporarily siding with one family member against another.
5. Constructively dealing with a family's strong resistance to change.
6. Negotiating collaborative relationships with other professionals and other systems who are working with the family, even when these groups are at odds with each other.

therapists (Winter, 1989; Crouch, 1987) believe that these roles can be advantageously combined. A sophisticated continuing discussion within academic family medicine is exploring the role of family therapy in medical practice.

The Knowledge Base of Medical Family Therapy

The fundamental tenet of medical family therapy is that *all human problems are biopsychosocial systems problems:* there are no psychosocial problems without biological features and no biomedical problems without psychosocial features. All therapeutic issues involve complex systems dynamics at biological, psychological, interpersonal, institutional, and community levels. We have added the term *systems* to Engel's (1977) biopsychosocial model to go beyond using that model simply as a framework for arranging biological, psychological, and social levels hierarchically and to help explain the interactions across the levels of the multiple social systems involved in health and illness (Doherty, Baird, and Becker, 1987). We emphasize that family therapists apply their sophistication in social systems analysis to biopsychosocial assessment and treatment.

To reduce the complexity of these issues to manageable levels, it is necessary to create areas of focus in professional work. Thus, health professionals often refer to "medical illness" or "physical illness" as distinguished from "mental illness" or "psychosocial problems." Similarly, professionals make distinctions between family problems, psychological problems, physical problems, and community problems. Some professionals concentrate nearly exclusively on the biomedical dimension and others on the psychosocial dimension, while a growing subset is working at areas of overlap between these two traditional domains. As practical as these distinctions may be for everyday discourse, physical and psychosocial problems do not exist as discrete, boundaried domains of reality. Professionals in these fields are dealing with biopsychosocial systems issues in research and practice whether they are aware of those systems issues or not.

Expertise in all aspects of the biopsychosocial systems domain is beyond the ability of individuals and specific professional groups. Given our cultural bias toward believing in a mind-body split, it is not surprising that most health professionals specialize in either the biomedical side or the psychosocial side of the divide. To work in the overlap area stretches health professionals beyond their traditional training and requires a degree of interprofessional collaboration that runs counter to the trend toward autonomy of professional groups, an autonomy newly won and especially treasured by nonphysician mental health professionals.

Contemporary medicine provides a good example of collaboration within its own ranks. Neurologists, for example, know that they cannot practice medicine without closely collaborating with neurosurgeons, radiologists, and other medical specialists. Psychotherapists and family therapists, on the other hand, often treat clients in relative isolation from other professionals. They may consult with therapist colleagues and may collaborate with a psychiatrist for medication purposes, but most therapists, outside of mental hospital settings and occasional cotherapy arrangements, do not work in collaborative teams on cases with other professionals. Because therapists tend to collaborate only with other mental health professionals, rather than with medical professionals, it is relatively easy for therapists to remain narrowly focused on a psychosocial conceptual framework and practice. When the culture splits the mind and the body, professionals tend to line up on either side of the gap—and mistrust the other side.

Medical family therapists operate in the biomedical-psychosocial overlap area of professional activity and must acquire knowledge that is generally inaccessible in their psychosocial systems training. To acquire this knowledge, they must learn from the work of other health professionals, biomedical scientists, and social scientists. Furthermore, since knowledge changes rapidly in the biopsychosocial area, medical family therapists must collaborate with physicians and other health professionals who practice different skills and read different kinds of professional literature.

MAJOR CHRONIC ILLNESSES AND DISABILITIES

Medical family therapists need to have an adequate working knowledge of the major chronic illnesses and disabilities and the resources to learn more basic biomedical facts when faced with specific cases. For therapists to work meaningfully with family medical problems, they need to be as informed as motivated patients are about their diseases.

The basic list of diseases and disease complexes is not long; it includes diabetes, heart disease, hypertension, lung diseases such as asthma and emphysema, the major cancers, plus the most common degenerative diseases such as multiple sclerosis and the muscular dystrophies. Beyond these and several common disabilities such as cervical spinal cord injuries, the therapist should read and consult with medical and nursing colleagues about the particular problems displayed in specific cases.

In addition to understanding common medical problems, the medical family therapist should be informed about the major treatments and their psychosocial implications. For example, a medical family therapist needs to know the following:

- Hypertension generally has no symptoms, and certain antihypertensive medications cause erectile dysfunction.
- Juvenile-onset diabetes involves the failure of the pancreas to produce insulin, and the patient requires lifelong insulin shots and careful attention to diet. Noninsulin-dependent diabetes, with onset generally in adulthood, may or may not require supplementary insulin injections and often can be controlled by weight loss and diet.
- Multiple sclerosis often involves repeating periods of relapse and remission and emotional lability that may be independent of the patient's social situation at the moment.

Medical family therapists are not expected to have expert knowledge about these common diseases but must know enough to be able to work realistically with patients and families experiencing them. They can obtain instruction from three overlapping sources—physicians and nurses; medical encyclopedias and continuing education articles intended for primary care health professionals; and patients and families, many of whom become quite knowledgeable about their health problems. For example, a woman with multiple sclerosis taught her therapist an important fact about the disease when she said, "These tears are my disease talking; I'm actually doing pretty well today." Similarly, reading about genetic predispositions to breast cancer can disabuse a therapist of a simplistic belief that such cancers are caused mainly by a "cancer-prone personality."

RESEARCH IN BEHAVIORAL MEDICINE AND OTHER SOCIAL SCIENCES

Behavioral medicine has produced a significant body of research knowledge about health and illness since emerging as a specialty in psychology in the 1970s. Also called *health psychology* in some circles, this field—in combination with other traditional disciplines, such as social epidemiology, medical sociology, medical anthropology, and nursing—offers bedrock information and perspectives for medical family therapy. Little of this material is available in traditional family therapy education or training. The following areas are particularly relevant to medical family therapy:

- *Stress and illness.* A voluminous body of literature attests to the deleterious effects of psychosocial stress on physical illness (Anatovsky, 1979).
- *Social support and health.* In a review for the journal *Science,* James House, Karl Landis, and Debra Umberson (1988) propose that there is now enough research evidence to assert with confidence that social relationships are a central factor in health and mortality. In fact, the authors concluded that poor social support is a stronger predictor of mortality than cigarette smoking.
- *Health behaviors.* Behavioral medicine and other researchers have explored the strong relationships between health and diet, exercise, and cigarette smoking (Gentry, 1984). Two behavior-related diseases, heart disease and cancer, currently account for 75 percent of all deaths in the United States. The federal government estimates that half of all premature mortality in the United States stems from unhealthy behaviors (U.S. Department of Health, Education, and Welfare, 1979).
- *Cooperation with medical regimens.* Lack of patient "compliance" with medication and other prescribed regimens is a major cause of illness and mortality. The National Heart, Lung, and Blood Institute (1982) estimates that most patients are not taking

enough of their prescribed medication to achieve blood pressure control. Behavioral medicine researchers have examined this issue in depth from psychological and behavioral perspectives.

- *Gender issues in health.* Perhaps because women researchers have been active contributors to the behavioral medicine literature, a rich body of work has examined gender aspects of health, illness, and health behaviors (Blechman and Brownell, 1988). Women have special health issues and concerns about reproductive health, breast cancer, alcoholism, cigarette smoking, care for ill family members, and treatment within the health care system.

Although they have contributed substantially to the understanding of individual behavioral factors in health and illness, social scientists from behavioral medicine have paid less attention to family issues.

FAMILY AND HEALTH RESEARCH

A substantial body of research about families and health now exists. In their book surveying this literature, Doherty and Campbell (1988) used the Family Health and Illness Cycle (figure 2.2) as a model for organizing this research. The cycle delineates the phases of a family's experience with a health problem, beginning with family health promotion and risk reduction and moving clockwise to adaptation to illness or recovery:

1. *Family health promotion and risk reduction.* There is now widespread consensus that most health behavior patterns are learned in and sustained by families. Cigarette smokers tend to marry other smokers (Sutton, 1980) and to smoke similar numbers of cigarettes as their spouses (Venters et al., 1984). Adolescents tend to smoke if their same-sex parent smokes (U.S. Department of Health, Education, and Welfare, 1976).

2. *Family vulnerability and disease onset or relapse.* The most widely used measurement of psychosocial stress, the Holmes and Rahe Social Readjustment Scale (Holmes and Rahe, 1967) contains a weighted list of fifty stressful events that require life readjustment by individuals. No fewer than ten of the fifteen most stressful events are family events, such as divorce, death of a

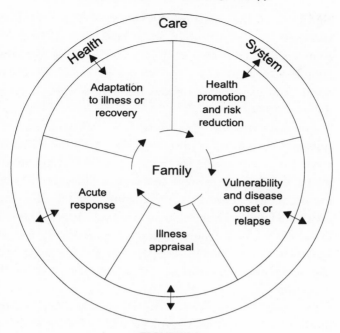

FIGURE 2.2
Family Health and Illness Cycle
Source: W. Doherty and T. Campbell (1988), *Families and health*
(Newbury Park, CA: Sage). Reprinted by permission.

spouse, and major change in health of a family member. Biopsy-chosocial research has begun to discover biological markers for family stress. Kielcolt-Glaser and colleagues (1987) have found that lower marital satisfaction is associated with poor immune system responses. And John Gottman and Lynn Katz (1989) showed that children's stress hormone levels (specifically, cortisol levels) were calibrated to the level of marital distress in their parents. Thus, increasing evidence shows that family-related stress leads to physiological changes that are associated with increased illness.

3. *Family illness appraisal.* In the family sciences, more and more attention has been paid to families' beliefs about health events. In Doherty and Campbell's (1988) words, families tend to have their own "epidemiology" based on their experience with cer-

tain illnesses, their relationship with health care professionals, and their level of education about health issues. Family health activities such as visiting a physician tend to flow from complex consultative processes in which family members share their beliefs and expectations about a family member's symptoms (Litman, 1974).

4. *Family acute response.* This research investigates families' reactions to the immediate onset of a disease or disability, such as a heart attack, a diagnosis of cancer, or a cervical spinal cord injury. Families at this stage of a serious illness tend to become more cohesive immediately following a potentially fatal episode of a family member (Steinglass et al., 1982). This is a time in which medical family therapists occasionally become involved with the family, especially if the therapist is working directly in a medical setting where the acute reaction is occurring.

5. *Family adaptation to illness or recovery.* Medical family therapists are most apt to become involved with a family at this phase. Many families handle the acute phase of an illness well but find the chronic, readjustment phase more problematic. A large body of research has examined how families cope with realigned roles, new interaction patterns, changed social support, and the ongoing stressors of family life (Doherty and Campbell, 1988). Understanding the constraints and opportunities faced by families with chronic illness is a cornerstone of medical family therapy.

SYSTEMS THEORIES ABOUT FAMILIES AND HEALTH

The pioneering contribution to family systems and medical issues was Minuchin, Rosman, and Baker's (1978) psychosomatic family model. This model is based on structural family therapy theory and clinical and research observations of families of children with uncontrolled childhood diabetes for whom organic explanations had been ruled out. Minuchin's team proposed that these psychosomatic families were characterized by patterns of enmeshment, overprotection, rigidity, poor conflict resolution, and triangulation of the child. Although this model has sometimes been misunderstood to imply that family patterns cause disease, the psychosomatic family model posits a circular process whereby family patterns and disease mutually maintain each other (Wood et al., 1989). This model was given initial research support in a study by Minuchin et al. (1978), which showed a link between family interaction and blood glucose levels in certain diabetic children. Although there were methodological problems with this original study, Wood et al. (1989) later found support for some elements of the psychosomatic family model, particularly triangulation and marital dysfunction, in accounting for disease activity in children with Crohn's disease.

A second area of pertinent theory comes from the work of David Reiss, Peter Steinglass, Jane Jacobs, and colleagues at George Washington University. With theory and research that began with mental illness, alcoholism, and the hospital environment, these scholars have shown how families organize around health problems. David Reiss (1981) and Reiss, Sandra Gonzalez, and Norman Kramer (1986) have described how the family's paradigm for coordination is an important factor in its ability to handle serious illness and relationships with the health care system. *Coordination* refers to the family's level of readiness to experience themselves as a single unity, especially in times of stress. Peter Steinglass's model of the alcoholic family (Steinglass et al., 1987) has proved useful in conceptualizing how families with other chronic illnesses can fail to buffer their daily routines and rituals from the illness, thereby allowing the illness to become an organizing principle of the family system.

A third theoretical contribution is John Rolland's (1984, 1988) psychosocial model of illness type and family life cycle. In his 1984 paper in *Family Systems Medicine*, Rolland made the case for a typology of illness that would facilitate the examination of individual and family dynamics in chronic disease—in other words, a psychosocial typology of chronic illness. His proposed typology used four categories—onset, course, outcome, and degree of incapacitation. For the purposes of a medical family therapist, these dimensions directly affect the family's everyday experiences and are likely to be more important than the particular pathophysiology of specific diseases. For example, both Parkinson's disease and rheumatoid arthritis have a gradual onset, have a progressive course, are nonfatal, and are incapacitating. Families with these illnesses will have a different set of challenges than families who have members with illnesses showing a different psychosocial profile, such as ulcerative colitis, which is a relapsing disease that does not follow a constant progressive course. Rolland (1988) integrates this illness typology with phases of the family life cycle, showing how the interaction between the characteristics of an illness and the family's developmental needs can derail a family from its natural course. For example, a parent's cervical spinal cord injury can make it difficult for a young adult child to leave home physically and emotionally.

The biopsychosocial approach to schizophrenia and other mental illnesses offers a fourth relevant theoretical contribution to medical family therapy. Family systems researchers have embraced concepts such as genetic vulnerability, stimulus overload, family communication effects, and expressed emotion. Expressed emotion, which refers to negative criticism and intrusiveness by a parent toward a mentally ill family member, is a particularly strong predictor of relapse and rehospitalization after treatment for schizophrenia (Leff and Vaughn, 1985). Because of their genuine biopsychosocial orientation, family systems theories emerging from the study of schizophrenia offer great potential for being adapted to other medical illness. Lyman Wynne (1989, pp. 507–508) indicates the complexity of this biopsychosocial systems model as applied to schizophrenia:

> What we see clinically in schizophrenic illness is not the simple consequence of an ultimate "etiology" but, rather, that the precursors, onset, and later course are part of a complex developmental, epigenetic process . . . that involves multiple systems levels—genetic and nongenetic biologic factors; rearing and developmental variables, both intrafamilial and extrafamilial; variations in the fit, integration, and developmental time of intrapsychic processes; and the responsiveness of the therapeutic systems that interface with the family systems and the identified patient.

A fifth theory useful for medical family therapy is the family adjustment and adaptation response (FAAR) model (McCubbin and Patterson, 1982; Patterson, 1988), which combines family stress theory and family systems theory. Applied to medical problems, the FAAR model builds on the adjustment and adaptation phase of the family health and illness cycle and examines families' efforts to manage the demands of chronic illness and disabilities in light of their resources, coping patterns, and beliefs. The outcome of this coping process is a level adjustment or adaptation. The FAAR model has been operationalized by a number of self-report instruments and has been applied successfully in research on how families cope with chronic and handicapping medical conditions (Patterson, 1989).

Finally, the Family FIRO Model, an extension of Schutz's fundamental interpersonal relations orientations model (Doherty, Colangelo, and Hovander, 1991) was originally developed by Doherty and Colangelo (1984) for family therapy and later applied to the family dynamics of health behaviors and chronic illness. The model offers three core dimensions of family interaction—inclusion (structure, connectedness, and shared meaning), control (power and influence), and intimacy (close personal exchanges). Publications on cigarette smoking (Doherty and Whitehead, 1986; Whitehead and Doherty, 1989), obesity (Doherty and Harkaway, 1990), and chronic illness (Doherty and Campbell, 1988) have postulated that health behaviors and disorders can serve as ways for family members to be included or excluded from each other's lives, to create battlegrounds for control, and to open or close opportunities for intimacy.

Conclusion

In sum, an important body of literature provides the knowledge base for medical family therapy but is not routinely included in the training of family therapists in the early 1990s. This knowledge base is extensive and better grounded empirically than most of the traditional literature in family therapy. Practicing medical family therapy, then, involves more than "parachuting" into the medical domain with one's existing knowledge. It involves grappling with new and exciting research and theory and in the process expanding the paradigm for treatment.

CHAPTER 3

Collaboration with Medical Providers

COLLABORATING WITH MEDICAL providers plays a central role in the practice of medical family therapy. The partnership between medical providers and family therapists represents an integration of the biological and the psychosocial processes with which our patients struggle. Together, medical providers and therapists can implement an integrated biopsychosocial approach to health and illness. When a patient is struggling with a medical illness and the therapist does not communicate or collaborate with the medical provider, the therapy is very likely to be incomplete or even destructive: doing medical family therapy without collaborating with medical providers is analogous to doing marital therapy with only one spouse.

Achieving a collaborative partnership with medical providers requires therapists to exercise their skills in joining, networking, consulting, and providing large systems assessment and intervention. Developing these skills provides the medical family therapist with opportunities for learning more about physical and biological aspects of problems and for preventing the rigidity, burnout, or "psychosocial fixation" (McDaniel, Campbell, and Seaburn, 1989) that can come from working in isolation. Therapists and physicians can draw on their different perspectives and areas of expertise to share the care and responsibility for challenging, multifaceted cases.

Contexts for Collaboration

Where do medical family therapists practice? Where does collaboration take place? Medical family therapy has only recently been conceptualized as a family therapy specialty, and most of the literature has addressed its presence within primary care medical settings. We have observed collaborative medical family therapy being practiced in the following settings:

1. *Primary care medical and training settings.* Family therapists serve as on-site consultants, referral resources, and cotherapists for physicians and nurses. The employment of family therapists in family medicine residency programs is now quite common. Involvement in primary care practice settings outside of residency training appears to be growing, although reliable figures are not yet available. Some family physicians and pediatricians are recruiting family therapists to spend one or more days per week practicing in their offices. Many payment and other logistical and territorial issues, however, remain uncharted in this form of collaborative practice (Glenn, 1987).

2. *Specialty medical settings.* An increasing number of specialty medical settings are involving family therapists in their work. Medical family therapists have been employed, for example, by a diabetes center to work with children and families, a rehabilitation-fitness center in a neurology clinic to work primarily with back pain patients and their families, and a children's hospital to work with children and families facing serious medical illnesses. These family therapists develop in-depth knowledge of a limited range of medical illnesses and form ongoing collaborative relationships with the medical teams.

3. *Private practice and mental health settings.* Some family therapists in private practice and agency work have developed knowledge and skill in biopsychosocial systems therapy. Often these thera-

pists have medical professionals in their families or extensive personal experience with illness and the health care system. When they begin to receive referrals from physicians, they find it natural to collaborate with them, read about families and health issues, and eventually develop an expertise in medical family therapy. They generally work with a wide range of family problems in addition to medical problems.

Although medical providers and family therapists have much to offer each other in these various contexts, not until the 1980s did close collaboration between the two groups became common. William Doherty and Macaran Baird's (1983) description of their early collaboration inspired other professionals to explore new relationships with colleagues working in hospitals, offices, and agencies. This early enthusiasm also uncovered differences between family therapists and medical providers in their approaches to similar problems—differences that if allowed to go unrecognized or unacknowledged can inhibit successful collaboration.

Challenges to Effective Collaboration

Physicians in primary care see a large number of patients whose primary problems are psychosocial. One study suggested that 15 to 40 percent of primary care patients have a diagnosable mental disorder (Hoeper, Nycz, and Cleary, 1979). Even though some physicians and therapists treat patients with similar problems, both parties report that straightforward and positive relationships between the two groups have been rare. Family therapy, in the early stages of establishing itself as a field, often mistrusted or disapproved of medical approaches to problems. In the early 1980s, when family therapists began to apply systems theory beyond the family to the treatment system and the larger systems relevant to the family, they often viewed medical professionals as part of the problem.

An important article published in 1980 by Mara Selvini, Luigi Boscolo, Gianfranco Cecchin, and Guiliana Prata drew attention to the

TABLE 3.1
*Differences in the the Working Styles of Primary Care
and Mental Health Professionals*

	Primary care professionals	Mental health professionals
Language	Medical	Humanistic, psychoanalytic, or systems
Traditional paradigm	Biomedical	Psychoanalytic
New paradigm	Biopsychosocial	Family systems
Professional style	Action-oriented	Process-oriented
	Advice-giving M.D. takes initiative	Avoids advice
Standard session time	10–15 minutes	45–50 minutes
Demand for services	Around the clock	Scheduled sessions except for emergencies
Use of medications	Frequent	Infrequent
Use of individual and family history	Basic	Extensive
At risk for	Somatic fixation	Psychosocial fixation

Source: S. H. McDaniel, T. L. Campbell, and D. Seaburn (1990), *Family-oriented primary care: A manual for medical providers* (New York: Springer-Verlag), 346. Used by permission.

importance of attending to the referring person in the treatment system. However, the article's title—"The Problem of the Referring Person"— indicated that the referring professional was seen as a part of the patient's difficulties and as a target for intervention by the family therapist. Instead of promoting collaboration, this approach perpetuates the underlying fear of medical providers that therapists will blame them for patients' problems and "shrink" anybody who dares approach them. This is not to say that medical providers or therapists do not become embroiled in their patients' problems; this can and does happen to both kinds of professionals. In fact, part of the value of collaboration lies in the opportunity for collaborators to provide an alternate point of view that can help other professionals recognize their biases and become more effective. Collaboration is not a relationship in which the family therapist is hierarchically superior to the medical provider, or the medical provider is hierarchically superior to the family therapist. It is a partnership of two or more practitioners who respect each other's skills and communicate in a way that enhances the care of mutual patients.

Differences in training, language, theoretical model, and culture have traditionally made it difficult for mental health professionals and medical providers to build successful collaborative relationships (Hepworth and Jackson, 1985; McDaniel and Campbell, 1986). Table 3.1 lists some of the marked differences in working styles that lead to tensions between the two groups of professionals (McDaniel, Campbell, and Seaburn, 1990). These differences, if not acknowledged, impede collaborative work. In a book for medical providers on family-oriented care, Susan McDaniel, Thomas Campbell, and David Seaburn (1990, pp. 346–347) use the following extreme and stereotypic scenario to illustrate how these differences in style, language, and expectations can interfere with collaboration:

DR. P: Hello, this is Dr. Psycho.

DR. M: Hi, Sue? This is Dr. Medic at the Family Medicine Center. I have this patient I'd like you to see, but I just have a minute to tell you about her as I'm already 45 minutes behind in my appointments. She's a 16-year-old primigravida at 34 weeks gestation complicated by some intrauterine growth retardation and mild preeclampsia. The problem is that this lady just won't come in for her prenatal visits or any of the tests she needs. I've tried everything to get her in. She's really impossible! I keep telling her that the baby is going to die if she doesn't do what I tell her. Can you see her? Maybe you can convince her that she's got to come in for these appointments.

DR. P: Well, Dr. Medic, I can hear you're really upset. What do you think is going on? Could she be depressed?

DR. M: I don't know; that's your department. She doesn't look very happy, but who would in her situation? Say, if you want to put her on an antidepressant, let me know so I can be sure it's a safe one for pregnancy.

DR. P: Seems like you're jumping to medications rather quickly, Dr. Medic. I feel I need to know something about the patient, you know, her history and her family, before we rush into pharmacotherapy. What do you know about her family?

DR. M: I don't have time for that stuff. It's hard enough dealing with all her medical problems. All I know is that I've seen her boyfriend and I'm sure he's on drugs. I've checked the lady for AIDS and she's okay so far, but she's not cooperating with me.

DR. P: Boy, sounds like this case is really getting to you. You're pretty angry at her, you know.

DR. M: I am not the patient here. Will you see this patient or not? Just convince her to come back for her tests.

DR. P: Calm down, Dr. Medic. I'm going to need some time to do a complete evaluation on this patient. I've got an opening in two weeks.

DR. M: Two weeks—she'll have a dead baby by then! Besides she probably won't show up. I'm calling now to get an appointment for her, which I'll give to her social worker so I can be sure she'll get there.

DR. P: That's being too directive. We need to use her ability to secure an appointment and get to my office as a measure of her motivation for change. I can't badger her to come. That's her decision.

DR. M: Look, I don't have time for this. Forget about seeing the patient. I'll just call Child Protective. They'll do something about this.

DR. P: I'm sorry, Dr. Medic. I'm trying to be helpful to you. I have to tell you I'm concerned you're falling back on strong-arm tactics instead of demonstrating the caring and sensitivity that's supposed to be part of being a health professional.

DR. M: Big help. Thanks a lot.

DR. P: Good-bye.

Implicit in this satire on physicians' and therapists' styles are differing assumptions about the theory and practice of these two helping professions. Misunderstandings can arise because of differences in the use of language, theoretical paradigms, and the working styles of medical providers and therapists. Professional competition and turf issues also can impede the development of a successful collaborative relationship.

NEGOTIATING LANGUAGE BARRIERS

The language used by professional disciplines reflects the world view of its members. It is useful to remember that some of the language used by family therapists is as incomprehensible to physicians as medical language is to nonmedically trained therapists. In addition, different professions use the same words with different meanings, creating still further opportunities for miscommunications to multiply. An example is the inconsistent usage of the terms *illness* and *disease*. A. Kleinman, M. Eisenberg, and B. Good (1978) distinguish illness, which is the patient's experience, from disease, which is the biomedical understanding of the patient's illness. It may be simplistic, but accurate, to generalize that physicians attend to disease and therapists attend to illness. Professionals need to communicate the focus of treatment and negotiate differences in language or miscommunication can continue.

CLARIFYING THEORETICAL MODELS

In successful collaborative relationships, differences in theoretical models or paradigms are acknowledged and investigated. Physicians are trained in a biomedical model and generally are concerned with identifying pathology and eliminating or halting the pathological processes. This mechanistic orientation has wide utility. Family therapists are trained in a systems model, but many would love to be able to operate from a mechanistic model—to pinpoint the initiation of a dysfunctional pattern and eliminate the process. Common beliefs about etiology in family therapy, however, focus on circular interactions and personal and family belief systems rather than linear, cause-and-effect processes. The different models used by physicians and therapists can result in predictably different assessments of a patient and family.

A physician referred a family to a family therapist because he felt that the parents were neglectful in their management of their child's asthma. The physician recognized that the parents cared about their child, but he felt frustrated that they did little about moving from an apartment in a housing project with flaking concrete and large amounts of dust. He attributed their inaction to laziness. The therapist agreed that the parents were concerned and caring but felt that a great sense of helplessness precluded their changing any aspect of their surroundings.

Differing assessments usually result in differing treatments. In the above case, the physician focused on educating the parents about how their living conditions affected their child's breathing. The therapist, on the other hand, focused on how the parents might make changes in other aspects of their lives so they could gain the confidence to make changes in their living situation. This physician and therapist needed to communicate about their views of the disease and the illness and their goals for treatment in order to support one another, clarify their roles, and negotiate a joint treatment plan.

DIFFERENCES ABOUT MAINTAINING CONFIDENTIALITY

Many therapists are trained not to share the details of therapy with medical professionals, a practice that is often resented by primary care physicians who provide ongoing psychosocially sensitive treatment for their patients. In medical family therapy, therapists and medical professionals need each other equally—for information, consultation, and support.

This problem of sharing information arises because medicine and the therapy disciplines socialize their trainees differently about their roles as helping professionals who maintain patient confidentiality. Therapists and medical providers are committed to respecting the patient's privacy, yet their practices differ. Generally, therapists are taught that the therapy relationship is unlike the patient's relationships with other professionals and that patient confidentiality is sacred. To encourage the patient and family to safely discuss embarrassing or personal material that might help them improve their situation, therapists do not communicate with others about the patient or family without a signed release from the relevant parties.

Medical providers, on the other hand, are trained to work within a health care team that shares relevant information to facilitate patient care. Confidentiality is important and is protected by sharing information only with other members of the team—such as the primary care physician, a nurse practitioner, and specialists involved in the case. When medical providers make a referral to a therapist, they assume that the therapist then becomes part of the team who is sharing information about the patient. A referral may include a detailed letter or a phone call describing a patient, the patient's problem, the physician's assessment of the problem, any treatments that have been tried, and the request for help. The physician would have discussed the referral with the patient and would never consider a communication of this kind with a therapist to be a breach of confidentiality. Medical providers ask for signed releases from patients usually only when asking for past records to be sent to another provider.

Given these differences, it is common for physicians to complain that therapists do not provide them with feedback or interim reports on patients they have referred. It is possible, and essential, for medical family therapists to become part of the treatment team and collaborate with nurses and physicians to provide the patient and family with an integrated treatment experience. To do so—and still remain true to the code of ethics so important to excellent mental health care—therapists and medical providers must negotiate with the patient and family so that they can share information with other professionals working on their behalf. Therapists may wish to obtain signed releases from patients agreeing to this collaboration. Usually patients are pleased to have their providers communicate with each other and coordinate their treatment plans. When this is not the case, the therapist needs to determine whether maintaining confidentiality around a particular topic is reasonable because it does not affect the patient's medical care or whether the issue represents triangulation, is part of the patient's interactional problems, and needs to be handled like any other destructive secret in family therapy.

Sometimes systems organize themselves and manage confidentiality in ways that make collaboration unlikely:

Professionals working at an employee health center for a large corporation wished to have a closer relationship with the group providing mental health services to employees. The two services were geographically separated and used separate charting systems, and health providers at both bemoaned the lack of collaboration. Physicians and nurse practitioners felt that the mental health services group kept their own "shop," would not communicate with them once they referred a patient for therapy, and were of little help in general. Therapists felt that the medical providers were not interested in mental health services and wondered why they received so few referrals.

When the director of the mental health unit and the director of the medical unit discussed this problem with a consultant, issues around confidentiality were identified as a major barrier to collaboration between the two units. Confidentiality in any employee health unit is a major concern, and the mental health services did not release information of any kind about their patients to avoid adversely affecting the employees' work status. If a patient self-referred to a therapist, the policy was that the patient would decide whether to inform the medical provider that he or she was in therapy. This rarely was encouraged, and therapists never negotiated with patients about collaborating with a medical provider. The medical providers, for their part, referred only those patients who requested therapy or were in the process of decompensating.

The discussion with these competent and well-meaning directors heated up when the consultant asked about psychotherapy patients who had medical problems. For example, did the units collaborate when a patient needed to have an HIV test? The director of the mental health unit said that patients occasionally were referred to the medical unit but that AIDS raised such important confidentiality issues that they recommended that patients be tested by the Health Department to ensure privacy. The director of the medical unit became enraged at this and said that the therapists' actions were unethical, since this medical issue was directly related to these patients' medical care. This policy meant that unknowingly some of his staff could be treating patients who were HIV positive, resulting in inappropriate care for these patients. Clearly a nerve had been struck.

The directors eventually calmed down, and the consultant praised both leaders for their strong commitment to caring for patients. Over several sessions they examined practices on both sides that undermined collaboration and then developed policies that protected patient and family confidentiality while allowing for collaboration around joint medical and mental health issues.

WORKING WITH DIFFERENT TIME CONSTRAINTS

Medical providers and family therapists need to acknowledge and accommodate the differences in their working styles to facilitate each other's effectiveness. Therapists entering collaborative relationships can discuss these differences in relatively brief meetings.

Perhaps the most obvious difference in professional working styles is the use of time: therapists typically see patients for fifty to sixty minutes, and physicians are likely to spend ten to twenty minutes with most of their patients. This is not because physicians are arrogant or do not care, but is due to efficient medical practice patterns that allow physicians to treat many patients per day. The time allowed for any single medical patient or family is determined by the goal of the interaction. The length of interaction time naturally affects the quality and the quantity of psychosocial information gathered by each professional. Medical family therapists need to understand the time pressures experienced by their medical colleagues and the conventions for highly efficient communicating with medical providers (to be discussed later in this chapter).

Medical providers and therapists may also differ in their expectations regarding length of treatment: family therapists generally anticipate gradual improvement over time rather than a quick cure, whereas both patients and physicians expect cures to come when a patient interacts with the medical system, and the sooner the better. At the time of referral, the family therapist should communicate with the medical provider about expectations regarding length of family therapy treatment to prevent misunderstandings between professionals or with the family.

Finally, medical providers are taught to give advice, and therapists are taught to eschew that role. Again, this difference arises from the differing functions of the two professionals. The physician is a biomedical expert from whom patients and families seek medical advice, and advice giving is part of the medical ritual through which the physician shares information and shows that he or she cares. Patients also seek advice from mental health professionals. Part of the art of therapy is helping patients and families arrive at their own solutions without frustrating their need to feel an expert is advising and caring about them.

COMPETING FOR TURF

Physicians and therapists easily are drawn into competitive struggles about who best understands or is most effective in caring for patients. These struggles are rooted in the differences in training, language, and theory that have already been discussed, as well as the economics of health care and the cultural hierarchies that affect each profession. Family therapists may resent the financial and social power that physicians typically have. Physicians perform necessary and valued work, and other people often make allowances so that work can be done. When one of us was detained in a hospital elevator by two physicians who held open the door while conversing, another physician asked them to complete their conversation outside the elevator. He then explained to the passengers that the physicians appeared inconsiderate but that "doctors who are involved with the care of a patient are not aware of anything else." The physicians' conversation could have been about gardening, but their bad manners were to be excused by their medical responsibilities.

Stories of physician abuse of power abound, but the stories also may reflect intimidation or perhaps envy of the privileged status of physicians in some settings. Without open acknowledgment of differences in cultural prestige, associated power, and salary, however, these inequities will remain barriers to effective collaboration and cooperative care for families.

Therapists also have been known to behave badly. Family therapists sometimes respond to financial or power differentials with physicians by either acting deferential and eventually passive aggressive, or acting competitive and actively aggressive. Both of these defensive patterns can lead to undesired physician behavior and initiate a sequence of competitive rather than collaborative interactions. Unresolved disagreements based on actual interaction or general resentment result in poor contacts for referral, increased likelihood for triangulation by families, and less successful treatment.

Inequities do exist in the way health care is reimbursed in the United States, but large-scale financial issues are best addressed by active participation in our professional organizations. One-to-one interactions between physicians and therapists around patient care work best when founded on mutual support and respect. John Sargent (1985) emphasized the importance of the therapist valuing his or her own work, performing as a professional who exercises a set of skills and not as an adjunctive provider following the physician's lead. Clarifying roles and responsibilities helps the family therapist support the physician in providing successful medical care for the patient and helps the physician support the family therapy. Respecting the professional territory of the physician without giving up our own space provides the foundation for healthy collaboration between professionals.

Fostering Collaborative Relationships

Family therapists are uniquely equipped to overcome barriers to collaboration with medical providers. They understand systems and the multiple perspectives that occur in any one context and therefore can position themselves to understand the experiences of patients, families, and members of the medical treatment team. Accessibility to the treatment team and systems consultation skills are the prerequisites to effective collaboration.

ACCESSIBILITY

In 1990 the Task Force on Family Therapy and Family Medicine, composed of representatives of the American Association for Marriage and Family Therapy and the Society for Teachers of Family Medicine, conducted an informal survey of sixty family therapists and physicians involved in collaborative relationships (Campbell and Williamson, 1990). The major themes that emerged from these questionnaires were that therapists wanted respect from their medical colleagues and that physicians wanted therapists to be accessible when they needed them. (Physicians also wanted therapists to respect their time constraints and skills as physicians, and support the physician-patient relationship during psychotherapy.)

All agreed that the easiest way to be accessible is to share office space, and many therapists now practice in a physician's office either part- or full-time. This arrangement allows therapists easy access to referrals, physicians easy access to consultation, and patients easy access to mental health treatment. Whether medical family therapists work in the same building or across town from their medical colleagues, being accessible means having a secretary, an answering service, or an answering machine; promptly returning calls; and arranging to be available on the hour, for example, so that medical colleagues can communicate as needed. It also means meeting with medical providers.

Nothing substitutes for knowing a referral source personally: it can be as essential to the overall success of medical family therapy as is joining with the patient and his or her family. Macaran Baird, a family physician, described how he developed a personal network when he began his practice by meeting with physicians, therapists, police, and social service workers in his community (Doherty and Baird, 1983). Once he had invested this relatively small amount of time joining with the professional members of his community, he then was able to pick up the phone and collaborate, refer, or request help from many of these people in an efficient and effective way.

Therapists are often reluctant to ask for time from physicians and might find it helpful to secure an introduction from a respected medical colleague. Even without this, many physicians welcome an invitation to lunch or a direct request for time to discuss common interests because their patients need therapy services and they themselves need professionals who are reliable and competent and do not undermine a patient's medical treatment. At these meetings physicians and therapists can discuss treatment philosophies, common treatment strategies, and preferences for how to communicate once a referral is made, and thus form the cornerstone for subsequent collaboration.

THE ETIQUETTE OF COLLABORATION: A SYSTEMS CONSULTATION MODEL

Traditionally, primary care medical providers consult with specialists about their patients. Etiquette about this consultation includes brief letters of referral from the referring physician, one or more letters from the consulting physician documenting diagnosis and treatment of the patient, an understanding that the consultant will deal only with patient concerns in his or her own area of expertise, and support for the relationship between the patient and the referring physician. Many physicians make mental health referrals just as they do referrals for oncology or opthamology, and they expect family therapists to conform to traditional medical etiquette.

A systems consultation model (Wynne, McDaniel, and Weber, 1986) allows family therapists to merge systems theory and techniques with a consultative role that conforms to medical etiquette. The systems consultation model identifies the consultee, the consultee's concern, the preferred outcome, and the anticipated duration for the consultation. Systems consultation emphasizes brief treatment that respects the primary responsibility of the consultee.

Susan McDaniel, Thomas Campbell, Lyman Wynne, and Timothy Weber (1988) distinguish consultation from supervision by who takes responsibility for the case. In supervision, the supervisor retains ultimate responsibility for the case, whereas in consultation, the consultee initiates the consultation and retains the ultimate responsibility. The three common forms of collaborative relationships that build on these principles of systems consultation are consultation, cotherapy, and limited referral (Hepworth and Jackson, 1985; McDaniel, Campbell, and Seaburn, 1990).

Consultation

With consultation, therapists and physicians are available to one another to provide information, suggestions, and support. The "informal hallway" consultation (Hepworth and Jackson, 1985) is available to practitioners whose paths cross because of geographic proximity to each other or because the providers have easy telephone access to each another. A physician may call a therapist before she sees an adolescent and mother for a follow-up visit because she wants to know how to screen this patient for anorexia. A therapist may stop a physician in the hall to ask whether a medical evaluation is appropriate for a particular symptom. Such discussions may or may not result in follow-up discussions, formal consultations, or referral. They reflect an ongoing, mutually respectful relationship between colleagues.

Formal consultations are also common. Consultations may occur between the therapist and physician or among therapist, physician, and family. Formal consultations frequently occur in medical training programs or hospital settings in which therapists are on site and available for lengthy discussions and follow-up. Tom Andersen (1984), from Norway, does not have his own office but travels to offices of general practitioners where he consults with the physicians and sees their patients. Family therapists as consultants are responsible for clarifying the nature of formal consultation, contracting for it, and negotiating appropriate boundaries and roles (Wynne, McDaniel, and Weber, 1986).

Cotherapy

In cotherapy both physician and therapist meet in one room with the family and negotiate a division of labor according to their respective skills. The division of labor distinguishes this relationship from a cotherapy relationship involving two therapists, but as with any cotherapy arrangement, the physician and family therapist must negotiate roles, hold frank discussions of the relationship between the collaborators, and continue evaluating the process and content of sessions. Cotherapy treatment teams are very effective with families in which medical problems are chronic and variable or families who are inappropriately focused on somatic problems (McDaniel, Campbell, and Seaburn, 1989). For these concerns, the simultaneous involvement of medical and family therapy providers allows for a closely integrated biopsychosocial approach in which biological and psychosocial processes can be discussed together, information can be shared, and triangulation can be minimized.

Cotherapy teams occur in a number of contexts. Cotherapy is easily available in medical training programs where family therapists are involved in teaching and clinical care. Thomas Campbell and Susan McDaniel (1987) describe family systems treatment by their cotherapy team for chronic illnesses and somatization disorder. Cotherapy occurs less frequently in private practice, but some fascinating experiments are being conducted by pioneers in the private practice setting.

Barry Dym and Stanley Berman (1986) describe a joint health care team of a family physician and a family therapist who together hold an initial meeting with all patients. After evaluating the symptoms and stressors from a systemic perspective, the two practitioners often work separately but with frequent, brief joint meetings. Based on his own practice experience as a family physician, Michael Glenn (1985) proposed a similar collaborative model in which the family physician and the family therapist form the core of a primary health care team that involves other health personnel as needed.

Limited Referral

In limited referral, the most common form of collaboration, the family therapist and the physician both treat the family but in different settings and with varying degrees of communication and cooperation. Limited referrals are those referrals in which care is not transferred from one practitioner to the other; instead, different kinds of care occur simultaneously. With these referrals, all providers are responsible for their respective treatments, and role clarification is essential.

Many collaborative relationships between family therapists and physicians are limited referrals. Family therapists in hospital settings are rare (McCall and Storm, 1985), but as members of the health care team, they generally accept referrals and are in close contact with other members of the health care team. Charts are shared, patients and families are discussed, and treatment plans are coordinated. Family therapists in medical training settings (Hepworth et al., 1988; Seaburn et al., in press) also frequently work as limited referral sources with separate sessions, but with much contact between physician and therapist providers.

Limited referrals are common in private practice. Most family therapists receive some referrals from physicians or nurses but may not think of themselves as collaborative partners. However, interest in increasing collaboration is high. The joint task force of the American Association for Marriage and Family Therapy and the Society of Teachers of Family Medicine was commissioned in 1990 to study and advance collaborative models in practice (Tilley, 1990).

Models for these relationships have been described for pediatricians and family therapists, who discuss cases throughout treatment and include a joint initial session if possible (Frey and Wendorf, 1984; Sargent, 1985). Although they work in different physical locations, the providers inform families that they communicate and function as a team. Michael Glenn, Linda Atkins, and Robert Singer (1984) believe that therapists and physicians who share office space increase the likelihood of referrals and provide more comprehensive care for families. Therapists and physicians in this model practice discuss cases frequently but generally do not see families together.

Location of practice may increase the rate at which referrals turn into contracted therapy sessions, but working in close proximity does not guarantee effective collaboration. Crane (1986) detailed her expectations and experiences working in a health maintenance organization with medical providers. She described how limited time for discussion and lack of role clarification between providers led to adversarial and conflictual relationships among providers and frustration with patients. Crane's experience underlines the importance of communication and role clarification for successful collaboration with limited referrals.

Communicating with Medical Providers about Referrals

Regardless of the structure of the collaborative relationship, communication about shared patients is at the center of collaboration and begins when either the therapist or the medical provider requests help. In this section we focus on communicating with the medical provider around a limited referral, but many of the principles discussed here are also relevant for cotherapy and consultation.

EXPLORING THE REFERRAL QUESTION

When a medical provider makes a referral to a medical family therapist, the therapist needs to solicit information about the referral. A phone call is usually necessary to clarify why the physician referred the patient, the stage of the patient's illness, the initiator for the referral (was it the provider, the patient, or the family?), and how the physician wishes to remain involved. Medical providers should be encouraged to call the therapist before they speak with a difficult patient about a referral so that the family therapist can help the physician to phrase the referral to sound noncritical, nonblaming, and nonabandoning.

The timing of a referral can be critical. When a referral is premature, the physician may be more motivated for the treatment than either the patient or the family. In these cases, the family is most likely not to appear for their appointment with the therapist. The medical family therapist may wish to attend the patient's next medical appointment, so that all parties can discuss when and if to agree to the referral. Or the therapist may suggest how the physician can better manage the patient in his or her practice and slowly seed the idea of a therapy referral (Seaburn et al., in press). With many patients, the referral process requires the medical provider to cultivate a complex set of assessment and interviewing skills while being supported by the medical family therapist.

Sometimes the referral comes from the patient or the physician when considerable stress accompanies the diagnosis and treatment of a serious illness. Other times the patient or family has become embroiled in a struggle with the medical treatment system. Most physicians are trained to cure diseases but not to treat the experience of illness (Shields, Wynne, and Sirkin, 1992). The patient or family may diagnose the problem one way and the physician another, leading to conflict and an eventual referral. Sometimes family therapists are consulted when the patient's experience of illness may not be recognized or validated by the medical team.

Exploring the referral question begins the process of ecosystemic assessment of the problem (Auerswald, 1985) so that a comprehensive therapy treatment plan can be devised that includes support for the patient's medical care. If the first step in this process—soliciting the referring person's point of view about the problem—is ignored, problems for the case may arise.

One of our first medical referrals was from an obstetrician who requested a "psychological evaluation" of a thirty-nine-year-old single female patient who was requesting a donor insemination procedure to have her first child. The obstetrician said he always asked any nontraditional OB patients to see a therapist, both for his own protection and for the patient and her family to have the opportunity to discuss the request and its likely consequences.

The therapist thought that this request sounded straightforward and scheduled a session with the patient, her mother, and her sister to discuss the procedure. During the session, it became clear that the patient was quite ambivalent about the procedure and was more interested in proving to her family that she was an "adult" than she was in actually raising a child. The session ended with the woman realizing she did not want to proceed with the insemination and the family agreeing to open communication and increased contact among themselves.

When this outcome was reported back to the referring physician, he became angry and implied that the therapist had "talked this woman out of her last chance to have a baby." The therapist then realized that she had not explored the physician's view of the problem when he made the referral. It was several years before this physician made another referral. This therapist learned to spend time in the early phase of the referral soliciting the physician's view and discussing the possible outcomes of a consultation.

CLARIFYING ROLES

Successful collaboration requires negotiation and role clarity. Lyman Wynne, Susan McDaniel, and Timothy Weber (1986) note that role confusion in the consultative relationship results in ambiguities in the therapeutic relationship. Patients may bring biomedical complaints to therapy and psychosocial complaints to their physician. Thus clarification of the nature of the consultative relationship is one of the most important requirements of effective collaboration. The physician and the therapist need to have a coordinated plan about how to treat the patient. For a patient with chronic headaches, the physician may wish to order tests and prescribe medications, leaving the stress reduction and counseling to the family therapist. Then, when the patient's husband questions the therapist about the medication being given to his wife, it is relatively easy to refer him back to the physician. Similarly, therapists must communicate to physicians the particular areas they wish to handle. Sometimes it is helpful to suggest that patients or families who raise a particular emotional issue with the physician be encouraged to raise their concerns in their next therapy session. Such role clarity limits destructive patterns of triangulation.

Medical providers and family therapists need each other. Physicians, particularly primary care physicians, are taught to feel responsible for attending to all the patient's complaints. By making a successful referral, many physicians feel they can respond to the patient's concern without having to treat the patient themselves in an area in which they do not feel skilled.

Sometimes colloboration in medical family therapy also includes other mental health providers. A depressed patient may require a medication evaluation from a psychiatrist or a primary care physician. A patient with chronic pain may benefit from acupuncture or biofeedback. Some patients with chronic illness benefit from psychoeducational multi-family groups (Gonzalez, Steinglass, and Reiss, 1987). Many avenues are available for the psychosocial treatment of patients with physical illness. However, multiple treatments and multiple providers open the door for multiple iatrogenic* problems.

The key to developing a sound medical family therapy treatment plan is to use the *minimum number of providers* to accomplish the maximum number of goals for treatment. When multiple mental health providers participate in one case, the family therapist needs to negotiate clear expectations regarding who is to do what and to maintain close communication with the other therapists. A network session with the mental health providers, the family, and the medical providers is usually important to achieving these goals (Speck and Attneave, 1972).

THE JOINT INITIAL SESSION

It is courteous and helpful to extend an invitation to the first therapy session to the referring physician and any other care provider very involved in the treatment of the patient. In one recent case a cardiologist and a marital therapist needed to coordinate their treatment plan with a couple who had experienced sexual and marital dysfunction after the husband's heart attack. Some physicians are interested in closely collaborating with a family therapist out of intellectual curiosity, dedication to their patients, or conflicting personal issues that are impeding treatment. Other medical providers may decline the invitation either because of the time demands of their practice or because they do not believe that a meeting is necessary. Many times the limited referral model is sufficient for successful collaboration.

It can be essential to have the referring person or relevant medical providers available for the intake if the referral concerns a case in which there is considerable doubt or disagreement about the diagnosis ("illness ambiguity") (Shields, Wynne, and Sirkin, 1992), a severely somatizing or resistant patient, or a problematic doctor-patient relationship. Without direct contact among all involved parties, the chances for lasting change will be minimal.

*_Iatrogenic_ is commonly used in medicine to mean symptoms caused by medication or treatment rather than by disease.

For situations requiring close collaboration in which the medical provider seems reluctant, the therapist may suggest holding the joint session at the physician's office. Sometimes it is not necessary for the physician to attend the entire interview. The physician may join the therapist at the beginning or the end of a session to describe a diagnosis or procedure, answer questions, and emphasize the collaborative nature of the treatment. When the therapist and the physician are unable to be in the same place at the same time, many medical providers are willing to speak by phone because it takes little time away from their patient care. By scheduling a phone call and using a speaker phone, it is possible to have the referring provider speak to the therapist and the family during the first part of an initial session to relate the reasons for the referral and discuss any issues of mutual concern.

An initial network session with the professional care providers, the patient, and family members is the most powerful way to begin a difficult medical family therapy case. It allows all parties to discuss the reasons for the referral, the goals for treatment, and the interaction between the medical and the therapy treatment plans. Professional roles can be clarified immediately. Compatibility between the medical and the psychotherapy goals can be ensured. This visible collaborative effort demonstrates to the family that the physician and therapist will work together to help them reach their goals. It helps to mitigate against any feeling by the patient that the referral represents criticism or abandonment by the physician. A network session begins the process of openly clarifying and negotiating what Shields, Wynne, and Sirkin (1992) have described as the differing perspectives of illness that are inevitably represented by patients, family members, and health care professionals.

REPORTING TO THE REFERRAL SOURCE

Many physicians report that they receive *no* communication from therapists to whom they refer. Therapists, of course, complain that physicians are busy and difficult to reach, but most physicians will respond to a persistent attempt to communicate. Treatment without communication is like two blindfolded drivers on a racetrack; not colliding is a matter of luck. Communication is the foundation of successful collaboration.

At medical school physicians learn to use a straightforward, concise style of communicating about patient care that highlights important issues and saves time so they can treat as many patients as possible per day. Many family therapists find this style of communicating formal and dry and instead are interested in lengthy descriptions of patient and family dynamics and debates about possible treatment strategies. Some physicians who are psychosocially oriented may enjoy such details, but many find them unnecessarily time consuming. Until the therapist and physician develop a personal relationship and negotiate the specific kind of information to be shared, the therapist should conform to the medical culture and communicate in a brief and timely fashion.

Most physicians send letters to therapists describing the patient and the reasons for referral, as is the custom with referrals to any tertiary provider. In return the physician expects pragmatic letters from the therapist regarding assessment, treatment, and recommendations for the physician. These letters may communicate information valued by the traditional medical model (for example, a mental status report) as well as information about systems dynamics that might be useful in the medical care of a patient. Physicians appreciate a written report for the patient's chart. Phone calls are sometimes also necessary but should be brief during physicians' patient hours when time is already pressured for the medical provider. Early in a collaborative relationship, the therapist may wish to clarify the kind and the frequency of communication both physician and therapist desire, such as when each feels that discussion of a case is necessary.

Jeffrey Harp, a family physician with family therapy training, has described three categories of referrals and the expectations that a referring physician is likely to have regarding communication from the therapist (1989) (see table 3.2). Assessment of the nature of the doctor-patient relationship is necessary for successful collaboration. For many patients, appropriate communication includes a routine letter following intake to describe initial impressions and treatment plan, and a termination summary at the end of treatment. These cases may be referred by a physician who prefers not to handle psychosocial problems or by a patient who prefers not to discuss a problem with the physician. Physicians in the midrange group are well versed in their patients' psychosocial problems. They may have attempted primary care counseling and reached an impasse. Typically they desire greater involvement, like to be consulted about their assessment of the patient and family and to

TABLE 3.2
*Physicians' Expectations Regarding Communication
after a Mental Health Referral*

Physician closeness to patient	Who initiates the referral	Expectations of own role	Expectations of therapist
Distant	Physician or patient	Minimal	Intake and termination letters
Mid-range	Physician	Assess patient, remain involved	Support prior work, monthly feedback
Intense	Physician	Treat patient, co-author treatment plan	Frequent feedback, consult on treatment, "cure"

Source: This table was constructed from ideas presented at a talk on "Physicians' Expectations from Therapists" given by Jeffery Harp, M.D., at a Division of Family Programs meeting in the Department of Psychiatry, University of Rochester School of Medicine, April 25, 1989.

describe the treatment to date, and are likely to want interim reports regarding treatment, in addition to the intake and termination notes. It is important for the family therapist to identify cases falling in the final category—the intense doctor-patient relationship. In these cases the patient may have stimulated the physician's own personal issues so that the physician is angry with the patient or is more motivated for the patient to begin therapy than is the patient or family. The physician in these situations is likely to have high expectations for therapy and may send a message that "the therapist must fix this patient as soon as possible." Close communication between this physician and the therapist is essential; in fact, the physician may wish to attend some or all of the therapy sessions.

Conclusion

Medical family therapists collaborating with medical providers require persistence and creativity. Family therapists must find common interests with their medical colleagues, gain the trust of these medical providers, and show that medical family therapy can be helpful to them and their patients. Collaborators who overcome barriers created by training and professional rivalries can enjoy the professional stimulation and enthusiasm that results from working together to deliver high-quality care to families. This collaborative relationship between family therapists and medical providers forms the foundation for the successful implementation of medical family therapy techniques with the patient and the family.

CHAPTER 4

Techniques for Medical Family Therapy

MANY FAMILY THERAPY TECHNIQUES are available to promote agency and communion in families with a member who has a physical illness. This chapter describes seven sets of techniques that together operationalize the medical family therapy model (see table 4.1). The intervention approaches in medical family therapy go beyond generic family therapy techniques. We are not maintaining that the strategies described here are outside of the practice of many family therapists, only that, in some cases, these issues have not been emphasized in family therapy training and take on special significance in medical family therapy. These techniques integrate concerns about health and illness into a systems framework for psychotherapy and represent an approach to psychosocial aspects of illness that can be adapted and expanded by therapists with different theoretical orientations.

Referrals for medical family therapy occur at different points in the course of an illness. The stage of the illness (Rolland, 1984) at the time of the referral affects how medical family therapy techniques are implemented. Cases referred in acute crisis, either at the time of a disturbing diagnosis or when a patient enters a terminal phase, require active structuring until the level of anxiety in the family lowers and people can both speak and listen to each other. Cases referred in a chronic phase

TABLE 4.1
Medical Family Therapy Techniques

---

1. Recognize the biological dimension.

2. Solicit the illness story.

3. Respect defenses, remove blame, and accept unacceptable feelings.

4. Maintain communication.

5. Attend to developmental issues.

6. Increase a sense of agency in the patient and the family.

7. Leave the door open for future contact.

---

often have developed dysfunctional ways of coping with the illness and may require techniques that facilitate the patient and family becoming "unstuck." In all cases, support by the medical family therapist for an appropriate physician-family relationship is important.

Because of the challenges facing families and patients with physical illness, therapists need to be flexible and creative. The format of medical family therapy will vary with the illness and the family issues of each individual case. Typically, a medical family therapy case will involve sessions with individuals, the couple, the family, *and* the family plus the professional team. A family therapist who can conduct all these sessions is likely to provide the patient and family with the most efficient and effective care.

The case of Ellen F is used throughout this chapter to illustrate the implementation of medical family therapy techniques. Ellen F was a twenty-nine-year-old married woman who first came to psychotherapy for marital problems related to difficulties with in-laws. She was referred then by her gynecologist. The couple was seen for fifteen sessions and terminated successfully. Seven years later, Ellen returned for therapy when her father became ill and seemed to be demented and she was feeling internal and external pressures to take a central role in her family of origin:

> The first course of treatment occurred when Bob F's father was terminally ill (see figure 4.1). At the time of referral, Bob had been

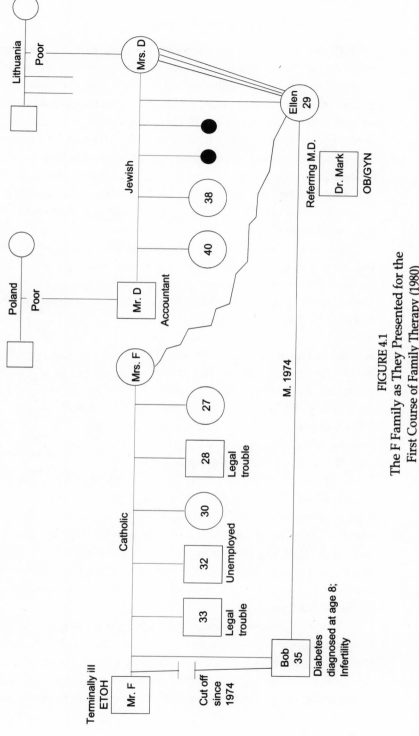

FIGURE 4.1
The F Family as They Presented for the
First Course of Family Therapy (1980)

cut off from his parents for six years, since his marriage to Ellen. Bob's father had a history of alcohol abuse; Bob and his five siblings had a difficult childhood fending for themselves while their mother worked to support the family. Bob was the oldest child in a Catholic family and now had the best-paying job, the most stable family life, and none of the scrapes with the law that his brothers experienced. Bob also had diabetes that had been diagnosed at and treated since age eight. He had infertility related to his diabetes and was resistant to his wife's plea for them to have children through donor insemination. This issue was central in many of their arguments.

Ellen came from a conservative Jewish family with whom she was very close. She was the youngest of three girls. All her grandparents were immigrants from Eastern Europe, and both her parents grew up poor. Her father was a successful accountant who had provided well for his family, although he was rarely away from his work. Her mother was a warm woman who Ellen felt always seemed be hungry for affection and attention. Ellen was special to her mother because she was born after two miscarriages, and as the youngest she held the same position that her mother had in her own family. Ellen's sisters were considerably older than she, so Ellen spent a lot of time with her mother during childhood. She described her relationship with her mother as "inverted—I took care of her more than she took care of me."

Late in adolescence, when Ellen and her mother frequently fought, Ellen sometimes fled to her older married sister's house. Finally, at nineteen, Ellen left home after "one more screaming match." Three years later she met and married Bob. He was six years older than she, and she was attracted to his seeming stability. After her marriage she became closer to her parents, and by the time she first appeared for therapy, she spoke to her parents by phone at least once a day.

The first course of therapy focused on leaving home and early marriage issues. During this treatment, Bob was able to mend the cut-off with his parents and reestablish a relationship with his sick father. As his parents learned more about Ellen, they were increasingly accepting of the match. They especially appreciated the way Ellen insisted that Bob take care of his health. Toward the end of this treatment, sessions occurred in which each family came in to bless the marriage and offer their advice to the young couple. These sessions were poignant because of the adversity the parents had experienced and because Bob's father was dying.

The couple managed to consolidate their commitment to each other and to attend to important issues in Bob's family after his father's death. Bob's feelings toward his family remained ambivalent, but he was able to interact with them and do what he felt he needed to do to stay connected. Soon after his father's death Bob agreed to donor insemination after exploring the issue in three therapy sessions, one of which was with the referring physician and the therapist at the physician's office. When they terminated from therapy, Ellen was pregnant with their first child. About a year later, they brought their baby daughter to the office to introduce her, and all looked very happy.

Now six years later, Ellen presented again feeling very stressed by the demands of her employment, her two children, and especially her mother, who seemed to become unglued as her father deteriorated. Ellen's obstetrician/gynecologist had suggested that she return to see a therapist because he felt that her gastrointestinal symptoms were reactions to stress (see figure 4.2).

Dr. Mark, Ellen F's referring physician, fell in the midrange in terms of his involvement in Ellen's difficulties (see table 3.2). He was Ellen's mother's physician; he had been involved in discussing Ellen and Bob's infertility issues; he had conducted the donor insemination procedures; and he had delivered the couple's two children.

When Dr. Mark called to refer Ellen for the second course of treatment, he knew her and her family well, and the concern in his voice was noticeable. His assessment of the situation was solicited, and he confirmed that Ellen's mother was decompensating in the face of her husband's deterioration. Ellen's mother had refused Dr. Mark's suggestion that counseling might be helpful to her, but he hoped that Ellen's mother might be engaged in some treatment through Ellen. He would monitor both Ellen's and her mother's physical condition closely and was happy to have a conjoint session or provide any other help that he could.

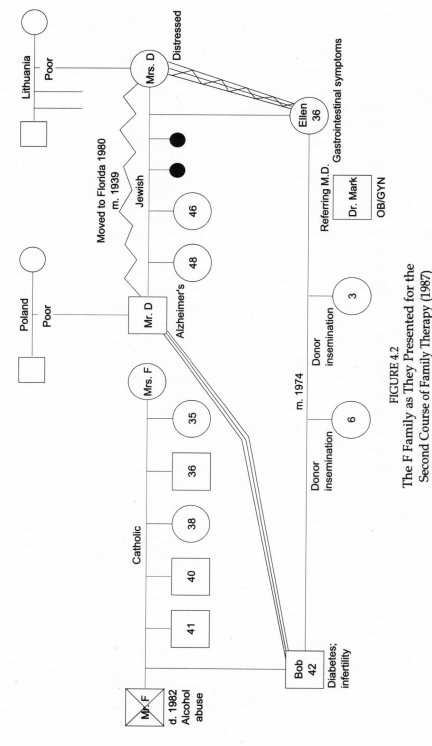

FIGURE 4.2
The F Family as They Presented for the
Second Course of Family Therapy (1987)

Recognizing the Biological Dimension

By working with physicians and families with medical problems, family therapists develop a more balanced approach to understanding human behavior. As we recognize and respond to physical as well as mental processes, we become more comprehensive and systemic in our practice of psychotherapy. When therapists ignore illness in patients, which can happen in traditional family therapy and psychotherapy, family members feel invalidated in their experience. Family therapists working in medical contexts need to feel comfortable with the physical domain and to be curious about the biological subsystem of the patient and sometimes other family members as well. Table 4.2 summarizes our approach to addressing the biological dimensions of illness.

FOCUS ON THE PATIENT

A principle underlying many standard family therapy techniques is that the label *patient* is used by the family to scapegoat one of its members. Many family therapists eschew the idea of a labeling one distressing family member as the patient. In medical family therapy, a patient *does* exist—it is the person with an illness. Part of joining with the family is accepting the medical provider, the patient, and the family's focus on the healing of this person. Family therapy eventually leads to discussing the coping strategies of all members of the family who are

TABLE 4.2
Recognizing the Biological Dimension of Illness

---

1. Start with a focus on the patient.
2. Use a psychoeducational approach to explain the difference between psychotherapy and other medical encounters.
3. Ask the physician to explain the patient's illness, its prognosis, and its possible course.
4. When there is ambiguity or disagreement about the diagnosis, maintain an open, exploratory stance.
5. Maintain humility about the possibility of biological change.

---

being affected by this illness, but the therapy needs to begin with a focus on the patient. Other family members are best approached as consultants in helping the patient deal with the illness (Wynne, McDaniel, and Weber, 1986). If, as in marital therapy, the family is encouraged to share responsibility for the problem, family members are likely to feel blamed for their loved one's illness—a feeling that therapy should remove rather than exacerbate.

EXPLAIN THE DIFFERENCE BETWEEN PSYCHOTHERAPY AND OTHER MEDICAL ENCOUNTERS

All patients hope for an easy cure—for physical problems, emotional problems, and interpersonal complaints. Medical family therapists who practice within a medical setting may discover that patients expect interactions similar to those they have experienced with physicians (Seaburn et al., in press): children may expect to get shots, adults may expect to get pills, and all patients expect to get answers and advice. Although medical care certainly benefits when the patient and family take responsibility for the illness and for implementing the treatment plan, empowering the patient and family is essential for successful psychotherapy. The medical family therapist must ask the patient and family in the first session, "What do you expect from therapy? What are your goals for treatment?" These questions begin the process of shifting the expectations they might have about coming to their physician to appropriate expectations for therapy. This reorientation educates them about the length of session, contact between sessions, the role of the therapist as facilitator or coach, and the role of the patient and family members as important players in this situation—the people who use their wisdom, strengths, and resources to face the challenges before them. It also should reassure children that therapy does not involve injections—or receiving stickers or toys after sessions. Once the patient and the family are oriented to the therapy setting, the therapist can ask questions that explore the patient's medical problems.

SOLICIT THE PHYSICIAN'S EXPLANATION ABOUT THE ILLNESS

The therapist needs to solicit from the referring medical provider an explanation of the typical course and prognosis for the illness and the way he or she views this particular patient's case. Typically, the physician and the patient have struggled with the illness over time, and the therapist needs to call and speak directly to the physician rather than receive medical information only from the family. With complicated cases, this conversation may happen in a joint first session or a later family conference (McDaniel, Campbell, and Seaburn, 1990) at which physician, therapist, patient, and family meet to hear the same information. These discussions help professionals develop and revise the collaborative treatment plan. In the therapeutic triangle between the medical system, the therapist, and the family, the therapist communicates directly with the medical system and with the patient and family to avoid any splitting or unhealthy coalitions.

REMAIN OPEN WHEN THE DIAGNOSIS IS AMBIGUOUS

Many patients with physical problems are referred to family therapists when the physician is unsure about the diagnosis and believes there may be a psychosocial component to the problem, or when the physician is certain about the diagnosis but the patient disagrees with it. In either case, a pull exists on the therapist toward psychosocial fixation—that is, toward explaining *all* the patient's problems in psychosocial terms.

Problems seen in medical family therapy almost always involve some organic process, even if it is a result of stress. At times depression or other behavioral symptoms signal the onset of an illness (such as cancer or Parkinson's) or a change in the course of an illness. By maintaining an open, exploratory stance toward physical processes, the therapist models for the patient and the family an openness and tolerance for the uncertainty inherent in dealing with medical problems. Even with somatization disorder—a common diagnosis in which patients express emotions through physical complaints—the physician is often unclear about the extent of the organic aspects of the patient's problems. Remaining open to biological, psychological, and social influences on medical problems allows for comprehensive and flexible treatment plans.

MAINTAIN HUMILITY ABOUT THE POSSIBILITY OF BIOLOGICAL CHANGE

Sick people are searching for hope and for answers: The job of the medical family therapist is to help the patient and the family respond in a healthy way to the challenge of illness. Therapists tend to patients' emotional health, but the effect of emotional or behavioral changes on a medical problem is usually unknown. Even with lifestyle changes such as losing weight or stopping smoking, the physician may most reliably cite the latest statistics or predict the effect that some behavior change may have on health, but in many areas, research on the effect of behavior change on health and illness has not been done. Therapists help the patient and family to *cope* with their particular problem: they do not, however, know the effect of psychotherapy on the course of a particular illness and so encourage patients to ask their physicians about the medical prognosis. Each patient and family can be encouraged to carry out their own "research project" to track what seems to be helpful or unhelpful and to work with the physician and family therapist to devise and carry out a treatment plan with the greatest likelihood of successful physical and emotional outcomes.

In the second phase of treatment Ellen F and her family focused on her father's symptoms, his uncertain diagnosis, and family members' own physical symptoms. Much of the therapy involved encouraging them to communicate with the medical providers, ask questions, and learn everything they could about the medical problems.

As frequently happens in medical family therapy, more than one member of Ellen F's family was experiencing physical symptoms at the time of her second referral. Ellen's own gastrointestinal symptoms were evaluated and found most likely to be stress related. Dr. Mark wanted to monitor her because he felt she was at risk for developing an ulcer. Ellen's father's prognosis was uncertain. His internist, a specialist on Alzheimer's disease, told the family he thought this could be early Alzheimer's but that only time would tell. The uncertainty was very stressful for the family. Ellen's mother's symptoms of increased despondency and dependency on her children seemed a potent reaction to the ambiguity of the situation and to the threatened loss of her husband.

Therapy began with Ellen and her husband, who told the therapist about the physical changes they recently had observed in Ellen's father. Therapy offered a place for them to express their distress and their fears about his condition. Ellen's parents had just moved to Florida for the winter. Ellen was encouraged to contact her father's physician in Florida and obtain as much information as possible from him, and to organize her family life so she could frequently visit her parents.

Ellen herself decided to refer her parents to a medical family therapist in Florida and solicited names of good therapists there. Once her parents began to see their therapist, Ellen felt relieved and was able to limit the number and length of family phone calls she made and received each week. With the agreement of her physician, Ellen's therapist suggested beginning this course of treatment by recording her gastrointestinal symptoms in a symptom diary and noting other daily events and stresses. Ellen and her husband monitored her symptoms for emerging patterns. Once Ellen set limits with her mother, her own symptoms disappeared. The rest of treatment focused on the couple's reactions to Ellen's father's illness and her feelings of responsibility and concern for her mother.

Soliciting the Illness Story

The joining process in treating patients with medical illness requires that the therapist solicit the illness story from the patient and the family (Kleinman, 1988). As with families with nonmedical problems, the therapist first gets to know the individual and the family independent of the illness or presenting complaint. Who are these people? Which family members work outside the home, and what is the nature of their work? What hobbies do they enjoy? How do they spend their couple and family time together? The family's ability to answer these early joining questions without moving into detailed discussion of the illness is an indicator of the extent that the family is organizing itself around the illness. Once a context is established, the patient and family should be asked to relay their experiences with the illness.

In addition to communicating the patient and family's experiences, the illness story allows the therapist to find a shared language for treatment with the family (Glenn, 1984; Goolishian and Anderson, 1987). Physical complaints may have both biomedical and metaphorical meanings for the patient and the family. By hearing and understanding the patient's illness story, the medical family therapist enters the patient's and family's world. This is the first step in the process of facilitating change.

LISTEN EMPATHICALLY

The medical family therapist needs to listen empathically to the family's illness story. The therapist asks about the onset of the illness, the symptoms of the illness, the experience of diagnostic tests and procedures, the diagnosis given by medical professionals (if it has occurred), treatments that have been tried by the family or the medical providers, the patient's emotional and practical responses to the illness, family members' emotional and practical responses to the illness, and the patient's current condition. In this part of the interview the therapist acknowledges that the medical domain is that of the physician and other medical providers but that the therapist wishes to understand the patient's *experience* of the illness. Questions or concerns raised by the patient or family about prognosis, treatment, or new symptoms need to be referred back to the medical provider, however tempting it may be to comment on or question the medical treatment plan when it is discussed with the family. The therapist may raise any serious concerns directly to the physician by telephone or in a joint family conference.

Table 4.3 lists a series of seventeen questions to be addressed to both patient and family members to elicit each person's perception of the illness (Friedman, 1991; Kleinman, Eisenberg, and Good, 1978; Seaburn, Lorenz, and Kaplan, in press; Shields, Wynne, and Sirkin, 1992). Because of the level of anxiety and concern exhibited in most families with sick members, it is especially important to respond to their story with empathy, respect, and a lack of blame and to emphasize the strengths exhibited by the family in their response to this crisis.

TABLE 4.3
Questions to Elicit Patient's and Family Members' Illness Perceptions

---

For the patient:

1. What do you think caused your problem?

2. Why do you think it started when it did?

3. What do you think your sickness does to you? How does it work?

4. How severe is your sickness? Will it have a long or short course?

5. What are the chief problems your sickness has caused for you?

6. What do you fear most about your sickness?

7. What kind of treatment do you think you should receive?

8. What are the most important results you hope to receive from this treatment?

9. Should we expect complications?

10. What has been your extended family's experience with illness?

11. Has anyone else in your family faced an illness similar to the one you have now? If so, what was its course?

12. What is your and your family's past history of recuperation?

13. What might make healing now a struggle for you?

14. Do you see yourself as having much to live for?

For family members:

15. What changes in family responsibilities do you think will be needed because of the patient's sickness?

16. If the patient needs care or special help, what family members are going to be responsible for providing it?

17. If the illness is already chronic or appears likely to become chronic, what are the patient's and family members' plans for taking care of the problem over the long term?

Source: The first eight questions are taken from Kleinman, Eisenberg, and Good (1978). Questions 9 and 10 are adapted from Seaburn, Lorenz, and Kaplan (in press). Questions 11 through 14 are adapted from Friedman (1991). Questions 15 through 17 are from Shields, Wynne, and Sirkin (1992).

TAKE A GENOGRAM WITH THE FAMILY TO TRACE
THEIR PARTICULAR HISTORY WITH ILLNESS AND LOSS

A genogram can be used to gather multigenerational information about illnesses in the family, the way the family has characteristically coped with illness in its various members, and the family's idiosyncratic health beliefs. Some families are fatalistic about illness; they believe that illness is part of God's larger plan, for example, and out of their control. Others feel very responsible for their health and believe that illness is a result of not eating the right foods and generally "not taking care of themselves." Often these themes can be traced through several generations. It is also important to place the family's reaction to this particular illness in the context of previous illnesses:

Ellen F and her family had a history of illness events that affected their reactions to her father's current condition. Ellen and Bob told the therapist the story of Ellen's father's illness from their first awareness that something was different in his behavior to his recent tests and questions about diagnosis. Then the therapist asked about the family's previous experience with illness.

Ellen said that her mother's father became demented around the time of Ellen's mother's marriage. This man, like Ellen's father, had been a patriarch—the clear leader of the family—and his role made it difficult for the family to reorganize to take care of him. Ellen's grandmother was unable to shift her position and become her husband's caregiver and became increasingly dependent on Ellen's mother, just as she was marrying. The family put the patient in a nursing home early in the disease process.

This information clarified the family's reaction to Ellen's father's potential diagnosis. Ellen clearly was concerned about her mother's increasing dependency on her and its effects on her own marriage. Ellen's mother was experiencing the challenge faced by her own mother—the challenge to become the primary caretaker and leader of the family—and was stressed by this as well as by her husband's deteriorating condition.

Bob's history also affected his reaction to his father-in-law's illness. Bob did not organize his life around his diabetes. Denial was a major part of the coping style he had evolved to deal with diabetes, allowing him to enjoy himself with friends and to function at work without most people even knowing about his illness. He had difficulty when others around him who were sick did not use the same coping style.

Ellen complemented Bob's coping style, in that she did the worrying for the family, much as his mother had done while he was growing up. Because of Bob's alienation from his own family in his early adulthood, Bob "adopted" Ellen's father as an important father figure in his own life. For him, his father-in-law's deterioration was like losing a father again. Fortunately Bob and his own father had experienced some reconciliation before his father's death, but Bob's father-in-law's illness reawakened many strong feelings for Bob of abandonment by important men in his life.

Bob's preference for working through painful issues quietly on his own resulted in marital difficulties because Ellen wished to talk at length about her thoughts, feelings, and anxieties about her father's condition. To help with this problem, Ellen was encouraged to talk to friends, talk in therapy, and join a support group for family members with Alzheimer's and similar disorders, in addition to talking to Bob about her concerns. The genogram session made it clear to Ellen that Bob was coping with strong feelings; his discomfort in talking about them was not a personal rejection of her.

Respecting Defenses, Removing Blame, and Accepting Unacceptable Feelings

Medical family therapy involves treating patients and their families who may face life-changing and sometimes life-threatening illness. It is especially important when working with these issues to maintain a healthy respect for the coping styles that patients and families evolve to deal with threats to their physical functioning or survival. In the face of serious illness, patients and families frequently have to shift their daily schedules, stretch their emotional and financial resources, and push themselves physically and mentally to meet the challenge of the illness.

75

It is not surprising under these circumstances that maladaptive coping styles may develop in some families. It is important not to intervene too quickly in trying to change these coping styles but rather first to focus on the strengths exhibited by the family in the way they have coped. Families facing illness need a large dose of support for the difficulties they have experienced and a generous amount of positive connotation for the adaptations they have made.

ACCEPT DENIAL

Denial is a common mechanism for dealing with illness. Sometimes patients deny they are ill or that they need to change the way they are living to accommodate an illness (like the patient who returned to a stressful job three weeks after having a serious heart attack). Sometimes one or more family members deny illness (like the wife who insisted her husband should continue to drive her to work after his physician documented that his vision was seriously impaired). People naturally resist change in themselves and their loved ones, particularly if it is a change that signals aging or death, and they may not admit or accommodate to an illness or disability in the way that appears healthy to the professional observer.

Accepting the denial—and providing support, positive connotation, and positive reframing—is the first step in helping the family move to a more realistic view of the illness and the patient's future. For example, with the patient who returned to work prematurely, the therapist and physician held a conjoint family session in which the therapist emphasized this patient's dedication to his work, then wondered aloud about how he might maintain this dedication and still take good care of his physical health. The patient and family then negotiated a plan for the patient to work mornings and attend a cardiac rehabilitation program in the afternoons. Without the initial support and positive connotation of his resistance to the medical treatment plan, the patient seemed likely to fight any alternative plan proposed by professionals or family members.

EXTERNALIZE THE ILLNESS

Some patients do not deny their illness but focus so entirely on their illness that their identity becomes organized around the illness.

They no longer talk about previous interests and show little concern for other aspects of their lives. They are frequently depressed and withdrawn. Sometimes family members, out of concern for the patient, also focus too much on the illness, protecting the patient from participating in activities they might enjoy out of fear for their health and generally restricting their interaction to exchanges about the illness. In this circumstance, it can be useful to help the patient and family "externalize the illness" (White, 1988; Wynne, Shields, and Sirkin, 1992)—that is, to separate the illness from the person who is ill.

With this technique the therapist might ask the patient to anthropomorphize the illness—to describe the illness as if it were another person or animal. What does it look like? How does it behave? What does it do to the patient? What does it do to other family members? What makes it act up? Does anything work to calm it? This creature can then be distinguished from the person who is the patient. When is the patient speaking as a person? When is it the illness talking? When are family members interacting with the illness, and when are they interacting with their loved one? In this way, both patient and family are encouraged to recognize and continue interacting with the person as they were before the illness, and as he or she is now apart from the illness.

REMOVE BLAME

Most people who come to a medical family therapist harbor some personal theories about who is to blame for the illness or disability. Personal habits certainly can influence illness and health, and current Western culture emphasizes individual responsibility for health. Popular books imply that with the correct diet and exercise and attitude, heart disease, cancer, and other dangerous diseases can be avoided. Although this approach is important for preventing preventable illness, it is easy to move from this position to one in which someone is always to blame for an illness or a death.

Many people cope with crises in their lives by trying to achieve mastery or a sense of control over the outcome. Illness challenges that sense of control. To recover a feeling of mastery, people may blame themselves, their families, and sometimes their medical providers. In families who have lost a baby to illness, family members will sometimes recite a family story that implies that perhaps the baby would have lived if the mother had taken the baby to the doctor sooner, the doctor had listened to the mother and diagnosed the illness earlier, or the father had not insisted on taking the baby out to walk on that blustery day. One such session occurred as follows:

> MOM: I *knew* it was too cold and wet to take Johnny out that day. But you insisted.
>
> DAD (defensively): The baby hadn't been out for almost a week. I thought it would be good for him. And you needed the break.
>
> MEDICAL FAMILY THERAPIST: One of the most difficult experiences anyone faces in life is the death of a child. It is so painful that we all naturally review everything that happened around the event to see if anyone could have prevented this tragedy. The doctors have said Johnny died of sudden infant death syndrome. As we've discussed, doctors don't understand SIDS very well at this point. All we know is that this illness happened suddenly and is unrelated, as far as we know, to anything you did with Johnny. We know how much you both loved Johnny when he was alive and how much you grieve now that he has died. It is hard to accept the uncertainty that we all feel about what happened, but it is important not to blame yourselves or each other for this tragedy. You both need each other's love and support now more than ever.

Families and medical providers face the uncertainty associated with the onset and outcome of illness. Medical family therapy encourages the emergence of real and imagined concerns about these uncertainties. The therapist's job is to help the family accept the illness or loss, remove blame when it is unwarranted, encourage rituals of retribution or forgiveness when appropriate (Imber-Black, 1989), and facilitate healing over time.

NORMALIZE NEGATIVE FEELINGS

Many feelings that occur routinely in families—such as anger, resentment, sadness, or guilt—may seem to become unacceptable when illness occurs. To some extent, this adaptation is constructive—as when petty transactions that typically cause a squabble appear unimportant in light of a serious illness or threat to an individual member's well-being. Sometimes, however, patients or family members isolate and do not express themselves in an effort to protect the ill person from the "stress" of their true feelings. Medical family therapy works to normalize the somewhat predictable negative feelings that occur for the patient and the family as a result of a serious illness.

In the case of Ellen F, Ellen and her family each had defensive reactions to the stress of her father's illness. The medical family therapist worked to help them accept these reactions, reframe them as related to how much they cared about each other, and stop blaming themselves and each other for an illness that was not in anyone's control:

Ellen F struggled most with her mother's response to her father's illness. Early in the diagnostic work-up, Ellen's mother took the position that she was sure her husband was "fine," that he was just forgetting things, and that he was being difficult because he knew he could rely on her to take care of him as she always had. From her perspective, this was just another way that her husband took her for granted.

Ellen had long felt frustrated by her mother's complaining to her about her father. Now she felt even more exasperated with her mother and secretly wondered whether her mother had "driven" her father to act this way. She knew her father enjoyed her company and regretted not visiting him more frequently. Since having children, Ellen and Bob had curtailed their traveling and usually did not see Ellen's parents during the winter months. Bob squirmed, became defensive, and justified these decisions, saying that he and their daughters needed her too.

The medical family therapist spoke to both of them about how difficult it is to have a parent with an undiagnosed problem and how trying it is to handle great uncertainty. Each family member was trying to cope with stress. Although it was understandable for Ellen to feel frustrated with her mother, the therapist said her mother's decision to believe that Ellen's father was being annoying was probably easier than thinking he might be seriously ill. Her mother must be very attached to him and afraid of thinking he might be sick. Ellen sighed when she heard this and said that her parents' arguments were difficult to deal with as an outsider but that she thought they cared about each other a great deal. The therapist added that it was tempting when coping with an ambiguous illness to find someone to blame for a process that may be outside of anyone's control. She recognized how much caring was behind all of Ellen's feelings for both her parents.

The therapist then noted the importance of Bob's reminder that her current family cared about her, and Ellen agreed that her husband helped her to maintain a balance in this difficult situation. After hearing these comments, Bob for the first time helped Ellen find a way to take more time away from home to visit her father. Prior to this, he had verbally supported the idea but found reasons why specific weekends were not good for her to be away. Bob also spoke in this session about how he valued the brief time he and his father had together after their reconciliation and before he died. The couple ended the session with a plan for the family to travel to Florida in several months so that Bob and the children also could see Ellen's father and mother.

Maintaining Communication

The art of medical family therapy includes encouraging honest communication throughout the family–health care network and respecting individual styles of coping with the stress of illness. Strengthening a family's sense of communion, or connectedness, during the time of an illness is an important goal of medical family therapy.

BETWEEN FAMILIES AND MEDICAL PROVIDERS

Honest and direct communication from the medical team about prognosis, disease course, and treatment plans provides the patient with critical information needed to decide how to respond to the illness. Physicians vary, however, in what they tell patients about the biomedical aspects of their disease: some medical providers provide a positive prognosis; some divulge extensive information about potential side effects or negative results; still others try to balance the amount of information that needs to be conveyed to the patient and family with the amount of information the patient and family seem to want. Often the medical team is uncertain about the course the patient may take with the illness and finds it difficult to discuss this uncertainty with the family. In these cases, the family therapist may encourage the medical team to answer questions and talk with the patient and family in clear language about the illness and its likely course.

To complicate the communication process further, patients or family members often do not hear the physician when news is bad or unexpected. This phenomenon plays a part in how much the patient and family feel they know about a patient's illness. Frequently, the medical team will have to communicate the facts about the illness on several occasions before they are heard and understood. Sometimes, the family therapist may signal the need for a conference in which the family may express concerns or ask questions of the medical team.

Not surprisingly, communication problems are common between ill patients and medical providers. Most patients with a chronic illness have had negative experiences communicating with representatives of the medical system during the course of the illness. This occurs because both family and medical provider are likely to be stressed during difficult phases of an illness and because many physicians and patients view disease from different perspectives—one focused on biology, the other focused on the human experience. Friedman (1991) poses the question for the patient: how do you take responsibility for your health without fighting medicine (that is, without fighting with your medical providers)? At network sessions that bring together all relevant parties, the family therapist helps to air the differing perspectives, resolve misunderstandings, and move the treatment forward (Speck and Attneave, 1972; McDaniel, Campbell, and Seaburn, 1990).

AMONG FAMILY MEMBERS

Protection can play a central role among family members in communication patterns about illness. Patients sometimes become secretive about their diagnoses because they do not want to "burden" other family members or destabilize the family structure. All patients and families deserve time to react and respond to new diagnoses, but some patients need support and encouragement to discuss the facts about their illness with others in the family. Families can be referred to their medical providers to discuss their questions, or the medical team and the therapist can convene a joint session to answer the family's medical questions.

For example, a patient with terminal cancer knew he was dying but did not wish to disclose this information to his children. His children said their father was dying but did not feel he could handle the information if he knew, given how depressed they felt he already was. In this situation, the secret that everyone knew acted as a barrier between the patient and his family at the very time when all parties were feeling most distressed and vulnerable. A session was called by the physician and the therapist for the patient and family. The physician discussed the patient's disease and its terminal course, responded to questions, and asked for the patient and family's input on the next stage of care. This approach dissolved any appearance of a secret, and with the therapist's support, the patient and family talked about how they felt and what they next wanted to do. In these kinds of circumstances, the family therapist can facilitate the communication that has been blocked and needs to take place.

Some patients or family members deny the reality of an illness or indicate they do not want to discuss details with each other or with the treatment team. It is important for the therapist to respect this protective shell of denial, be supportive of the patient, and wait for a signal of readiness to discuss the illness.

Gail Dakof and Howard Liddle (1990), in their research on cancer patients, found no single communication style that was most adaptive for all individuals or couples facing illness. Rather, they found the couples who had matching communication styles reported the least amount of conflict and distress: that is, couples who *both* wanted to talk about the illness and their feelings about the illness did well, and couples who *both* agreed they did not want to talk about the illness also did well. The couples with divergent styles, where one wanted to talk about the illness and the other did not, were more likely to report conflict and distress about the illness and their relationship. In this study, concordance in communication styles was more important than candor about the illness. Family members can be supportive of one another without focusing on the illness. Some family cultures value quiet acceptance of difficult life events over which they have no control; some value lively discussion of feelings when under stress.

Other family values can influence the family's reaction to the medical treatment plan. Values such as "we take care of our own," for example, can make a nursing home placement very difficult for a family even when all agree it is a sensible plan. Religious beliefs can make decisions about reproductive choice or continuing treatment for a terminal patient complicated. Family therapy can help elicit these concerns and values so that families can work with their medical team (as well as their spiritual advisors) to negotiate a treatment plan that all parties understand and support:

> During their summer trip to Florida to visit her parents, Ellen and Bob F decided to communicate again with her father's doctor and requested a meeting with him for themselves and the family. Her father's functioning had clearly deteriorated. He had lost more memory functioning and experienced more frequent periods of confusion. Ellen's mother hesitated to have this meeting because she did not want to "bother" the doctor. She also said that she should deal with this and that she did not want Ellen and Bob to worry more than was necessary. Ellen persisted because her mother was becoming increasingly nervous and perhaps was afraid of what she might hear from the doctor at a joint session. In a supportive way, Ellen asked if she might discuss the idea of a meeting with her father's doctor. Her mother agreed, and her father had no objections.
>
> When Ellen called her father's Florida physician, he welcomed the idea of speaking to the entire family. He agreed that her father's condition had deteriorated and that they needed to discuss what next to do. Ellen mentioned her mother's hesitation to the physician. A few days later, Ellen's mother said that her father's physician had called their family therapist and suggested that the therapist also attend the meeting so the overall treatment could be coordinated.
>
> At the meeting, the physician reported there was no longer any uncertainty about the diagnosis: Ellen's father had Alzheimer's

disease. The physician also said he seemed to have developed early Parkinson's. With regard to the Alzheimer's, the family heard what they basically already knew but had not yet openly acknowledged. The Parkinson's was a surprise, so the physician explained the illness and the ways it might affect Ellen's father. The family agreed that Ellen's father was still healthy enough to live with her mother and have her take care of him, and they agreed to get a home health care aide. They also talked about symptoms that might eventually signal a need for nursing home placement.

Both Ellen and her mother cried during this discussion. Ellen's father seemed confused. The family therapist scheduled a meeting for her parents and one for her mother alone at the end of the session. She also said she was glad to meet Ellen and Bob and encouraged Ellen's mother to bring either or both of them in to see her at any subsequent visits. Ellen was upset about the diagnoses but pleased and relieved to see how well coordinated her father's medical team was.

Attending to Developmental Issues

In addition to the standard emphasis on individual and family developmental periods, medical family therapy focuses on the developmental progression of the illness and its psychosocial corollaries, the interaction between the illness phase and individual and family developmental issues, and the interaction of the illness, patient, and family with the developmental dynamics of the caregiving system. Families coping with a serious illness, especially one in the chronic phase, face a balancing act. They need to adjust physical, emotional, and financial demands so they can respond to the needs of their sick member, attend and support that person, and help to implement the medical treatment plan. They also need to continue their own lives in some fashion. This is a challenge for all families, and some families have more difficulty achieving this balance than others. Penn (1983) has described the unhealthy coalitions that can become established in response to an illness, become frozen in time, and so prevent family members from moving on in their own development.

PUT THE ILLNESS IN ITS PLACE

Sandra Gonzalez, Peter Steinglass, and David Reiss (1989), in their discussion groups for families coping with chronic illness, describe the importance of "putting the illness in its place." This means that the family needs to attend to the demands placed on them by the illness but not allow the illness to dominate the family's schedule or organize the family's emotional life. Wherever possible, families should be encouraged to maintain day-to-day routines, family rituals, holiday traditions, and attend in general to other family members' developmental issues:

Ellen struggled to balance her commitments to Bob and their children with her concern for her father. Her emotional energy was really with her father, and she expressed hope that Bob would understand and take care of their girls. The couple reported that sometimes this strategy worked and sometimes it didn't. Over time Bob grew tired of doing the housework and child care and became what they described as "grumpy," or one of the girls would misbehave more than usual to gain more of her mother's attention. In therapy, the couple worked to identify the signs that Bob or the girls were feeling neglected so that Ellen could both tend to them and also feel their support.

After her father's diagnoses were clarified, Ellen had difficulty deciding how frequently to visit her parents when they were in Florida. She planned one of her first visits to coincide with the beginning of school for her oldest daughter, thinking this plan would involve less work for Bob. As it turned out, however, their daughter, Katy, was very disappointed that her mother was not going to take her to the first day of first grade. After discussing it in therapy, Ellen rearranged her flight plans to go the second week of her daughter's school. This plan worked well for everyone. She was able to entertain her parents with stories and drawings from Katy's first week, and Katy was much more accepting of her mother being away at that time.

Ellen and Bob had to communicate about and juggle their schedules throughout the time of her father's illness. This balancing act contributed to the stress of this period, but facing it directly prevented family members from developing powerful resentments and allowed them to continue with their lives after the crisis was over. With their therapist's encouragement, they worked especially hard to maintain birthday and holiday celebrations as usual.

Increasing a Sense of Agency in the Patient and Family

As we have discussed, illness is an out-of-control experience for most patients and their families. In Edwin Friedman's (1991) model of illness, the outcome is determined by a combination of biological factors, luck (or random events), and the response of the organism. This section on agency focuses on activating the individual and family response of the organism. Family therapy can help families increase their sense of competency and agency around factors over which they do have some control, and their sense of acceptance of factors that are out of their control.

EMPHASIZE THE PATIENT'S INPUT

At some level, most people feel helpless and vulnerable when ill. The family therapist, in collaboration with the medical team, can encourage patients to take an active role in making decisions about their treatment plans. The patient may ask for information from the medical team about the illness and weigh options for treatment in discussion with other family members. Norman Cousins, in his book *Anatomy of an Illness* (1979), exemplifies the patient who increases a personal sense of agency by taking charge of an illness and actively participating in a treatment plan. When patients are so sick that they are not mentally competent to participate in decision making, this role falls on family members, who need considerable support to fulfill this duty. Other patients may exercise their right to participate in their health care by consistently disagreeing with the medical providers and refusing treatment recommendations.

For example, a moderately obese middle-aged man rejected his doctor's recommendation that he lose weight and change his eating habits after he recovered from a mild heart attack. The patient said he would not change his diet because he enjoyed his wife's cooking and because food was one of his only remaining pleasures. The physician felt very frustrated with this patient and consulted a family therapist to negotiate a treatment plan that was acceptable to all parties. The therapist met with the patient, his wife, and the physician. The therapist emphasized her understanding that the patient did not wish to have another heart attack, and then negotiated a compromise food plan in which the patient continued to have many of the foods he enjoyed but in smaller quantities. He also agreed to decrease his red meat intake and experiment with eating egg and sugar substitutes, as long as he was in charge of planning his own menu. His wife agreed to try cooking with some of these new products. This plan was instituted for one month and was reassessed with the physician at the end of that time.

BRACKET PATIENTS' UNHEALTHY DECISIONS

Patients and families frequently choose not to follow the suggestions of their doctors. The medical recommendations may conflict with their own sense of themselves ("I don't need help, and I certainly don't need medication"), with strongly held family values ("We eat as our grandparents ate; this is part of our tradition"), or with the patient's world view ("If it's my time to go, then I'm ready; I don't need surgery or medications or any doctors making money off me").

When the medical team presents a treatment plan that the patient refuses, it may be useful to put a time frame around this decision. With the heart patient who loved his wife's cooking, the therapist suggested the couple try the modified diet for a month and then reconsider. With any serious illness, patients' feelings about their illness and the sacrifices that might be required to treat the problem often change over time. By bracketing the decision with a date for review, the therapist recognizes the patient's right to decide whether and how to comply with treatment recommendations and allows the patient and family time to digest information about the illness and to change their responses over time.

The same approach may be beneficial with behavior changes such as smoking. The patient who refuses to quit now may reconsider that decision in three months. Similarly the patient who quits may want to make an initial commitment to be reevaluated in one month. Because these behavioral changes always involve reevaluation, it may be useful to structure this period of questioning into the actual treatment plan.

> MEDICAL FAMILY THERAPIST: I'm impressed, Mrs. Ciano, that you have taken that first important step in making a commitment to stop smoking. And it sounds as if your husband has agreed to help you in a number of ways so that you can fulfill this commitment. It's usually difficult to maintain this promise to yourself to become more healthy. I have found it helpful with my patients to schedule a follow-up appointment to ask if they are prepared to continue the commitment not to smoke. So I would like to meet with you and Mr. Ciano in a month from now to review your progress and hear from you about the future. How does that sound?
>
> MRS. CIANO: That sounds good. It's a lot easier for me to give up smoking for one month than to think of giving up smoking for years to come. Maybe I need to try it one step at a time. We'll see you in one month, if I don't need to call you before that.

FACILITATE RATHER THAN ADVISE

To increase a patient's and family's sense of agency the therapist needs to communicate confidence in the family's ability to make good decisions. Although it is tempting in medical family therapy to offer patients advice when they are confronted with difficult treatment decisions, therapists are most effective when they support the patient and family in gathering as much medical information as possible, help them to discuss the possible options, and then facilitate as the patient or responsible party makes the best possible decision for now. This kind of decision-making process dominated the next phase of treatment for Ellen F and her family:

> Six months after Ellen and Bob met with her parents, their physician, and their therapist, Ellen's father continued to deteriorate. Ellen's mother telephoned her daughter at least daily. Her father was abusive at times, struck her mother, and wandered around their apartment at night. The couple had not returned north for the

summer because Ellen's mother felt the move would be too difficult this time. She was becoming more reclusive and distressed.

Ellen and Bob worked in therapy to balance their own family's needs with the need of Ellen's parents. Ellen focused on her sense of loss, her father's transformation from the man she once knew, and her ability to support her mother without overfunctioning herself. Ellen also asked the therapist if she felt her father should be placed in a nursing home. The therapist communicated her confidence in the family by saying that she knew this was a very difficult situation, that she could not know when placement would be necessary, but that she knew that the family and the medical team would act together when the time was right.

With the situation deteriorating, Ellen visited her parents in Florida, and the family met again with the physician and the therapist. Ellen asserted her view that her father should be placed in a nursing home because her mother was no longer able to care adequately for him and caregiving was eroding her mother's health. Ellen's mother rejected Ellen's plan, saying that the illness was difficult enough to cope with and she could not tolerate her husband living somewhere else. The physician said the illness had progressed to the point that placement in a nursing home was an option. He said he was certain that placement would be necessary unless her father became ill and had to enter a hospital, but that the timing of the placement was up to the family. Ellen asked her father for his input, but he was agitated and his verbal contributions were incoherent. Because Ellen's mother remained adamant that her husband remain home, the therapist said that she and the family knew best and eventually would reach agreement about placement. A follow-up meeting for one month later was planned, with assurance that the family could initiate a meeting sooner if necessary.

Before Ellen returned north to her own home, her father wandered out into the street in the middle of the night. Ellen awoke to the sound of horns blowing and ran outside to bring him back in. The next morning Ellen's mother agreed to a nursing home placement. They were able to arrange placement within days, much quicker than usual, and Ellen stayed to help her mother and father make the transition.

Leaving the Door Open

Medical family therapy typically begins during an illness crisis in a family. Therapy may help the family to cope with the demands of the illness and sometimes expands to help family members with other aspects of their lives. When a family no longer needs to consult with a therapist, a soft termination allows the family to feel a sense of accomplishment about the changes they have made, feel confidence about their ability to continue without therapy, and know that the therapist is available for further consultation should the need arise.

RECOGNIZE THE PHYSICIAN'S ONGOING INVOLVEMENT

Referrals for medical family therapy can come from primary care medical providers or from specialists. When they come from a primary care provider, therapists need to remember that primary care physicians and their patients have ongoing relationships. Most physicians view medical family therapists as tertiary care providers who provide specialized treatment in their areas of expertise, after which the patient returns to the primary care physician for ongoing care. The primary care physician may then refer the patient back to the specialist should other problems emerge. Once the problem is addressed, the patient may not return to the specialist for years, if at all, but the patient and the specialist have established a relationship that can be renewed if necessary.

PROVIDE PATIENT FOLLOW-UP

Therapists who do not have offices situated in a medical context may wish to follow up care by calling or writing to patients at six months to one year after termination. This information provides valuable feedback on the efficacy of medical family therapy.

Therapists who share offices with medical providers can see patients with whom they have terminated in the waiting room waiting to see their physicians. Therapists working in medical contexts are also likely to hear about their patients from the physicians they regularly work with (Seaburn et al., in press). These informal contacts offer opportunities for the therapist to support the patient and the physician in their ongoing work. Easy access should not imply that the patient needs further psychotherapy when the situation does not actually warrant referral. An open door is not the same as a revolving door.

Like Ellen and Bob F, patients may ask to return to family therapy when entering a new phase of a chronic illness, when dealing with the long-term ramifications of a threat to life, a disability, or a death, or when facing a new problem unrelated to a medical event. An open door allows patients to return for an occasional consultation or for a new phase of treatment:

Once Ellen F's father was settled into the nursing home, the crisis in Ellen's family abated. Ellen reported feeling that the family accepted her father's illness, although they were sad and missed the person her father had been prior to the illness. The relationship between Ellen and her mother was stable. Her mother now called several times a week at times previously negotiated to be convenient for Ellen. Ellen encouraged her mother to go out, see her friends, and take care of herself, as well as deal with Ellen's father. Ellen and Bob reported that their relationship was positive and supportive. Both agreed this was a stressful time in their family life but felt pride in how they were coping with it (see figure 4.3).

Even though the stresses remained, Ellen and Bob felt they no longer needed therapy. Because this was the second course of treatment, the therapist felt certain they would call if they needed help again. After reviewing their many accomplishments, the therapist wished them the best and asked if she could follow up in six months to see how they were doing. The therapist called Ellen's physician, as was their agreement, to let him know this phase of treatment was over.

At the six-month follow-up, the therapist learned that Ellen's father had deteriorated but the family remained stable. Two years later, a letter arrived from Ellen informing the therapist that her father had recently died. She said that the family had continued to cope well with the stress of the illness and that they were prepared for his death. After his death, her mother moved north to be closer to her children and grandchildren. Ellen reported that the limit setting she had done with her mother during her father's illness and the balance she had achieved with her own husband and

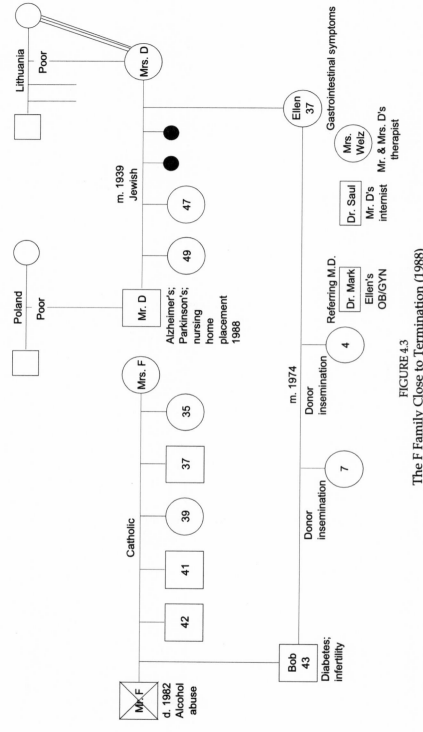

FIGURE 4.3

The F Family Close to Termination (1988)

children prevented this move from being the crisis it might have been prior to therapy.

Conclusion

Medical family therapy is a complex process that builds on the foundation of traditional family therapy intervention techniques and strategies and requires therapists to develop skills in collaboration, consultation, and assessing and intervening in large systems as well as families. The fundamental techniques of medical family therapy integrate concerns about health and illness into a systems framework for psychotherapy, and increase both agency and communion in families facing illness.

CHAPTER 5

Health Behaviors That Harm

W E HAVE BECOME enemies of our own health. Throughout much of human history, the great debilitators and killers were infectious diseases transmitted through air, water, and incidental bodily contact: a stray skin puncture could easily end in premature death from bacterial infection; water- and airborne diseases killed millions of people as Europe became densely populated. In the twentieth century, however, the greatest health scourges in economically developed countries arise from personal behavior, particularly smoking, diet, alcohol use, and sexual behavior leading to AIDS (Glazier, 1973; Matarazzo, 1984). As the *Surgeon General's Report on Health Promotion and Disease Prevention* attested, "Of the ten leading causes of death in the United States, at least seven could be substantially reduced if persons at risk improved just five habits: diet, smoking, lack of exercise, alcohol abuse, and use of antihypertensive medication" (U.S. Department of Health, Education and Welfare, 1979, p. 14).

Any discussion about health-related behavior is a discussion about families, since it is in families that we first learn health habits and then practice them throughout our lives. This is why medical family therapists have an important role in helping both families and medical professionals to deal with the complex issue of how to modify longstanding health behaviors. As family therapists, we have been trained to work with families to bring about change in interaction patterns that lead to psychosocial distress. As medical family therapists, we have learned to work with families around health behavior issues not normally dealt with by therapists. In this chapter, we discuss two of the major behavior problems encountered in health care—cigarette smoking and obesity.

Medical family therapists generally encounter these two problem areas in patients whose smoking and weight are complicating medical problems such as hypertension, diabetes, or lung disease. The referral to the medical family therapist may be made by a frustrated physician or family member who asks for help in changing a recalcitrant family member's behavior, and sometimes a patient approaches the therapist because of feelings of helplessness and shame about being unable to "control" his or her own behavior. The therapist's work with smoking and obesity thus is likely to be part of a larger set of assessment and treatment issues. This chapter complements the other discussions in this book on treatment issues in medical family therapy, particularly the chapters on chronic illness in adults and children. The medical family therapist addresses health issues as they come up in therapy, focusing on them for a time, defocusing at other times, and then returning at timely moments to deal with them again—always avoiding the trap of turning the therapy into yet another effort to force the patient to adopt different health behaviors.

Smoking and Obesity in Cultural Context

Smoking and obesity are not simply individual or family issues. Both are tied inextricably to larger social and cultural forces. This section discusses some of these forces from historical and psychocultural perspectives.

SMOKING IN AMERICAN CULTURE

Smoking was not a major public health problem until the twentieth century. Health historian Edward Shorter (1987) writes that in 1900 the average American teenager or adult consumed forty-nine cigarettes per year, whereas by 1962 the figure was 3,988 cigarettes per year. Since the latency time for cigarette smoking to cause cancer and heart disease is counted in decades, it was not until the mid-twentieth century that alarms began to be sounded in the medical community. Even in the 1950s, medical journals continued to carry ads from tobacco companies, and no experts pointed to lifelong smoking as a possible factor in President Eisenhower's much-publicized heart attack in 1955 (Shorter, 1987). The tide began to turn after scientists marshaled data on the links between smoking and cancer and heart disease, but even now the federal government provides subsidies to tobacco growers while condemning tobacco use as the leading cause of death in the country.

In the first three decades of this century, cigarette smoking began to symbolize for many young Americans personal freedom from the limiting traditions of the past. Recent Virginia Slims cigarette advertisements have replayed this theme for contemporary women: "You've come a long way, baby." In one 1990 magazine advertisement, for example, the caption under a purported 1904 picture states that "Mrs. George Hubbard found a clever way to sneak a cigarette while her husband still got the attention he demanded." The other picture is of a sleek, sexy contemporary woman holding a cigarette; she has clearly "come a long way"—toward a greatly increased risk of heart disease, cancer, and other diseases.

In the late twentieth century, smoking has become a cultural blend symbolizing personal freedom and self-indulgence and carrying a social stigma. This cultural split lends itself well to the kind of psychocultural analysis that cultural anthropologist Howard Stein (1985) has applied to alcholism. Stein views American culture as having "psychocultural splits" between excess and denial and between dependency and self-control. The split means that only one side of the polarity is accessible to individuals in the culture at one time; for example, we see ourselves as either dependent or fully in control, as either self-indulging or self-denying. Cigarette smoking, now viewed culturally and medically as a personal flaw, has become caught up in this psychocultural split. The increasing coerciveness of the antismoking movement is decreasing the popularity of smoking but also may serve as a vehicle that plays out the psychological and cultural dimensions of our wish to deny our dependencies and excesses. Just as the alcoholic is labeled a disease carrier and shunted off to specialized treatment programs, the smoker can become, for nonsmokers, a symbol of a feared road not taken. That road is one of risk-taking self-indulgence, of living for the momentary pleasure of a chemical, and of stubborn refusal to conform to the conventional wisdom of professionals and the majority of one's peers. Smokers, on their part, retort that they are fighting for their freedom for self-determination—thereby tapping another cultural split between community expectations and individual rights.

As members of this culture and inheritors of its splits and fixations, medical family therapists are at risk to fall into the coercive stance toward smokers that has been adopted by the medical profession and a growing number of social institutions. To the extent that smoking becomes viewed in the culture as a feared and potentially contagious moral flaw, the culturally unaware medical family therapist may relate to smokers in ways that actually make it harder to quit (Whitehead and Doherty, 1989). Since we all have aspects of our lives and behavior over which we feel uncertain control, therapists must be careful not to assume the moral high ground with smokers and work on personal self-control issues through "helping" the smoker. Although this type of countertransference naturally may occur in any area in the therapist-client relationship, Stein's psychocultural model alerts us to the increased risk of these distortions when the culture at large is permeated with splits and denials around the health problems our clients face.

OBESITY IN AMERICAN CULTURE

Much of the foregoing psychocultural analysis applies equally well to obesity, a problem associated with the abundance of goods provided in the industrialized world, coupled with a fear of overconsuming that abundance. Social historian Hillel Schwartz (1986) traces the history of "diets, fantasies and fat" from the Roman era till the present. Although he finds historical precedents to the faddish diets of modern times, Schwartz believes that in earlier eras most people consumed only what they needed to satisfy themselves. There appears to have been little confusion between appetite and hunger; when food is not plentiful, most people consume what they need and save the rest.

Contemporary America, on the other hand, has developed a powerful contradiction between the exhortation to eat and consume abundantly and to be slim and self-controlled. The natural desire for food has become tinged with self-reproach (Schwartz, 1986). These cultural contradictions affect women more seriously than men, since the cult of thinness is pressed more forcefully on women than men and the countervailing cultural message to indulge in sweets and fats is no less compelling. Indeed, Schwartz describes the current cultural ideal in the form of a frightening oxymoron—"the Weightless Body."

As with smoking, contemporary culture splits between the poles of self-indulgence and self-denial, which sets individuals careening back and forth between the two, like a battle waged with forays and retreats but no resolution. Eating, dieting, and the fear of obesity, then, become the screen on which the psychocultural splits are projected and played out.

Therapists have strong feelings and beliefs about weight, dieting, and obesity—feelings and beliefs influenced by families and personal experience and by the culture at large. One of the authors overheard two female therapists in heated argument over whether a shared female client was "just overweight" or "disgustingly fat." This was not just a clinical discussion. Unless they carefully examine their culture-based ideas about weight, therapists are apt to define as problems certain levels of weight that are not problems to clients, agree prematurely to help a client lose weight for the "wrong" reasons, attempt to work out their own issues around weight by vigorously helping a client lose weight, or form coalitions with family members and other health professionals to control a client into self-control—a dubious enterprise, to say the least.

The medical family therapist needs to tread carefully in the areas of smoking and obesity and be aware that sometimes the treatment for a cultural obsession can be worse than the "disease." Sometimes the best we can do is to help the client, family, or health professional accept the likelihood that no change may be possible at present. Other times, by carefully sifting out our needs, the cultural issues, and the issues of the patient, the family and the professionals, we can work with smoking and obesity in a way that leads to meaningful behavior change and improved physical and emotional health for all involved.

The Family FIRO Model: Inclusion, Control, Intimacy

As mentioned briefly in chapter 2, the Family FIRO Model, developed by William Doherty and Nicholas Colangelo (1984) and adapted from Will Schutz's (1958) Fundamental Interpersonal Orientations (FIRO) Model, has been used to provide a family systems perspective on obesity, smoking, and chronic illness (Doherty and Campbell, 1988; Doherty and Harkaway, 1990; Doherty and Whitehead, 1986; Whitehead and Doherty, 1989). We briefly describe the model and then apply it to smoking and obesity in families. The model's conceptual framework is described most fully in Doherty, Colangelo, and Hovander (1991) and is outlined in table 5.1.

The Family FIRO Model offers three core dimensions of family relationships—inclusion, control, and intimacy. *Inclusion* refers to interactions that relate to bonding and organization and shared meaning in the family. As indicated by the subcategories and descriptive terms in table 5.1, inclusion represents the "glue" of the family—how it is structured, how members are emotionally connected, and how the family creates shared meanings about itself and its environment. *Control* refers to interactions that relate to influence and power in the presence of conflict. In other words, the control dimension of family interactions represents how family members deal with overt or covert conflict or disagreement. *Intimacy* refers to interactions that relate to open self-disclosure and close personal exchange. It represents the in-depth dimension of open and vulnerable conversations between family members. In this model, intimacy interactions are distinguished from inclusion-connectedness interactions by the depth of self-disclosure; thus, a relationship can be highly bonded and committed but still have few emotionally intimate interactions as defined here.

The most important postulate of the Family FIRO Model for health behaviors is that inclusion, control, and intimacy constitute a

TABLE 5.1
Family FIRO Concepts

Categories of Family Interaction		
Inclusion (bonding and organization)	Control (influence and power during conflict)	Intimacy (self-disclosure and personal exchanges)
Structure (boundaries, role organization, alliance, membership, position)	Dominating (confrontation, coercion, manipulation, dictating, discipline)	Mutuality (sharing feelings, relating to each other as unique personalities, emotionally close sexual interactions, sharing vulnerabilities)
Connectedness (nurturance, involvement, commitment, belonging, affiliation)	Reactive (resistance, rebellion. submission, withdrawal, disobedience)	
Shared meaning (identity, loyalty, rituals, values, world view)	Collaborative (negotiation, compromise, balancing, give and take, working through)	

Source: Adapted from W. J. Doherty, N. Colangelo, and D. Hovander (1991), Priority setting in family change and clinical practice: The Family FIRO Model. *Family Process, 30,* 227–240.

developmental sequence for managing major family change, with inclusion coming before control and control coming before intimacy. Thus intimacy problems in families are difficult to resolve in the presence of major control struggles, and unresolved conflict pollutes the waters of intimacy. Furthermore, control problems are difficult to resolve in the presence of inclusion problems such as lack of commitment to the relationship, confused boundaries, or patterns of overinvolvement. These inclusion issues, which seed control struggles in the family, need to be addressed prior to the likelihood of meaningful progress on the control problems. For example, marital conflict over the patient's lack of compliance with a diet or medication regimen may flow from over-involvement by the spouse in the health behaviors of the patient coupled with the patient's underresponsibility for self. According to the Family FIRO Model, these inclusion issues related to roles and boundaries should be the initial focus of the therapist's effort to help the couple create positive change. Doherty and Colangelo (1984) believe that the Family FIRO Model's priority sequence is used implicitly by many experienced family therapists who know which issues to focus on in the early stages of therapy and which issues to postpone.

The primary therapeutic implications of the Family FIRO Model for medical family therapy lie in the areas of assessment and priority setting in treatment. For assessment, the model suggests that the therapist pay particular attention to inclusion issues, such as how a medical problem or health behavior issue has become incorporated into the structure of the family (such as in role patterns or alliances), how it has become a vehicle for bonding or disengagement, and how the family manifests beliefs around the problem; control issues, such as how the medical issue has become a battleground for power and influence; and intimacy issues, such as how the medical issue bars open dialogue or sometimes provides the starting place for open dialogue.

Perhaps the major advantage of the Family FIRO Model is that it offers guidance about priority setting in the face of multiple family problems. The model suggests that it is usually a mistake to focus on increasing emotional intimacy (as defined earlier) before treating coercive or passive-aggressive control patterns (because these problems will foul the waters of intimacy), and that it is usually a mistake to focus on modifying control or conflict styles before systematically addressing inclusion issues that are feeding the conflict (such as a sense of abandonment by the partner or a lack of agreement about the roles family members should play toward the patient). *Focus* is emphasized here in order to indicate that in particular sessions the therapist should not feel compelled by the model to ignore nonpriority issues that emerge. Sometimes in order to connect with the family the therapist must work on the family's presenting issue first—even if that order does not seem logical. For example, if parents insist on viewing their child's failure to take medication as a control problem, the therapist may have to initially accept this frame in order to engage the family in treatment. Skilled therapists, however, know how to work on presenting issues at the overt level and underlying issues at a less overt level.

Finally, the Family FIRO Model applies beyond the family group to the therapeutic system created by the therapist, the family, and the health professionals. These clinical systems have their own evolving patterns of inclusion, control, and sometimes intimacy. The Family FIRO Model offers a language and procedure for analyzing and intervening with clinical systems and larger systems as well. When a physician is behaving coercively and a patient reactively, for example, the therapist can look for underlying inclusion issues such as boundary problems and lack of shared meaning about the diagnosis or treatment plan.

A Family Perspective on Smoking

Over 400,000 Americans die each year from smoking as the smoking habits of the 1950s and 1960s take effect (Centers for Disease Control, 1991a, 1991b), and this number reflects a steadily rising trend from the 188,000 smoking deaths calculated for 1965. These deaths occur mainly from lung cancer, other cancers such as mouth and pancreatic, cardiovascular diseases like heart and arterial diseases, and respiratory diseases like bronchitis and emphysema. Two of the great pioneers of family therapy—Nathan Ackerman and Murray Bowen—died prematurely, probably from the results of cigarette smoking. The human cost is enormous.

Since the landmark 1964 Surgeon General's warning against smoking, the medical community has actively advertised the negative health consequences of smoking and helped reduce the percentage of American smokers from 40 percent in 1964 to 29 percent in 1990 (Centers for Disease Control, 1991a, 1991c). Unfortunately, rates of decline for women, especially young women, are lower than for men, and the death rate from smoking is higher for African-Americans than for white Americans. The good news is that quitting cigarettes, even after many years of smoking, leads to better health outcomes; but the bad news is that quitting is difficult for most people: 80 percent of smokers say that they would like to quit, but only a small portion succeed (Fielding, 1985). In the best smoking cessation programs, only 20 to 40 percent of smokers successfully abstain for one year.

Like most health behaviors, smoking has been considered largely as an individual decision and an individual behavior. This bias toward the atomic individual has held despite the clear research evidence to support a family perspective on the problem. Doherty and Campbell (1988) summarize this research as follows:

> We know that smokers tend to be married to other smokers (Sutton, 1980), and to smoke a similar number of cigarettes per day as their partners (Venters et al., 1984). An adolescent is mostly likely to smoke if the same-sex parent smokes (Bewley & Bland, 1977; U.S. DHEW, 1976). Smoking couples tend to quit smoking at the same time (Venters et al., 1984). Smokers are more likely to quit if they are married to nonsmokers (Price et al., 1981), and to remain abstinent longer if their spouses or friends do not smoke (Lichtenstein, 1982; Ockene et al., 1981). Several studies have demonstrated that support from the spouse is associated with successful quitting (Ockene et al., 1982).

Most theorists and researchers have regarded the family, particularly the spouse, as a source of social support for the smoker who wants to quit. In the mid-1980s, however, a new generation of family systems theorists and clinicians began to examine smoking from a systems-interactional viewpoint. The following discussion is derived from the work of William Doherty, a medical family therapist, and D'Ann White-head, a behavioral psychologist with expertise in smoking cessation. Together they applied the Family FIRO Model to cigarette smoking interactions and conducted a qualitative research study examining family interactions around smoking and smoking cessation (Doherty and Whitehead, 1986; Whitehead and Doherty, 1989).

Doherty and Whitehead conceptualized smoking as part of an interactional dance in close relationships. Focusing specifically on family relationships, they suggested that smoking may become part of various dimensions of family relationships—inclusion-connectedness, control, and intimacy. According to this interpretation, smoking is calibrated to the intricacies of family dynamics and serves as a way to be close or distant, to be in control or out of control, and to deal with the perils of intimacy. Following are examples taken from Whitehead and Doherty's (1989) interviews with thirty male and thirty female subjects, half of whom were current smokers and half exsmokers. Two-thirds were married, all were white, half had a high school education, and half had a college education. The median age was thirty-nine, with a range from eighteen to eighty-one.

SMOKING AND INCLUSION PATTERNS

Over half of the interview subjects described major inclusion issues surrounding their smoking. They used smoking to connect with relationship partners (they described socializing with friends who smoked and told the interviewer that "bumming cigarettes was a sharing thing") and to gain distance (one exsmoker said that smoking "was a substitute for conversation many times. . . . When I'd get into a frustrating or angry situation, I would tend to smoke at that time"). When it is used to withhold thoughts and feelings from a family member, then, in the words of one subject, "Smoking is a kind of shield against anything else." The following case illustrates how inclusion issues can complicate smoking cessation:

A family physician asked a medical family therapist to help him work with a couple who were in conflict over the husband's repeated failures to stop smoking cigarettes. He would abstain for a few weeks and then relapse. She wanted to become pregnant and did not want herself or the baby exposed to his "dirty" smoke. Exploring the context of the smoking revealed that the husband was not "allowed" to smoke in the house, went to the coffee shop located behind the couple's house to smoke after dinner, and there visited with his friends. At the times when he quit smoking, he also quit visiting with his friends, leading him to feel "boxed in" by the marriage. The medical family therapist pointed out that smoking served as a way for him to gain privacy and helped the couple negotiate new ways to obtain privacy without the presence of smoking.

Sometimes smoking can be associated with powerful issues of bonding in relationships. One research subject told the interviewer that she had been an avid nonsmoker but started smoking after her father died of lung cancer out of "anger because my father died" (Whitehead and Doherty, 1989, p. 269). Presumably her angry and ambivalent identification with her father led her to embark on the same deadly path that ended his life. This interview led Doherty to pay particular clinical attention to adult-onset smokers, who may experience major family events that precipitate the start of a behavior pattern they fully realize is self-destructive:

> A midforties couple with children ages sixteen and twenty came to therapy for help in dealing with the bulimia of the older child, who was in college and unwilling to attend therapy sessions. The therapist, noticing the huskiness of the father's voice and the presence of a cigarette pack in his shirt pocket, inquired about the husband's current and past smoking. The man had smoked since adolescence, was diagnosed with emphysema ten years earlier, but continued to smoke two packs a day. The therapist then asked the wife if she smoked. She replied that she had started to smoke ten years earlier when her husband was diagnosed with lung disease. She explained that she hoped that if "I started up, he would see that his smoking was hurting him as well as me." The therapist replied, "So you were thinking that if you started pushing yourself off the cliff, he would try to save both of you." She agreed with the analogy but said, "It didn't work; now I'm hooked too." This exchange was important in the therapist's assessment of the family's problems and required the therapist to be sensitive to health behavior issues that fall outside the traditional purview of mental health professionals.

For some individuals, then, smoking plays a role in patterns of bonding and connecting in the family. Issues of who smokes and who does not, who gains closeness or distance from smoking, are important barometers of family functioning and may be crucial elements in whether a smoker is able to quit and remain a nonsmoker. Smoking is a difficult habit to break even when it is not permeated with family interaction functions; but when it is associated with closeness, personal freedom, and family alliances, smoking can be nearly impossible to give up until these underlying issues are resolved.

SMOKING AND CONTROL PATTERNS

Like other addictive behaviors, smoking is defined in our culture as a problem of lack of self-control. It is not surprising, then, that smoking can become a family battleground over control. In the Whitehead and

Doherty (1989) study, about one-third of the subjects were rated as having moderately strong to very strong control issues in their social interactions around smoking. Some of these individuals reported intensely negative struggles with family members over their smoking: "[My family members react] violently, negative. [They say] 'You're going to die of that, it stinks, cut it out, you can do it' . . . [They are] extremely negative, which causes a little built-in resentment" (Whitehead and Doherty, 1989, p. 270).

People who feel that other family members are trying to control their smoking generally react negatively, either with overt or covert expressions of resentment. One male smoker told the interviewer that if nonsmokers complain about his smoking, he tells them to leave. Another man, an exsmoker, was still angry about his mother's refusal to talk to him when she caught him smoking: "It makes me angry because I figure it's my life, but they don't look at it that way."

When smokers become reactive to the efforts of family members because they experience themselves as losing control over their lives, the family system then becomes caught in the paradoxical hierarchical patterns described by Chloe Madanes (1981) as an incongruous hierarchy: the smoker experiences self as clearly out of control, which is proved by the smoking; family members who try to take control of the smoking behavior render the smoker even more out of control; the only way for the smoker to maintain or regain control of his or her life is to continue to smoke or to relapse from abstinence. In this paradoxical control struggle, the only way to be in control is to be out of control:

> In the case of the couple described earlier, where the wife wanted to become pregnant in a smoke-free environment and the husband used smoking to gain privacy, the control dynamic showed itself in a pattern whereby the wife nagged and criticized the husband about his filthy habit. He responded to her coerciveness by agreeing with her but saying that he was unable to stay off cigarettes. After the inclusion component of the smoking had been dealt with, the medical family therapist and the physician helped the couple to negotiate a more collaborative control pattern. This consisted of the husband promising to be straightforward and honest if he had a cigarette, and the wife resigning from the monitoring and criticizing role. They agreed that if the husband had a major

relapse—returned to regular smoking—then the couple would come back to the doctor's office for a discussion about what to do next. The couple expressed a sense that they were using the smoking issue to learn to deal with their boundary and control processes in their young marriage.

Occasionally, smoking becomes part of a virulent control struggle in a marriage or an exmarriage. One wife threatened to divorce her husband if he did not quit smoking; another woman tried to use her exhusband's smoking to deny him child visitation rights. In these cases, it seems best not to deal with the smoking itself but to address the underlying control (and inclusion) issues that are being played out here. When levels of coerciveness are extremely high, the therapist should not try to "help" the smoker to quit.

When control issues are paramount in smoking, then the smoker may be unable or unwilling to cede personal control to other family members or to health professionals. The dilemma for the smoker is that other people are "right" about the desirability of quitting—but they are extorting too high a price through their dominating behaviors. Some smokers would rather go to their grave as free individuals than yield to pressure to change. If a medical family therapist can help the family detoxify the control dynamics around smoking, then the smoker is free to make a personal decision to quit or to continue smoking for now. In the latter case, the therapist can help the family negotiate rules for buffering other family members from the smoke, if they wish, and to buffer the smoker from ongoing criticism from the nonsmokers. The goal is the healthiest family interactions, even in the face of unhealthy decisions by one family member. Since the medical family therapist's goal is not to convince the smoker to quit, respectful negotiations about family rules in the face of smoking can constitute the focus of treatment.

SMOKING AND SEXUAL INTERACTIONS

Doherty and Whitehead (1986) postulated that smoking may play a role in intimate sexual interactions among some couples. However, none of the sixty individuals interviewed in the Whitehead and Doherty (1989) study spontaneously reported such interactions, perhaps because no explicit questions in the interview were asked about this issue. On the other hand, smoking and sexual intercourse appeared to be linked in many movies in the midtwentieth century, before the antismoking movement took hold. Bernard Mausner (1973) observes that smoking can serve both as a tension release before intercourse for those who are anxious about the experience and as a relaxed communion after intercourse when both partners light up and quietly stare into space. He comments on how "versatile" smoking appears to be in human relationships.

TECHNIQUES FOR WORKING WITH SMOKERS AND THEIR FAMILIES

A number of specific techniques were implied in the foregoing case examples and discussion of smoking and inclusion patterns, control patterns, and intimacy interactions (see table 5.2):

Work with Family Members

The medical family therapist will not be asked to work with smoking unless the smoker already has experienced problems quitting; those who can do it on their own, or with mutually negotiated family support, do so. Therefore, negotiating with the smoker to expand the therapeutic system beyond the patient is a crucial first step. In our experience, patients who are seriously interested in quitting or who are seriously bothered by family interactions around smoking are quite willing to invite family members to participate. For married patients, the spouse is

TABLE 5.2
Techniques for Working with Smokers and Their Families

---

1. Work with mutliple family members if possible.

2. Emphasize the smoker's sense of agency.

3. Use behavioral contracting strategies.

4. Help negotiate alternative rituals.

5. Reframe failures and relapses as learning opportunities.

6. Avoid being too persuasive.

7. Support the smoker's decision to try a smoking cessation program.

---

essential; unmarried patients should include someone they interact with on a daily basis. Avoid using children and adolescents to help their parents quit because this reverses the generational hierarchy and may make the smoker resentful. Adult children, however, can be quite helpful. In general, we ask the smoker to choose whom to invite to the family sessions and request that the spouse be included.

Emphasize Agency

Emphasizing the smoker's sense of agency is the primary technique for working with family boundaries around smoking. Ask smokers whether this is a good time to try to quit, and stress that the decision is theirs. Ask the smoker if he or she wants help from family members or health professionals, and stress that only the smoker knows what might help. This process of interacting respectfully with the smoker models for the family (and often the health professional) a stance that respects the smoker's autonomy.

Use Behavioral Contracts

Behavioral contracting strategies can help the therapist negotiate explicit agreements about what the smoker, each family member, and the health professional (if one is present) will do in the days and weeks ahead. First ask the smoker to propose something that the family member could do to be supportive. Then ask the family member for agreement, disagreement, or modification and for some additional behavior either one might engage in. Using this procedure in alternating fashion, we have found that most couples and families can successfully negotiate support agreements that fit their idiosyncratic needs. For example, one wife asked her husband not to say anything when she reaches for a cigarette but only praise her for days when she successfully abstains. Another wife asked her husband to gently scold her if he sees her reaching for a cigarette; in this case, since he was "following orders," his critical behavior was supportive and not nagging. When both spouses smoke, the agreement might involve one spouse smoking outside the presence of the one trying to quit. We have not found contracting successful, however, if the supporting spouse also smokes.

Negotiate Alternatives

If smoking is connected with couple inclusion-connectedness, then the partners may need to develop different bonding rituals. In one case both spouses quit but reported the next week that they had spent no time together in the prior week. Because their companionship time focused around coffee and smoking after dinner, giving up smoking led them to go their own ways. The couple decided to go for an after-dinner walk together as a substitute for smoking-associated connecting. Similarly, families may need to decide how to handle smoking at the next family celebration if some people continue to smoke and others abstain.

Reframe Failures as Opportunities

Smokers who say they want to quit but continue smoking often feel like personal failures, an opinion sometimes shared by family members. The therapist who emphasizes the patient's agency can reframe failures and relapses as learning opportunities. The smoker has much to learn even from a failed attempt: (1) perhaps this was not a good time to try to quit; how will the patient know when a better time arrives? (2) perhaps the patient did not prepare himself or herself for the situation that led to the relapse; what strategies can now be applied in similar situations? (3) the patient or family had not realized that few people succeed on their first few tries to quit; how can they realign their expectations for a long-range effort? Repeated failures can be handled with the first option listed here by suggesting that the smoker may have decided that it is not a good time to quit smoking. In other words, the medical family therapist should keep focusing on the patient's sense of agency—of making ongoing decisions, even if those decisions are not popular with the doctor or the family.

Avoid Persuasion

Implied in the first three techniques for working with smokers and their families is a therapist stance we now make explicit. The medical family therapist's job is to help smokers quit if they *want* to quit and to work with them and their families and their health professionals toward supportive and healthy interpersonal processes. Therapists who are too enthusiastic about the smoker quitting or not relapsing easily enter the same coercive loops that families and health professionals often are caught in with the smoker. Few medical family therapists are neutral on the value of smoking cessation, but the therapist can be neutral in the sense of respecting the patient's autonomy and sense of timing. At the same time, the medical family therapist must respect the family's right to place boundaries around smoking, since passive smoking affects their health as well. Family sessions that deal with smoking should be approached not with eagerness for the smoker to quit but with a supportive stance toward the rights and boundaries of all parties involved.

Support a Decision to Try a Program

Key to supporting the smoker's decision to try a smoking cessation program is the medical family therapist's support of the patient's sense of agency in approaching smoking cessation—through whatever means he or she thinks may help. If the therapist makes a determined referral to a stop-smoking program, then failure in the program may damage the therapeutic relationship. Likewise, if the patient is being pressured by family members to join a program, the therapist's first priority should be to support the patient's autonomy. Success in the program can be a source of cautious celebration (because relapse is common), and failure in the program can be seen as an experiment that yielded information about the smoker's current level of interest or ability to quit smoking. In either case, the therapist remains in a supportive but not overinvolved mode with the smoker and the family.

Medical family therapists can work effectively with families and cigarette smoking only to the extent that they have resolved personal, familial, and cultural issues around smoking, an activity that is deadly as well as symbolic of dependence and self-indulgence. The leading trap is to become caught in coercive coalitions with either family members or health professionals. Smokers are accustomed to being coerced and know how to deflect it. A healthy dialogue about an unhealthy behavior is the only path to a healthy outcome.

A Family Perspective on Obesity

Medical family therapists generally encounter the issue of obesity when consulting or doing therapy with an adult whose weight complicates a chronic illness such as diabetes or when a child or adolescent is believed to be psychosocially impaired and medically threatened by overweight. In these situations, the weight problem is the primary impetus for the consultation or referral. In other situations, the obesity is not part of the original reason for therapy but emerges as a problem during the course of treatment.

Depending on how overweight or obesity is measured, the national prevalence rates are 19 to 27 percent for American adults, with rates nearly equal for males and females (Centers for Disease Control, 1988). Overweight tends to begin in childhood, proceed to become a lifelong problem for many people, and run in families. The causes of obesity are assumed to include genetic factors and family environment factors, with a smaller subset of individuals influenced by metabolic and endocrinological disorders (Sobal and Muncie, 1990). However, the medical research has been inconclusive on the subject of the negative health consequence of obesity alone, with many studies showing only a weak association between body weight and mortality (Manson et al., 1987). On the other hand, obesity does play a negative role in many common diseases, particularly hypertension, diabetes mellitus, coronary artery disease, and skeletal system diseases (Sobal and Muncie, 1990).

Dieting has been the principal means that individuals use to lose their excessive weight. However, the relapse rates from diets are high, and many scholars are concluding that biological mechanisms make it likely that dieters eventually regain more weight than they lose (Stunkard and Penick, 1979). In addition, major sociocultural factors are involved in weight gain and weight loss: obesity is higher in low-income groups, and there is a high degree of cultural stigmatization of the obese (Wadden and Stunkard, 1985). Interestingly, however, there is no evidence that obese people in the general population show more psychopathology than nonobese people (Wadden and Stunkard, 1985).

After Hilde Bruch's pioneering analysis of obesity and the family, nearly forty years passed until family systems and obesity issues were addressed (Bruch and Touraine, 1940). Behavioral psychologists' interest in spouse and parent support for weight loss led to a series of studies that suggested that family involvement could be helpful (Brownell, Kelman, and Stunkard, 1983; Epstein et al., 1990), and by the mid-1980s, family therapists were showing interest in obesity (Ganley, 1986; Harkaway, 1983, 1986; Hecker, Martin, and Martin, 1986; Stuart and Jacobson, 1987). The following discussion is based on the collaboration of William Doherty with Jill Elka Harkaway, a family therapist with expertise in working with families of children with chronic, serious obesity. Doherty and Harkaway (1990) organized the assessment and treatment of obesity around the Family FIRO Model.

We do not assume that obesity in children and adults invariably serves functions in the family system. In some cases the genetic load or personal eating and exercise habits make obesity highly likely, and the individual's weight becomes incorporated in nonproblematic ways into the family's interaction patterns. When these individuals try to lose weight, the family is supportive, does not feel threatened, and stays out of control struggles over food, eating, and weight. The medical family therapist's role with these families is to help the patient and family cope as best they can with the possible negative effects of the overweight on the patient's health and to minimize the negative self-image the patient might have developed because of social stigmatization. In this chapter, however, we provide assessment categories and treatment techniques for situations in which the therapist believes that the family has been organized around the obesity in a dysfunctional way—generally shown in serious psychological problems in the obese member, inability to master life transitions such as leaving home, obsession with food or weight, or continual conflict in the family over food or weight.

OBESITY AND INCLUSION PATTERNS

Obesity can serve the following inclusion functions in families:

Loyalty to the Family

In some families, obesity is a multigenerational theme that provides a sense of self-definition. In such families, obesity may demonstrate loyalty to the family, and losing weight can be perceived as an affront to the others, who continue their struggle alone. Loyalty can better be managed by trying to lose weight but failing. Doherty and Harkaway (1990) illustrate this dynamic with a family in which the highly obese adolescent boy was following the model of his uncle, who had held a world record for weight. All members of the family were overweight, and the uncle was the family star.

Coalitions in the Family

When one parent is overweight and the other thin, the child may be making a political statement by his or her weight. The child does not consciously choose a weight to correspond with one parent, but similarities in body shape and weight problems can indicate coalitions in the family. Pay particular attention to whether the thin parent criticizes the fat child for the same behaviors the obese parent engages in.

Delaying Entry into the Adult World

Because of the stigmatization of obese children in social groups, they often hold tight to the family for emotional support. For some families, this situation is considered acceptable and even encouraged. By delaying a child's entry into the adult world, obesity can protect the family's boundary. In fact, by staying out of the mating "market," the obese child never has to leave home.

Protecting the Marriage

A plaque one of us saw on the Ohio Turnpike read as follows: "A plump wife and a full barn never did a man any harm." This bit of sexist folk wisdom communicates the protective value of obesity in some marriages. Some couples admit that they feel that there is a protective value to obesity and that if one or both partners lost weight, they would worry more about extramarital affairs and the stability of their marriage.

OBESITY AND CONTROL PATTERNS

Obesity tends to be viewed culturally as a problem of self-control. Obese people are thought to overindulge in food, although no evidence shows that obese people in general eat more than nonobese people.

Because obese people are thought to be unable or unwilling to control their appetites, family members may try to perform the control task for the obese member, in which case weight control serves as a metaphor for relationship control. The following specific sequences of control interactions were observed clinically by Doherty and Harkaway (1990).

Maintaining Control by Losing Control

The paradoxical power struggle that is observed with smoking and nonsmokers also appears in families dealing with obesity. The partner tries to control the obese person, who agrees to "be good"—that is, to lose the unwelcome weight. Over time, however, the partner's helpfulness begins to feel coercive, and the obese person resists or rebels, prompting further efforts at control by the partner. Eventually, the obese person abandons the diet, and the partner gives up in disgust. The obese person has won the control struggle by making the partner back away but has lost the weight struggle one more time. This incongruous hierarchy can also be played out with health professionals, weight loss program staff, and therapists.

A Rebellion That Backfires

This paradoxical power struggle can occur with parents and children with obesity: the child's weight is too high; the parents tell the child to reduce sweets intake and not eat between meals; the child rebels by both refusing to eat less and perhaps even eating more; the more the parent tries to control the child's weight, the more weight the child gains. Although perhaps resembling a successful rebellion, this is a pseudorebellion: although the child is trying to maintain autonomy from an intrusive parent, the child actually becomes more closely tied to parents through both the preoccupying power struggle and the isolating social stigma.

The Obese Child with Too Much Power

Sometimes the child's weight does not have a strong inclusion function in the family. It is not tied to loyalty, connecting, or alliance issues but indicates a child with too much power. The battleground over control happens to be played out around food, with the child's tantrums being successful (often with one parent) in obtaining snacks. The parents are too divided to resist effectively, but they are not invested in the child's obesity. These cases are more easily treated than ones in which family inclusion issues are paramount.

OBESITY AND SEXUAL PATTERNS

Sexuality is closely tied to body weight and body image. Although sexual interactions can relate to inclusion (for example, fidelity) and control (for example, how the partners manage their differences), here we deal with emotionally intimate sexual encounters and obesity.

Weight can be used to manage sexual closeness and distance. For someone who is having trouble managing emotional closeness in the relationship, gaining weight (if thinness is seen as a barometer of attractiveness) can send a message that sexual intimacy is not desired. Conversely, the thinner partner may use the other's weight gain as an excuse to have fewer sexual interactions. In their research study of weight and marriage in a cross-section of American couples, Stuart and Jacobson (1987) found that wives who were mildly discontented with their marriages were most likely to use their weight to foster emotional and sexual distance from their husbands. Contented wives did not want sexual distance, and strongly discontented wives did not need any excuses for sexual distance.

TECHNIQUES FOR WORKING WITH OBESITY IN FAMILIES

The techniques for working with obesity in families have many similarities with those used for dealing with smoking issues in families: emphasize the agency of the patient, uncover and deal with inclusion issues, disentangle control issues through multilateral negotiations. Here we emphasize some special aspects of treating obesity in a family systems context (see table 5.3).

Attend to Personal Weight Issues

Therapists who fear personal identification with obesity—based on past experience, present assessment of their own weight or family members' weight, or concern about becoming obese in the future—are particularly prone to excessive enthusiasm about helping obese individuals or exces-

TABLE 5.3

Techniques for Working with Obesity and Families

1. Pay attention to your own weight issues.
2. Disassociate yourself from measuring successful treatment by numbers on the scale.
3. Focus initially on the patient's decision-making process about losing weight.
4. Distinguish between weight that creates medical problems versus culturally defined weight goals.
5. Accept weight loss failure gracefully.
6. Help the family stay supportive but not overinvolved in the weight loss efforts.
7. For individuals involved in major control dynamics, encourage attendance at community programs.

sive pessimism about the possibility of change. For the unaware therapist, the therapy becomes a way to work on personal or family issues around weight, self-indulgence, and self-control—and be paid for it. However, when the patient begins to regain any weight lost (many patients oblige the doctor and the therapist by losing a few pounds at the outset of treatment), the therapist is apt to become coercive and eventually give up in disgust.

Do Not Measure Success by the Scale

Other professionals before you probably fell into the trap of trying to measure successful treatment by numbers on the scale. Focusing on weight goals keeps alive the cycle of preoccupation with the scale and prevents an exploration of the personal and family issues that may keep the obese person from making a mature decision about his or her weight, eating, and exercise.

Focus on the Patient's Decision

By focusing initially on the patient's decision-making process about losing weight and being neutral about whether the patient loses weight, the medical family therapist is in a position to help the patient analyze the reasons for trying to lose weight and avoid attempting the drastic changes that often accompany dieting. Obese people and their families tend to have magical beliefs about how wonderful life will be if the weight is lost. Sometimes the obese individual is basing the decision on self-loathing or pressure from others—neither of which is likely to lead to a desirable outcome. During the decision-making process, often by taking a "go slow" approach, the therapist can work effectively with the inclusion issues surrounding obesity: Who will the patient be disloyal to if he or she loses weight? What relationship might be disturbed? Who will the patient stop having meals with? How will he or she handle new sexual possibilities?

Separate Medical and Cultural Issues

The therapist needs to distinguish between weight that creates medical problems and culturally defined weight goals. A patient's diabetes might be controllable with a fifteen-pound weight loss, but the patient may want to lose forty pounds to regain the weight she had as a nineteen-year-old. The therapist can identify with the health goal—if the patient genuinely embraces the goal of controlling the diabetes—while being neutral on the patient's choice to lose a larger amount of weight. Patients who have encountered health professionals who pressure them to calibrate themselves to the idealized norms of the weight charts sometimes find it liberating when a pragmatic therapist concentrates on losing only enough to get out of medical danger.

Accept Failure

The therapist can discuss these weight loss failures in terms of timing in the patient's life—always emphasizing the patient's sense of agency. People have multiple priorities in their lives, and controlling a chronic illness may not necessarily be near the top of the list. The medical family therapist, preferably in conjunction with the patient's physician and nurse, can help the patient and family become clear about these priorities, even if that means that everyone accept the likelihood that the patient's weight will remain higher than is medically indicated, say, for safe blood sugar levels. In these cases, the patient might be encouraged to set a more realistic goal of not gaining more weight.

Help Families Stay Supportive But Not Overinvolved

There is growing evidence that one of the best ways for spouses to support weight loss in the obese partners is to be *quietly* supportive and to stay out of the way. Talking about food, dieting, and weight can create inclusion and control dynamics that complicate matters for the obese person. Leslie Faricy (1990), in her study of twenty-five couples in which one partner had successfully lost over twenty-five pounds in a weight loss program, found that in most cases the partner was supportive from a distance and was not involved in the process. In the most successful treatment program for obese children, parents were taught ways to deal with their own weight and were taught, along with their child, certain behavior modification approaches (Epstein et al., 1990). This highly effective program helped parents and children achieve a moderate level of involvement during the weight loss process, with parents concentrating on themselves as well as on the child.

Encourage a Decision to Try a Program

For chronically overweight people who struggle with major psychological and family control issues over eating and weight, Overeaters Anonymous offers a potentially helpful approach to eating and weight. The program's use of Alcoholics Anonymous principles helps individuals to shortcircuit control issues around eating by emphasizing the "powerlessness" of the individual over food. This reframe sometimes reduces the sense of struggle, and the group cohesion helps to reduce social isolation. Unlike most commercial weight loss programs such as Weight Watchers, the goal of OA is more personal growth than weight loss. For patients who are interested in the commercial weight loss programs, the therapist can support their personal choices about joining but also their choices about quitting without guilt.

The following two cases of medical family therapy with obesity are taken from the work of Jill Harkaway, as described in Doherty and Harkaway (1990):

Joan was a twelve-year-old girl referred for obesity and compulsive overeating. She had become symptomatic with a rapid weight gain after her parents divorced and her father remarried. The family believed that the father was the only one who could understand and manage her behavior, since he himself was obsessive and a compulsive overeater.

The apparent loss of control over her eating and subsequent rapid weight gain led to the father's continued involvement with Joan and her mother. Every day after work he stopped at their house for dinner, rather than going home to his new wife, in order to ensure that Joan was not bingeing and was eating a proper diet meal. He called daily and spent time on weekends with Joan and her mother. Thus the father, who would otherwise be drawing a clear boundary and aligning himself with his new family, was included in the "old" family because of the child's problem.

The therapist's goal was to help the family manage its inclusion issues around the formation of a new set of boundaries that would allow the family transition to be completed. The outcome was that the family allowed the father to give up his old role and find a different way to connect with his daughter without the need for the daughter to be obese and compulsively overeat.

Linda, age thirty-five, sought treatment for lifelong severe obesity. She was involved with a man who loved her but wanted her to lose weight. She agreed with him that she was too heavy and promised to lose weight for him. They had become locked in an unfortunate sequence: the more he tried to help her lose weight, the more weight she gained. She said she desperately wanted to lose weight, not only for him but for herself as well.

The therapist learned during the second interview that the couple had been discussing marriage for some time but that their concerns about weight and its meaning in their relationship had become a source of pain and confusion for them both. The confused messages were, "If she loved me, she'd lose weight," and "If he loved me, he wouldn't care what I weighed." The conflict over the weight kept them at once overinvolved and emotionally disconnected.

Although the struggle over weight was the couple's "ticket"

to therapy and weight was a major battleground for control, the therapist saw the primary issue as one of commitment (inclusion) and focused treatment accordingly. When this issue was handled successfully, the woman was free to handle her weight as a personal issue concerning health and self-image and not as a metaphor for marital commitment. In cases such as this, the "success" of medical family therapy is not in the pounds lost but in reducing emotional trauma and salvaging a relationship.

Conclusion

The systems orientation to health behavior problems that are typically defined as individual is a strikingly new approach for both patients and professionals. It offers not only a new technology for behavior change but a broad and complex view of health behaviors and the goals of treatment. From a family therapy perspective, an effective therapeutic intervention can be defined as one in which any member of the system (the patient or a family member) or any relationship in the system (a marriage relationship, a parent-child relationship, or a relationship involving the physician, a nurse, or therapist) changes in a healthy direction. Sometimes the overweight diabetic patient keeps the weight on and the blood sugar high, but the family and physician learn a lesson about who is ultimately responsible for the patient's health. Sometimes the smoker, freed from the burden of family inclusion and control dynamics, feels free for the first time to choose to quit smoking cigarettes. The victory here is not merely in the abstention or the improved lung or heart functioning but also in the promotion of agency and communion in the patient and those who care for the patient.

CHAPTER 6

Somatizing Patients and Their Families

SOMATIZATION DISORDER, hypochondriasis,* and somatic fixation are common problems that frustrate primary care physicians, drive medical costs skyward, and contribute to patients' and families' feelings of being misunderstood. Somatization is a process whereby people with difficult life situations present not with anxiety, depression, or relationship problems, but with numerous physical symptoms. Somatizing patients frequently do not differentiate between emotional and physical experience and do not use emotional language to express emotional distress. Instead, they use somatic language to describe all difficulties, whether physical or emotional:

> PATIENT: My back hurts. My head is throbbing. And I can't eat because my throat is closed up. I think I may have cancer. Could there be a tumor in my throat?
> THERAPIST: I understand that you are very uncomfortable today,

*In this chapter, we address all conditions listed in the *Diagnostic and Statistical Manual III-R* under somatoform disorders. See the *DSM III-R* for the currently accepted definitions of these and other related terms. For purposes of psychotherapeutic intervention, we do not find these distinctions clinically useful.

Mr. Brown. I know your physician does not currently believe you have cancer, but you should discuss any new symptoms with him. A few minutes ago, when we were drawing your genogram, you said that two of your babies died soon after birth. Can you tell me some more about this?

PATIENT: They are gone. I had to be hospitalized soon after because my back was killing me. I had surgery on a disc in my back. It's never really been right ever since. I haven't been able to work, and my wife accuses me of being lazy. Do you think that new medicine that's in *Newsweek* this week might help me?

Somatizing behavior is a prevalent problem that can occur not only in hypochondriasis or psychosomatic disease but also in any illness or injury. For some people, somatization is part of a lifelong coping style that functions like a chronic illness that ebbs and flows depending on other physical and emotional stresses and strains. Mr. Brown, in the case just cited, experienced a ruptured disc soon after the death of his second son. The emotional components of his problem played a significant role in his inability to recuperate fully.

Somatizing patients experience most of their problems as physical and frequently seek medical attention, but they challenge the traditional medical model. Their physical symptoms either do not make physiologic sense or are grossly in excess of what would be expected from physical findings. Typically somatizing patients vociferously deny any emotional component to their problems.

Medical providers often become enormously frustrated with these patients. Many physicians have been taught to be somatically fixated in their approach to medicine—that is, to focus exclusively and inappropriately on the somatic aspects of a complex problem (Van Eijk et al., 1983). A somatically fixated medical approach renders physicians much less capable of helping somatizing patients. Patients often believe these doctors do not understand them, cannot find out what is wrong, and seem not to want to care for them. Family members, who may share the same somatically fixated health beliefs as the patient, may express their own frustration at the traditional medical system for not curing their loved one's symptoms.

Traditional mental health approaches have also failed these patients. Psychodynamic theory understands somatization as part of the patient's character structure—part of the way the patient defends against frightening emotional experiences. Because somatization is seen as deeply rooted, and because traditional therapists recognize the difficulty in establishing a working alliance with somatizing patients, these patients are usually thought of as "poor candidates for psychotherapy" (Greenson, 1967). We have received referrals from a primary care physician, desperate for help, accompanied by a letter from a psychiatrist saying that the patient is basically untreatable.

Somatization is a problem that begs for a biopsychosocial, family systems approach. Treating these patients in individual therapy can become a losing battle between the patient's symptoms and the therapy. Dealing with context and interactional issues around the somatizing behavior can provide the leverage and the necessary intensity for successful treatment. Several uncontrolled studies found family therapy successful with somatizing adults (Hudgens, 1979) and children (Mullins and Olson, 1990).

Collaboration is a crucial ingredient for a biopsychosocial approach to somatization. Although some somatizing patients can be managed exclusively by their primary care physician, many benefit from a team approach that includes a medical family therapist. This team approach includes close collaboration between the medical family therapist and the medical providers, and between the treatment team and the family. (See Taplin, McDaniel, and Naumburg, 1987, for an example of this collaboration.) Because somatizing patients initially do not accept the emotional component of their problem, collaboration by the therapist with the physician plays a role in the treatment of somatizing families that is even more pivotal than the one played with patients with other medical problems. Without this close collaboration, the patient and family rarely accept the referral and usually do not continue in the early stages of treatment with a medical family therapist. Once collaborative relationships with the medical providers and the family are established, the therapist can help to develop an integrated approach that allows the medical team to understand the patient's symptoms and treat the somatic components of the problem, the family to support the patient's health and well-being, and the patient to develop competence and confidence in monitoring and managing his or her physical and emotional needs.

Cultural Support for Somatization

The notion that a physical symptom must have a primarily organic cause, or that an emotional feeling is primarily determined by some psychological experience, is widely accepted in our society. The Cartesian mind-body dichotomy pervades the structures and the meanings we construct to describe our illness experiences. The idea that mind and body are an integrated, related, communicating whole has only recently and tentatively been considered by mainstream Western society. The complex disorder of somatization symbolizes our culture's struggle to recognize the integration and interdependence of physical and emotional aspects of life.*

Our culture also struggles with the relationship between individual responsibility and illness. Again we dichotomize. We tend to hold people responsible for their emotional problems, while believing on the whole that they are *not* responsible for disease or illness. Framing a problem as "physical," as is true for somatizing patients, allows for a passive-dependent patient role that is sanctioned by most people. Medical anthropologist Arthur Kleinman describes somatization as "culturally authorized, socially useful, and personally availing" (1986, p. 151).

The fields of medicine and psychotherapy struggle with the mind-body dichotomy, as does our culture as a whole. Medicine's worship of biotechnology seduces physicians and patients alike into becoming somatically fixated and concluding that biomedicine *is* medicine rather than only one important component of the diagnosis and treatment of a patient. As we demonstrate, exclusive application of the biomedical model to somatizing behavior is likely to escalate the symptoms, frustrate the patient and physician, and increase medical visits and costs. In the psychotherapy field, likewise, exclusive focus on psychosocial issues often results in rejection of therapeutic treatment by the somatizing patient and rejection of the patient by the therapist.

A biopsychosocial approach to somatizing behavior counteracts

---

*Somatization is a behavior pattern that occurs worldwide, but it varies in prevalence across cultures. Asian cultures, even less accepting of psychosocial explanations than Western cultures, appear to have a higher incidence of somatization than does the West (Bhatt, Tomenson, and Benjamin, 1989). Hispanic people also tend to have a higher incidence of somatization than do Anglos (Koss, 1990).

this cultural support for the mind-body dichotomy. It allows both the physician and the therapist to assume that every physical symptom has some biological, some psychological, and often some social component to it. The biopsychosocial model avoids the reductionism of trying to discover whether some symptom is "organic" or "all in your head." Somatizing behavior is most often a complex blend of physical, emotional, and interactional processes.

Recognizing and Understanding the Somatizing Patient

The somatizing patient is extremely sensitive to bodily cues (Barsky, 1970). Using a diary to record physical symptoms, Robert Kellner and Brian Sheffield (1973) found that 60 to 80 percent of healthy people experience some somatic symptoms in any one week. Of course, most of them do not label those symptoms as problems that require physician intervention. However, individuals' perceptions of a symptom are quite variable. Several studies have shown that the same amount of tissue pathology produces varying degrees of functional impairment and subjective distress in different individuals (Eisenberg, 1979). Those who are sensitive to bodily cues and experience greater impairment and distress are more likely to label their symptoms as problems in need of treatment.

THE EXPERIENCE OF SOMATIC FIXATION

Figure 6.1 is a continuum of somatic fixation presented by patients, ranging from somatic denial at one end to somatic delusions at the other.

Somatic denial	Sensitive to bodily sensations	The "worried well"	Obsessed by symptoms	Somatic delusion

FIGURE 6.1
Range of Somatic Fixation by Patients
Source: Adapted from S. H. McDaniel, T. Campbell, and D. Seaburn (1990),
Family-oriented primary care (New York: Springer-Verlag).
Used by permission.

Somatizing patients have an unhealthy and uncomfortable relationship with their bodies. This discomfort is often expressed in sexual inhibitions or problems:

Suzie presented as a twenty-eight-year-old separated woman with multiple somatic complaints. Her head and arms ached, and she had shooting pains in her head and her legs, frequent stomach distress, and early morning awakening. Suzie was convinced that she had a serious, potentially life-threatening illness that had not been discovered by her physician. She requested all the blood tests and diagnostic procedures she knew of (including an expensive magnetic resonance image) to discover the problem. Of great concern to her was her five-year-old son, who she felt was manifesting many of the same symptoms she had. She worried that her "disease" was communicable and she had given it to him. On several occasions, Suzie wondered whether she should be quarantined to ensure that no one else got the disease.

Most of the time Suzie functioned extremely well. She was a highly valued and productive employee at the large company where she worked. She also worked out and went to a strenuous aerobics class five days a week. Frustrated with the difference between this patient's internal experience and her external appearance, her physician referred her to a medical family therapist.

It took several months in therapy to uncover Suzie's story. Her symptoms, she said, began around the time of her marital separation. Suzie left her husband partly out of dissatisfaction with the relationship and also because of a blossoming relationship with a man at work. After the separation, this man continued his sexual relationship with her but made it clear that he did not want a serious commitment. After hearing this, Suzie had a rapid succession of affairs, two with men who were casual acquaintances, but then quickly felt distressed about these experiences. Soon after this, Suzie contracted a viral infection.

Suzie asked her doctor to check for any sexually transmitted diseases. Her tests were negative, but the viral symptoms persisted and developed into symptoms that she worried might be life threatening. At first she was concerned her "disease" was some-

127

thing similar to AIDS, sexually transmitted and eventually fatal. After she experienced symptoms for about a year, articles on the symptoms of chronic fatigue syndrome began appearing in the media. Suzie then described herself as having "chronic fatigue syndrome without the fatigue."

She denied any lingering stress or emotional difficulty with her separation or subsequent affairs. The "stress" was experienced, she said, because no one could diagnosis or treat her illness. She accepted a referral to a medical family therapist to try to alleviate the stress she experienced in receiving medical treatment.

Suzie is typical of many somatizing patients in her experience of her illness and her frustrations in trying to obtain treatment for her problems. She was also typical in that she had many of the physical symptoms of depression and anxiety, even though she denied any mood disorder. (Suzie fervently believed that she never experienced any depression, "only relief," after her separation.) Some somatizing patients benefit from treatment that includes antidepressants. Suzie eventually agreed to a trial of antidepressants because of their successful use with chronic fatigue. Although the medication did not cure her problems, she did report that it was helpful in diminishing her pain.

Like Suzie, all somatizing patients should be screened for major depression and panic disorder. Both conditions are very common in these patients, often are missed by referring physicians, and respond to antidepressant treatment (Katon and Russo, 1989). Family therapists who do not prescribe medication can collaborate with the patient's primary care physician or consulting psychiatrist to facilitate this aspect of the treatment plan.

How does somatizing behavior develop? Robert Kellner described the cycle he believes occurs with many somatizing patients: "[A] common sequence in a hypochondriacal reaction is the experience of new somatic symptoms at times of anxiety or depression followed by a selective perception of bodily sensations, motivated by fear of disease and subsequent increase in anxiety with more somatic symptoms; these elements become linked in a vicious cycle, by frequent repetition are overlearned, and the chain becomes predictable" (1986, pp. 10–11). It is not difficult to imagine the interactions with both family members and medical providers that might reinforce this behavior.

FAMILY FACTORS IN THE DEVELOPMENT AND MAINTENANCE OF
SOMATIZATION

Many family factors can encourage or support somatizing behavior. Some family cultures lack any language for emotional experience: all family members may be alexithymic and allow only language about physical experience; children receive attention for physical pain but no attention for emotional pain. This approach conditions children to experience any need or problem as physical, and physical symptoms become their language for a range of experiences. Abuse is not uncommon in emotionally impoverished environments. Several studies have uncovered a relationship between severe somatizing behavior and early deprivation, physical or sexual abuse, or trauma (Katon, 1985). For these patients, early emotional trauma has a significant physical component.

No research, as of yet, has focused on families of somatizing patients. Clinically, it seems that families with severely somatizing members share patterns of interaction that seek to avoid or anesthesize emotional pain. A significant number of somatizing adults are married to other somatizing adults. These couples share a language of bodily discomfort. Other somatizing adults marry caregiving partners. The caregivers may not themselves be ill, but they, too, privilege communication about physical events and deny most emotional experience. Somatization also occurs frequently in association with alcoholism or a family history of alcoholism. Returning to our case example, the family factors in the development of Suzie's somatizing behavior were significant:

Suzie denied any history of physical or sexual abuse. However, her childhood had been difficult. Her father was alcoholic and quite unpredictable. Her mother, she said, was "always sick." Suzie learned about somatizing behavior quite early. Then she married a man who also seemed to be always symptomatic. He requested frequent nurturing from Suzie because of his illnesses and the many accidents that occurred on his job as a lineman. Suzie came to resent her role as caregiver, and the couple argued about whether she nurtured him enough when he was sick. After separating from her husband, her next boyfriend was physically healthy but had a tendency to drink too much. In this relationship, she became the patient and her boyfriend the caregiver.

Including the family and friendship network in the treatment of patients like Suzie can be essential for interrupting communication patterns based solely on physical symptoms, and in creating space and obtaining permission for additional communication based on emotional experience. One significant session with Suzie late in treatment included her boyfriend and two friends from the chronic fatigue support group. At the end of the session, Suzie announced her resolve to drop out of the group with this comment: "This group just isn't meeting my needs. I want to maintain my friendships, but I'm too busy to listen to everyone's depressing stories." Several weeks later, she also broke up with her boyfriend who had refused treatment for his alcoholism.*

Family members may also act as resources to treatment. Family members of somatizing patients often worry about both the physical well-being and the unhappiness of their symptomatic loved ones. Because of this concern, family members may provide important support for therapy, especially in the early phases when patients may be most resistant. Suzie's sister and mother brought her to the early sessions because they worried "that she might die if we don't try everything." In reality, the life span of somatizing patients is no shorter than that of the general population (Coryell, 1981). However, the life of the patient and the lives of other family members can be dominated by physical symptoms, interpersonal struggle, and an excess of medical care.

Somatization and the Experience of the Referring Physician

If the problem of persistent physical symptoms is frustrating for the patient and the patient's family, the experience of the physician whose satisfaction comes from healing is also intensely frustrating. Consider the following poem, written by a physician who was moved to question his career choice after an afternoon encounter with a somatizing patient:

*At a one-year follow-up, Suzie had a new boyfriend, a new job, a new house, and only occasional headaches.

SECOND THOUGHTS

It's five o' five
day's almost done.
All the patients seen
but one.

I stand outside
the exam room door,
read the nurse's note
with horror.

"New patient says
teeth itch at night,
stomach aches when shoes
too tight.

"Numbness starting
in the knee,
dizziness
since '63.

"Food goes up
instead of down,
always tired,
lies around . . ."

Tears start to fall,
I just can't hide 'em.
The note goes on
ad infinitum:

" . . . climbing stairs
causes gas,
no sense of smell
when driving fast.

"Left hand hurts
and right hand's weak,
sneeze sends pain
from hands to feet.

"Last week had
a pain in the chest . . ."
Stop! No more!
Can't read the rest!

I think business school
would have been wiser,
'cause they don't have
somaticizers.

—Tillman Farley, M.D.

Somatizing patients are extremely common in the offices of primary care physicians like Dr. Farley. One study found as many as 60 percent of all primary care patients present with somatic complaints that are an expression of psychosocial distress (Cummings and VandenBos, 1981). Many of these patients are those referred to as the "worried well" (see figure 6.1). These patients require some reassurance and time from medical providers, but it is the small group of patients with serious somatizing disorders that most challenge the technical skills of providers and escalate costs of the medical system. Frank deGruy, Lisa Columbia, and Perry Dickinson (1987) found that patients with a diagnosis of somatization disorder had a 50 percent higher rate of office visits, 50 percent higher charges, charts close to twice as thick as the average chart, and significantly more diagnoses than matched controls. These patients may have expensive, potentially dangerous, and unnecessary procedures and treatments. It is not unusual for patients with somatization disorder to have a history of numerous hospitalizations and surgical procedures (Zoccolillo and Cloninger, 1986). The overall cost of these patients to the health care system is staggering. Kellner (1990) estimated that one-fifth of the medical budget is spent on somatizing patients.

Somatization disorder has been termed medicine's "blind spot" (Quill, 1985). Many physicians misunderstand the indirect communication conveyed by somatizing behavior and use a biomedical frame to understand and treat the complaint. When somatizing patients are told by these physicians that they are healthy or given a relatively benign explanation for their symptoms, these patients feel misunderstood and react with persistent complaints and demands. (In contrast, most other patients react with relief to this news [Pilowsky, 1978]). The biomedically oriented physician, feeling incompetent, then may react to the patient's demands with anger ("This is all in your head"), distancing (for example, not returning phone calls), more diagnostic tests, or referral to a specialist. Figure 6.2 describes this somatically fixated physician-patient interaction.

The way out of this cycle for the physician is to take a biopsychosocial approach to patient care from the beginning. In this approach, the physician does a comprehensive evaluation by conducting an interview that intersperses biomedical and psychosocial questions (Doherty and Baird, 1983). He or she establishes a collaborative, rather than authoritarian, relationship with the patient and the family, models tolerating uncertainty, and may ask a family therapist to join the treatment team. Together, the physician and therapist set limited goals and monitor patient functioning rather than symptoms. The physician continues to be available after the family has terminated with the therapist.

In addition to providing comprehensive care for these patients, a collaborative relationship can be cost-effective. G. Richard Smith, Roberta Monson, and Debby Ray (1986) found that a psychiatric consultation coupled with recommendations for the primary care physician reduced the medical costs of patients with somatization disorder by 53 percent. F. J. A. Huygen (1982) also found that referrals to a family therapist in his office resulted in much less overutilization of medical services.

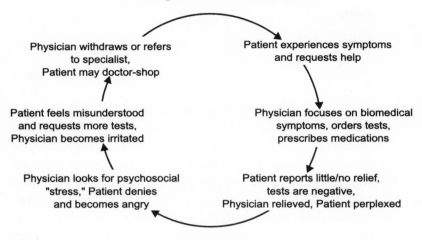

FIGURE 6.2
Somatically Fixed Physician-Patient Interaction
Source: Adapted from S. H. McDaniel, T. Campbell, and D. Seaburn (1990),
Family-oriented primary care (New York: Springer-Verlag).
Used by permission.

Clinical Strategies for Treating Somatizing Patients and Their Families

REFERRAL

Every aspect of the referral of a somatizing patient is challenging for the referring physician and for the therapist who accepts the referral. Somatizing patients who easily accept a referral to a mental health specialist by definition do not have the problem. The contract for treatment early on is with the referring physician. The patient and family members are usually somewhere between skeptical and actively resistant to seeing a therapist, so the referral usually requires creativity, patience, and extra energy on the part of the physician and the therapist.

Much of the work for the therapist with these referrals involves consulting with the physician, as early in the process as possible, to build a close collaborative relationship. It is easier with other kinds of medical referrals to use a traditional, limited referral format for collaboration. (See chapter 3 for a discussion of the different kinds of collaborative relationships.) Success with a somatizing patient and family, however, is more likely to require close collaboration. The following suggestions can help the therapist work with the medical provider during the referral of a somatizing patient:

Empathize

First allow the physician to express the frustration he or she typically feels by the time the referral is made. Empathize with the physician about how difficult it is to tolerate the uncertainty of managing these patients medically. As every primary care practitioner knows, somatizing patients can develop serious diseases like any other patient. The physician always feels he or she is walking a fine line in terms of not missing an important medical diagnosis and yet not playing into the somatizing behavior and giving the patient an expensive biomedical work-up for an emotionally based problem.

Integrate Treatment

Suggest an integrated treatment approach in which physician and therapist have regular and continued involvement with the patient and family (see figure 6.3). Some physicians may want to "dump" these patients after a long series of frustrating encounters; the physician becomes convinced that the primary problem is "in the patient's head" and, as such, is the therapist's responsibility. Emphasize the importance of the physician's role in evaluating and reassuring the patient and family about any new or intensified symptoms, especially while therapy is progressing. The physician needs to understand that success is most likely if both professionals continue to see the patient on a regularly scheduled basis (so they do not have to become symptomatic to be seen). This understanding often prevents the physician from withdrawing. It may also help the physician to view the patient's demands for a "cure" as demands for continued caring (Kaplan, Lipkin, and Gordon, 1988).

Ask for Support

Ask the physician to support the referral actively with the patient and the family. Ongoing support from the physician is often crucial to the success of the referral. For an example illustrating the importance of this support, see Taplin, McDaniel, and Naumburg (1987). It should be

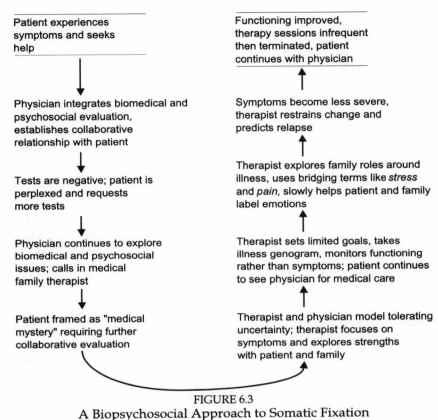

FIGURE 6.3
A Biopsychosocial Approach to Somatic Fixation

suggested, however, that the physician not promise too much while trying to convince the patient to accept the referral. Rather, he or she may say something like, "My colleague is a therapist with a special interest in working with patients who have mysterious medical problems. Many patients and their families have found working with her to be helpful. You and I have tried many things; I would like you now to see her and find out if she can be helpful as you try to live with these symptoms and regain some of your enjoyment of life."

Meet Conjointly

For severely somatizing patients who are resistant to the referral, offer to go to the physician's office and have a joint session (or sessions) with the physician, the patient, and the family to accomplish the referral. These sessions are needed more frequently for referral of somatizing patients than for other medical patients. Somatizing cases can be similar to those referred by the courts in that the motivation for treatment is typically much higher in the referring person than in the patient. Joint sessions allow the physician to express support directly for the family to seek therapy. In the context of such support, the sessions also allow the patient and family to demystify the therapist and the therapy experience so that trust may begin to develop. Frequently after one session with both providers, the family is willing to see the therapist on its own. For physicians and therapists with a special interest in collaboration and somatizing patients, tough cases may be treated effectively and efficiently by the therapist and physician acting as a cotherapy team throughout treatment. For an example of this approach, see McDaniel, Campbell, and Seaburn (1990).

The case of Mr. Stuckey illustrates many of the clinical strategies outlined in this chapter:

> Mr. Stuckey, a sixty-three-year-old retired plumber, was active until diagnosed with prostate cancer. Mrs. Stuckey had a history of bilateral breast cancer in remission. Dr. Gale, a family physician, was very attached to Mr. Stuckey and his wife. "He reminds me of my father," she said in referring him to the therapist.
>
> Dr. Gale had not pursued some early diagnostic testing when Mr. Stuckey became symptomatic and so felt guilty when the cancer was found. Once the diagnosis was made, Mr. Stuckey quickly had surgery. After surgery there was some confusion about whether Mr. Stuckey required radiotherapy or not. The surgeon first told them that Mr. Stuckey was "cured" and then reversed this and told them that he needed radiation. Mr. Stuckey had a psychotic episode in the hospital in reaction to some pain medication. He had no previous psychiatric history, and his mental status cleared when the medication was withdrawn.
>
> During the radiation treatment, Mr. Stuckey became profoundly depressed and had to be psychiatrically hospitalized for a week. His psychiatrist reported that the patient had been close to catatonic and would not be responsive to psychotherapy.

The referral for family therapy was made by the primary care physician six months after surgery. At that time, the physician said Mr. Stuckey was fixated on his scar, reporting soreness and a conviction that the surgeon had not removed all the cancer. The therapist had two phone conversations with the physician about this patient, mostly listening to the physician talk about her guilt over not picking up symptoms of the cancer earlier. The therapist also learned the patient had other somatic complaints and was extremely reluctant to see another mental health specialist. His problem, he said, was his cancer, not his mental state. The referral was easier than some, however, because the couple had a long-standing and close relationship. The patient agreed to go to therapy at the urging of his wife and his physician.

EARLY PHASES OF TREATMENT

The joining phase with somatizing patients like Mr. Stuckey needs to be extended because of the patients' caution, distrust, and reluctance to acknowledge any emotional aspects of their illness. Communicating respect to these patients is of utmost importance, in part because of their experiences with frustrated medical providers. It can take months to develop a mutually agreeable contract.

Early in treatment, patients often wish to schedule sessions far apart, hoping that a biomedical cure will occur in the meanwhile. Sometimes a medication metaphor will facilitate negotiations about when to return: "You need to come frequently enough so that you're experiencing a therapeutic dose." This period—when the patient or family is highly resistant to therapy and will not (or cannot) discuss their emotional lives—can seem very slow moving. A systems approach, with close collaboration with the medical providers and a large dose of patience and persistence, can often be successful in helping these families through this phase.

The most important technique in joining with these patients is some acceptance of their definition of the problem. Many early sessions are characterized by patients trying to convince themselves, their families, and especially their therapists that they do not need therapy because the symptoms represent a *medical* problem. The following are strategies that can help therapists deal with this presentation:

137

Focus on Symptoms

It is important for the therapist not to be intimidated by the patient's numerous symptoms; in fact, focus on them in the session by listing them on poster paper, having the patient draw pictures of physical problems, and generally soliciting information about the symptoms. Also ask the patient to keep a symptom diary outside the session to help with the assessment of the illness. The symptom diary may be formatted so that physical symptoms are recorded on the left side of the page, and life events and emotional reactions on the right. This format foreshadows recognition of the interweaving of physical and emotional processes. Family members who are involved in the patient's illness may also keep a diary about their observations of the patient.

Hear the Illness Story

Solicit the patient's and each family member's descriptions and diagnosis of the problem. Hear their story and their experiences with the symptoms, the illness, and the medical system. Work to understand the meaning of the symptom for each person. The patient and the family members all need to have the experience of feeling understood.

Collaborate with the Family

Use a collaborative approach that emphasizes the unknown, mysterious aspects of the patient's illness. Begin to enlist the patient and family's help in discovering what seems to yield even small improvements and what seems to make the symptoms worse.

Solicit the patient's and family's strengths and areas of competence. These can be useful resources to treatment. Patients with severe somatic fixation and a history of deprivation or abuse need a huge dose of support.

Note the extent to which the family's health belief system is the same as or conflicts with that of the physician or the therapist. Over the time of treatment, the goal is to work toward mutually acceptable explanations of the symptoms for the patient, family, medical providers, and therapist.

Take a Genogram

Use a genogram first to take a family medical history. Gather information about any transgenerational meaning for the patient's symptom by asking, "Has anyone else in the family had an illness that in any way resembles this one?"* Over time ask about recent stressful life events. When the trust level has increased, assess the patient and family for childhood abuse, deprivation, unresolved grief, substance abuse, and workaholism or other forms of overfunctioning.

Identify Role Changes

Listen for how the illness may have changed the typical roles or balance of power in the family. In one couple, both members' somatizing behavior brought them together after an affair threatened their marriage. In another, the illness gave the husband a "job" as a patient when he had been at loose ends after retirement. In another family, the wife's illness forced the husband to help with housework and parenting after years of his wife's overfunctioning at home and working on the family farm.

Use Medical Language

Use medical language and physical interventions—such as relaxation tapes, exercise, and attention to sleep and diet—in the early phase. Many of these interventions become family projects and represent a different, healthier focus on the body. At a minimum, the therapist must work to have family members support, or at least not sabotage, these interventions.

Refrain from Emotional Language

Emotional language, reframes, and in-depth emotional exploration are premature during this phase. The therapist must wait for the family and the patient to signal their readiness. Frequently, important aspects of family history are withheld for months until the family is ready and able to discuss them. This should be respected.

*Mullins and Olson (1990) found modeling to be a significant factor in the development of somatizing disorders in children.

Tolerate Uncertainty

Stay in touch with what is not known about the illness; at times biological components to the problem emerge and require biomedical treatment. Like the physician, the therapist must communicate that he or she does not fully understand the symptoms, does not have a quick answer or pill that will solve the problem, and is able to tolerate the uncertainty while continuing to work on various aspects of the patient's problem.

> In the early phase of treatment, Mr. Stuckey attended therapy with his wife but believed it to be "a waste of my time and your time, doc." He was polite but not engaged. On a few occasions when Mrs. Stuckey was unable to attend a session, it was difficult to maintain a conversation with Mr. Stuckey except when listing and describing his symptoms. He fixated and perseverated on several symptoms and gave monosyllabic answers when asked about any other topic. He kept a symptom diary that was highly repetitive and had a few paragraphs a day on the left side for physical symptoms and only an occasional word on the right side for stressful events or emotional reactions.
>
> Mr. Stuckey believed his symptoms were due to a recurrence of his prostate cancer, a recurrence that physicians were unable to detect. Mrs. Stuckey believed her husband's symptoms were due to anxiety and not cancer. She frequently reassured him that he was okay and that the doctors were trustworthy.
>
> Mrs. Stuckey drew from her own experience with breast cancer to deal with her husband's illness. At one time, after her first mastectomy, she became quite depressed for six months and withdrew from her family and her community. She felt the same was happening to her husband. After several months, Mr. Stuckey compared his illness to his father's experience in his last years when he seemed to be deeply depressed and perhaps even catatonic. His father did not recover emotionally before a heart attack resulted in his death in 1971. See figure 6.4 for a genogram of the Stuckeys' case.
>
> Mr. Stuckey had been very close to his father, who also "held things in." He was less close to his mother. Mrs. Stuckey had been

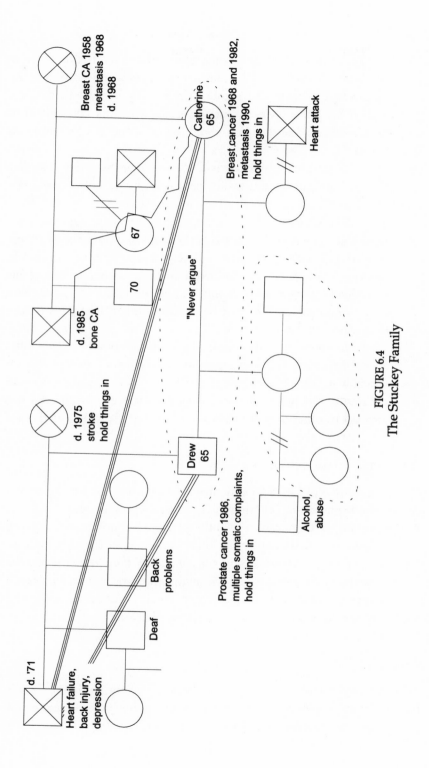

FIGURE 6.4
The Stuckey Family

Breast CA 1958
metastasis 1968
d. 1968

Breast cancer 1968 and 1982,
metastasis 1990,
hold things in

Heart attack

d. 1985
bone CA

70

67

"Never argue"

Catherine
65

d. 1975
stroke
hold things in

Drew
65

Prostate cancer 1986,
multiple somatic complaints,
hold things in

Alcohol
abuse

Back
problems

Deaf

d. '71

Heart failure,
back injury,
depression

physically abused by her father. She said she married because of her love for Mr. Stuckey's father. Both Mr. and Mrs. Stuckey agreed that they never fought—Mr. Stuckey because he admired that in his father, Mrs. Stuckey because she was determined to have a different kind of household than the one in which she was raised.

Mr. and Mrs. Stuckey had many strengths. They had two grown sons and several grandchildren, all living out-of-state. Mr. and Mrs. Stuckey described their marriage as close and were supportive of each other, although they had kept separate bedrooms for years. Both seemed to have an uneasy, uncomfortable relationship with their own and with each other's bodies. Mr. Stuckey had been especially active in the community before his retirement, going to church and visiting with sick friends. He was action-oriented and had not been successful in filling his leisure time after retirement.

The couple was likeable, though they exhibited somewhat flat affect, anxious moods, and appeared rather passionless. Mr. Stuckey was able to use a relaxation tape that focused on breathing to ease the discomfort he felt at the site of his surgical scar. He did not respond to other muscle relaxation tapes, but his wife used them.

THE MIDDLE PHASE OF TREATMENT

The middle phase of treatment with a severely somatizing family can extend for as long as six months to several years. During this phase it is important to judge progress in the patients by monitoring changes in their level of functioning rather than in their symptoms. Symptom-free living (a "cure") occurs occasionally but is unlikely in these patients. More realistic goals involve a decrease in symptoms and an increase in functioning in areas such as work and family relationships. Several strategies are commonly useful during this phase of treatment:

Negotiate a Definition

Work toward a mutually acceptable definition of the problem. This is frequently accomplished by listening for and suggesting language that can bridge physical and emotional explanations:

"Mr. Stuckey, it sounds as if your body has been under a tremendous amount of *stress* given all you and your wife have been through in the last several years. You have a sensitive body, and these symptoms seem to act as *warning signals* to you. We must learn to pay attention to them and understand what they are trying to tell us."

"Your husband's heart attack is a serious matter, Mrs. Gonzola. And now, six months later, you lose your grandson in this terrible accident. You must feel as if your heart is broken. We must have your physician evaluate your chest *pain,* and we all must evaluate the effects of the other painful experiences you have had recently."

"Mr. Easterly, it is as if your body is no longer sick but has sustained some internal *scarring* as a result of all you have been through. We must work to protect these scars and your other old wounds so that you may continue to live your life with the least amount of distress possible."

Express Curiosity

Express curiosity about, and help the patient and family determine, their individual responses to stressful life events and chronic difficulties. Introduce the possibility of both physical and emotional responses. Continue with the diaries to help the patient and family members begin to differentiate physical from emotional sensations.

Introduce Emotional Language

Once bridging terms have been mutually agreed on, slowly use emotional language for emotional experience and very gradually have sessions that become less somatically fixated.

Reinforce Engagement and Explore Risk

Help family members to reinforce each other's interest and attempts at a higher level of activity and engagement in relationships, and to withhold reinforcement for symptomatic behavior (Hudgens, 1979).

Explore the risk of change by asking how family life would be different if the patient's symptoms disappeared or improved. When somatizing is a chronic problem, the risk of change is most substantial:

> For the couple who both began somatizing behavior after facing a marital crisis because of the husband's affair, both members of the couple felt their illness helped them reestablish their priorities and brought them closer together. They were fearful of what might happen if they became well enough to return to work and interact more with friends outside the family. Also, the husband stopped a substantial drinking habit because of his illness; both worried that he would resume it if he got better. It was important to address these issues in the middle phase of treatment.

Avoid Psychosocial Fixation

Avoid psychosocial fixation by continuing with an integrated biopsychosocial approach. Continue to refer patients to their physician when they have a new or different symptom. The best interventions with somatically fixated patients are those that combine the biomedical and the psychosocial—that is, biomedical interventions that make psychological sense and psychological interventions that make biomedical sense (McDaniel, Campbell, and Seaburn, 1990). Collaboration with and information from the physician make these interventions most likely. One case, for example, was clearly embedded in unresolved grief about the deaths of two babies. Each time grief over the deaths was mentioned in couples therapy, the husband described an increasing number of physical symptoms. Finally, a conjoint session with the physician was held in which the physician read the babies' death certificates line by line, and the medical significance of each sentence was discussed. This intervention took an hour and was the first time the couple was able to converse about the loss. They had many questions about what had happened. The session was a turning point in the treatment.

Occasionally during the middle phase of treatment a power struggle between the patient and family and the physician may escalate as the patient continues to be symptomatic and fires the physician (or a series of physicians). In these cases, the treatment team has been disrupted, and the therapist may be the only one providing continuity of care for the patient. When the problem with the physician is unresolvable, the therapist may refer the patient to a physician who has experience in treating somatizing patients—in listening and setting limits in the context of a caring relationship. Returning to the case of Mr. and Mrs. Stuckey and the middle phase of treatment:

Very slowly Mr. Stuckey began to believe that his symptoms might not be life threatening. He saw his surgeon and his oncologist, who continued to tell him that there was no recurrence of his cancer. His diary began to have more entries on the right side. He also discussed his commitment to church and how he felt peaceful and calm when attending a service.

Mr. Stuckey began to describe his problem as one of "anxiety" and joked about how he always focused on the worst-case scenario. He also began describing "discomfort" in his surgical scar as evidence of overactivity, rather than as a recurrence of his cancer. The therapist also suggested he consider it a signal that something was bothering him and that he had to figure out whether it was physical or emotional. Early in this process of relabeling, Mr. Stuckey pressed the therapist for solutions to his "anxiety," much as he had pressed his physicians for solutions to his somatic symptoms. The therapist maintained her uncertainty about his illness but affirmed a belief in his ability to function better if he and his wife collaborated in finding a treatment plan that could work for him.

Mrs. Stuckey began to use the same language to describe her husband's problems. They agreed that Mr. Stuckey did not have enough to do and that he became "depressed" when sitting around and "worrying about his illness." She suggested he again take up woodcarving as a hobby, which he soon did. Therapy focused on increasing Mr. Stuckey's level of activity. Mrs. Stuckey agreed to make his favorite meal on days when he was able to visit his old bowling buddies. It was also agreed that when Mr. Stuckey was feeling bad, he needed to be quiet. Therefore, he would retire to his room rather than lying in the living room where his wife tried to nurse him back to health.

The therapist slowly began to talk to this couple about

giving themselves permission to recognize negative feelings, disagree, express themselves, and still feel safe with each other. This process occurred in conjunction with paying tribute to Mr. Stuckey's father, who bore his anger and disappointments in silence. Both Mr. and Mrs. Stuckey began to question whether his father's depression in his last few years might have been related to his inability to talk about what bothered him. Over time. Mrs. Stuckey began to distinguish between "healthy discussions," as they called their arguments, and the abuse that seemed to characterize any conflict in her childhood home.

Mr. Stuckey's functioning fluctuated considerably for much of this phase of treatment. Each time he experienced a new symptom, he returned to his physician. During one phase he became very angry at the surgeon who he believed "lied" to him about getting all the cancer out. He considered going to another doctor but decided against it after discussing his complaints with the surgeon.

At another point in treatment when he had fixated for a particularly long time on his scar, the primary care doctor and the therapist held a joint session to evaluate the problem. The patient was encouraged both to return to his oncologist for another evaluation and to pray more. The fixation eased within weeks.

Before retiring, Mr. Stuckey had been an avid gardener. During this phase of treatment, Mr. Stuckey started with one tomato plant (which threatened to die on several occasions) and moved to a small plot with a variety of vegetables during the next season. These vegetables provided an invaluable metaphor for treatment. The first tomatoes from the first plant were enjoyed and greeted with great fanfare by the couple and the therapist.

As Mr. Stuckey began functioning better, several sessions focused on the risks of his improvement. As with many cases, the couple agreed that the illness had brought them closer together. It had also given Mr. Stuckey a "job." The couple discussed what they would need to do to remain close if he was not so ill. They also discussed some hobbies and volunteer activities he might engage in to keep him active and entertained. The therapist agreed that Mr. Stuckey seemed to be the kind of person that is happiest when he is busy. However, she cautioned the couple to move slowly on these new projects and to pay attention to how he was feeling so as not to aggravate his "scar."

LATER PHASES OF TREATMENT

In the early and middle stages of treatment, the therapist explores the risk of change, and the patient learns to regard his or her symptoms as "warning signals" or as communications about a problem that needs attention. Once the patient and family are functioning better, the therapist can help the patient feel a greater sense of control over the symptoms by exploring at length what makes them worse. Family members may act as consultants about what they observe.

Successful completion of these experiments means that termination may be considered. As in all medical family therapy cases, termination involves returning the patient to the exclusive care of the primary care provider. In somatizing cases, it is important to terminate slowly and with much reassurance about remaining available to the family if the need arises. When somatization is a longstanding, pervasive coping style, it is not unusual for the therapist to see the family again for a brief period of treatment when it encounters some new stress. Usually there is a recurrence of increased somatizing behavior, but the therapist is able much more quickly to focus on the emotional aspects of the problem. The following strategies for the late phase of treatment for somatization are often helpful:

Predict Setbacks

As the patient begins to have fewer and fewer symptoms, expect and predict setbacks. In one case where difficulties were not predicted, a patient became symptomatic while the therapist was on vacation. The patient called her family physician, who provided reassurance about her newest ovarian tumor fear but did not ask her to come in. The patient ended up seeing her obstetrician and finally felt slightly relieved. When the therapist returned, the therapist told the patient that it was great the patient only had to go through this process once (a huge improvement over the past). But the patient might have been spared some of the disappointment if the therapist had predicted problems as the patient began to improve. Predictable setbacks can occur when a patient's family member or friend receives a new diagnosis, when someone important dies, or as a result of any significant stress.

Write a "Prescription for Illness"

Write a "Prescription for Illness" with the family, detailing what the patient and each member would have to do to bring back the patient's symptoms or make them worse. For one family's "Prescription for Headaches," the patient said she would have to deny she had any problems, fight every possible battle with her husband, not keep in touch with her parents, stop exercising, and not get enough sleep. Her husband said he would have to ignore his wife except when she was sick, not talk to her about what he was thinking or how he was feeling, and leave all the childrearing to her. Their ten- and twelve-year-old boys said they would have to keep yelling and fighting even when their mother asked them to calm down.

Terminate

Consult with the primary care physician about the timing of termination. Make sure the patient has an appointment with the physician soon after stopping therapy.

Terminate slowly, seeing the family once a month, then once every three months, until the family itself wants to stop. Remain available, but set the expectation that future contacts are likely to be "consultations" (Wynne, McDaniel, and Weber, 1986) rather than another course of therapy—unless an entirely new issue arises. Such was the case with the Stuckeys:

> Slowly, over a nine-month period, after discussing the risks of change and the important transgenerational issues involved in his illness, Mr. Stuckey began to have fewer and fewer symptoms. He was more active, looked healthier, and enjoyed (rather than dreaded) time spent with family and friends. Mr. Stuckey raised the

possibility of stopping treatment. At first, Mrs. Stuckey opposed him as she feared he would again become incapacitated. In response to her concern, the therapist helped the couple to write a "Prescription for Mr. Stuckey's Pain and Anxiety." They each agreed that what could make his symptoms worse were inactivity, lack of exercise, not seeing a trusted physician regularly, not talking honestly to each other, and the onset of a new illness. The therapist suggested that they do an experiment to see if they could make the symptoms worse by intentionally not talking to each other the next time one of them was annoyed about something. The couple was unable to complete the assignment because they kept teasing each other about not talking whenever an annoyance arose.

After this experience, with Mrs. Stuckey's support, the therapist scheduled the sessions for once every three months for a year and then terminated. Both Mr. and Mrs. Stuckey had regular appointments with their family physician during this time. The physician reported to the therapist that he saw no increase in symptoms or decrease in functioning, so both agreed it was time to stop the therapy.

The Stuckey family was not seen for about a year, until they were referred because of Mrs. Stuckey's depression after she received a diagnosis of metastatic cancer. With this news, Mr. Stuckey's functioning improved even more as he was needed to take care of his wife. His wife described her diagnosis as "shock therapy" for her husband. The couple was seen once every month or two to support them and keep their communication open during this stressful period. After an initial block in their communication, the terminal illness brought them even closer. They were able to talk about their joys and their sorrows, Mrs. Stuckey talked about her fears about death, and Mr. Stuckey talked about his fears about life without her.

After Mrs. Stuckey's death, Mr. Stuckey experienced an acute recurrence of some of his symptoms, as had been predicted, but he was also aware of his intense feelings of grief. The intensified somatic symptoms lasted only about three weeks and remitted within two months as he successfully reorganized his life.

Challenges Therapists Face in Treating
Somatizing Families

"The somatizing patient confronts us continuously with our own vulnerability to physical illness, the aging process, deterioration, and ultimate death" (Chabot, 1989, p. 133). This is perhaps true for all medical family therapy but is especially true in work with somatizing patients whose fears about illness and death are intense. The somatizing patient often expresses the family's fears of dying, fears of living, and general unease with uncertainty of any kind. Therapists who enjoy working with these patients must develop spiritual and emotional resilience to be able to confront these basic challenges of living. The therapist also may be able to help the physician and medical team feel more comfortable in the face of their uncertainty about the symptoms. When the treatment team can move forward in the face of uncertainty, it provides a model for the family about remaining active while acknowledging and living with the unknowns of life.

In addition to challenging the therapist on an existential level, the somatizing patient and family also frequently challenge the therapist on a technical level. As mentioned earlier, the joining phase can be difficult and extended, and require patience on the part of the therapist. It is easy to get pulled into a power struggle over whether the patient's symptoms are entirely organic or not. Focusing on the symptoms and the family's explanations diminishes this problem. The middle phase of treatment can be tedious while the patient's emotional life remains impoverished. Curiosity about the symptoms as metaphors can help the therapist through this period.

Collaboration with the medical provider can also be an important outlet for support. We regularly bring somatizing patients to a consulting group of physicians and therapists (McDaniel, Bank, et al., 1986) during the middle phase of treatment, when the therapist's experience has been alternating between satisfaction, hope, frustration, and boredom. Sometimes the difficulty is a "boring" family; sometimes it is frustration with the treatment team. The support and the input from others with differing points of view usually help the therapist to develop new strategies and bring new energy to the case.

Although working with somatizing patients and their families

150

almost always includes phases of frustration or difficulty, it is also intellectually stimulating and personally rewarding. This work is important conceptually because it occurs precisely at the interface of our struggles to understand the constructs we label *mind* and *body*. Patients are often extremely grateful to find someone who "understands" and someone who can help them better negotiate the medical system. It is poignant to experience the patient and the family as they begin to develop a language and an ability to experience emotional events. With these developments come more significant connections with the therapist and, more important, with each other. Sessions can move from flat, sterile, biological discussions to warm, humorous, and expressive exchanges. These experiences are a testimony that medical family therapy can make a difference in people's lives.

CHAPTER 7

Pregnancy Loss, Infertility, and Reproductive Technology

Fertility is revered in almost all cultures, and pregnancy is a milestone in adult development. It is the bridge between generations, rich in symbolism and central in human experience. M. Notman, "Reproduction and Pregnancy"

BIRTH AND DEATH are the most basic of human events. Reproduction signals the survival and continuity of the family and the species. For many, children represent a small piece of immortality—an extension into the future. Having children is a much anticipated goal for most women and men. A 1985 Current Population Survey found that only 10 percent of American women ages eighteen to thirty-four did not expect to have biological children at some point in their lives (U.S. Bureau of the Census, 1986, p. 20). However, adults in their childbearing years face a range of possible outcomes with regard to becoming parents (see figure 7.1). The continuum of parenting possibilities runs from those who voluntarily become parents, to those who do not wish to become

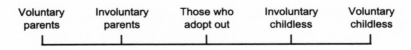

| Voluntary parents | Involuntary parents | Those who adopt out | Involuntary childless | Voluntary childless |

FIGURE 7.1
Continuum of Parenting Possibilities
Source: This figure is an expansion and reorganization of a continuum proposed by L. L. Schwartz (1991), *Alternatives to infertility* (New York: Brunner/Mazel).

152

parents but find themselves pregnant and choose to raise their children, to involuntary parents who surrender their children for adoption, to the involuntarily childless who experience pregnancy loss or infertility, to the voluntarily childless who choose either to abort their pregnancies or never to become pregnant. This chapter examines one end of the continuum and discusses the medical and psychosocial issues and clinical strategies for couples for whom childbearing does not come easily— couples who experience pregnancy loss, abortion, infertility, and the reproductive technologies that attempt to treat infertility.

Many professionals and laypeople view the reproductive stage of the life cycle as a prominent marker of adulthood. It is an extended family event that immediately changes the new parents' relationships with their parents, offering opportunities for reparation or reconciliation after the turbulence of adolescent separation. Ivan Boszormenyi-Nagy and Geraldine Sparks (1973) said, "Familial loyalty is characteristically based on biological, hereditary kinship." Emotional and biological continuity from generation to generation forms family identity, family legacy, and family myths. Consequently, many women and men experience both internal and external pressures to have children.

Little girls are taught from as early as they can hold a doll to value caregiving and raising the next generation. Women often anticipate this event for years. Socialization and biology combine to make them acutely aware that they do the childbearing, they often assume the largest share of child rearing obligations, and their options are time-limited as their reproductive potential ends in their midforties. Men also are taught to put great value on having children. In ancient Jewish law, a man who is not a father is incomplete. Often, men are expected to carry on the family line, and, traditionally, children signal a man's virility (Stotland, 1990). Many men look forward to the joys and challenges of child rearing.

With both genders, socialization works to continue the species. Some feminists object to what they believe is a romantic, idealized view of childbearing and see pressures to have children as another way for society to subjugate women. Some couples choose to remain childless for emotional or lifestyle reasons. But the overwhelming majority of couples desire children and assume their ability to have them.

However, the reality is that about one in seven couples, or close to 14 percent, learn they have some infertility problem that may prevent them from having biological children (U.S. Office of Technology Assessment, 1988). Ten to 15 percent of couples in the United States who want to conceive cannot conceive. Another 5 to 10 percent are plagued by repeated spontaneous abortions. The rate of infertility has risen since the end of the 1970s due to increased use of birth control and delayed childbearing, as well as the increased prevalence of sexually transmitted diseases that affect fertility (U.S. National Center for Health Statistics, 1982). New options from modern technology for couples with reproductive problems have resulted in the medicalization of what was previously primarily a psychosocial crisis. A medical diagnosis now can be established for approximately 90 percent of infertile couples (American College of Obstetricians and Gynecologists, 1989), and about half of these who seek treatment can be helped to conceive through reproductive technology (Kraft, Palombo, Mitchell, et al., 1980). Even for those couples who are able to conceive without difficulty, approximately one in five of all pregnancies ends in miscarriage (U.S. Office of Technology Assessment, 1988).

For these couples and their families, the biology of reproduction is not a straightforward process involving selection of a partner, sexual expression, pregnancy, and delivery. Instead it can involve traumatic loss and grief, feelings of inadequacy and envy, and a potentially long period of interaction with medical providers who become intimately involved in the couple's life. In addition, issues around sexuality, control, and loss either may be shared or divisive for any couple experiencing the stress of pregnancy loss or infertility.

Medical family therapists can play an important role in supporting couples and families through these developmental crises. Referrals may come at any stage of the process—from the initial diagnosis of a problem, through stressful treatment procedures, to seemingly unrelated problems that stem from unresolved issues around infertility or pregnancy loss. Some clinics routinely refer patients with reproductive problems for counseling, but they are in the minority. Other obstetricians and fertility specialists will refer patients who exhibit acute emotional reactions to a diagnostic work-up or a loss. Some patients will self-refer either because they recognize a need for professional support during a stressful period or because they want help in considering their treatment options. Collaboration with medical providers can enable the therapist to help patients negotiate the medical system. It may also provide some reciprocal support and relief to physicians and therapists who do this difficult work.

Patients with reproductive problems can stimulate strong reactions in the therapist related to gender, reproduction, and loss. Female therapists may see more of these cases than male therapists because of the biological and cultural biases that make reproduction more the responsibility of women than men, and because of a belief by many patients that female therapists may be more empathic and supportive about these issues. However, as society recognizes the importance of both women and men in childbearing and child rearing, and as male therapists indicate their interest in these areas, opportunities may increase for many systems-oriented therapists to help with these problems.

Couples who experience difficulties with reproduction present complex and challenging personal, interpersonal, and ethical dilemmas that strike at the core of family life. The technology for treating infertility, especially, is new and constantly changing, and the psychosocial impact of infertility, loss, and reproductive technology is only beginning to be researched and understood. Medical family therapists can help couples, families, and medical providers to develop an approach to these problems that maximizes the couple's communication and sense of control over the decisions they face.

Pregnancy Loss

When any desired pregnancy ends in loss, the event results in both physical and emotional upheaval for the woman and some degree of stress for her family. Psychologically pregnancy represents an opportunity to prepare for parenthood, including reworking previously unresolved developmental conflicts. Unplanned termination of a pregnancy results in a painful loss and interferes with this developmental process as well.

THE GRIEVING PROCESS

Only since the 1970s and 1980s has our society begun to recognize the importance of miscarriage and other pregnancy losses. Prior to

155

that time, and sometimes even now, denial of the importance of this loss has resulted in isolation for the couple and those who care about them. These situations were often ignored in obstetrics. Now many physicians and hospitals actively try to facilitate a healthy grieving response (Kirk, 1984; Leff, 1987; Leppert and Pahlka, 1984). In many cases, parents experience powerful grief over pregnancy loss that takes months to years to resolve. DeFrain (1991) found the average recovery time for families after a miscarriage to be nine to fifteen months and for stillbirth or a SIDS death three years.

Grief over a pregnancy loss will differ depending on how much the pregnancy was desired, the length of the pregnancy, the amount of medical and social support available for the couple, the ability of the couple to offer each other support, and the couple's ages and fertility histories. If the loss occurs to an older couple whose pregnancy was a result of lengthy infertility treatment, it may have a different meaning than to a relatively young, healthy couple.

Family therapists may see couples in the acute stage just after a pregnancy loss or as a result of a complicated grief reaction. Because of the historical lack of social support for pregnancy loss, this "forgotten grief" (Kirkley-Best and Kellner, 1982) can result in a range of individual and interactional problems that may or may not be recognized by patients as related to the loss. Consequently, therapists taking a geno-gram and family history should always ask specifically about dates and information regarding miscarriages, stillbirths, and other reproductive problems, to assess the impact of pregnancy loss and any delayed grief.

Miscarriage

Miscarriages, or spontaneous abortions, are especially common events. As mentioned earlier, a conservative estimate is that one in five pregnan-cies ends in miscarriage. (It is difficult to obtain statistics on the preva-lence of miscarriage because some women may miscarry before they even realize they are pregnant, while others may not seek medical attention after a miscarriage.) A late miscarriage may be experienced differently than an early miscarriage, but either experience represents a loss and must be processed with recognition of the meaning the couple gives to it. For some couples, early loss is very painful and made more so by the lack of support extended them by family and friends who either did not know about the pregnancy or do not appreciate the significance of the loss. Some women and some partners experience the due date for the lost pregnancy as a time of great sadness. Family therapy can normalize the experience of the loss and facilitate rituals that may further the grieving process. As with any crisis, it can be an opportunity for the individual and the couple to pull together, examine their life goals, and work through the experience (Elkin, 1990).

> One couple presented for marital therapy soon after Tracy, age twenty-eight, miscarried their first child. Tracy was distraught, not sleeping at night, and had experienced considerable weight loss in the six weeks since the miscarriage. Bob, age forty-nine, focused on his wife's distress. This was his second marriage, a relationship that began as an affair during his first marriage. Bob had two teenage children from his first marriage and said he agreed to have one child with Tracy only because she wanted so badly to be pregnant and be a mother. After an initial negative reaction to the news of the pregnancy, Bob bought several baby items, began to build a cradle, and had been speaking positively about the baby just prior to the miscarriage. However, after the loss he worried out loud that his ambivalence had "caused them to lose the baby." During treatment, the couple decided to hold a private memorial service. Both Bob and Tracy wrote messages to the child they lost. Close family and friends came with food to share for dinner. Tracy's serious symptoms remitted soon after. Therapy then moved to dealing with trust issues that were unresolved from early in the relationship.

Fetal Death in Utero

Fetal death in utero (FDIU) resulting in stillbirth is a loss that occurs late in a pregnancy, when much time has elapsed for the woman and her partner to bond to the fetus and develop hopes and dreams for their unborn child. FDIU is a particularly stressful experience because in many cases the woman must continue to carry the pregnancy after she is aware that the fetus is dead. She must then endure labor and delivery without the reward of a living baby at the other end. For those unaware of an FDIU, a stillbirth comes as a shock at the end of labor and delivery. It can be an acute and unexpected loss accompanied by predictable feelings of anger, depression, and guilt. Many times the cause of fetal demise or stillbirth is unknown, contributing to the couple's sense of despair.

Some hospitals now have "bereavement teams" to provide crisis intervention and support around this kind of loss (Cohen et al., 1978; Leff, 1987). For those who do not, the medical family therapist can provide invaluable consultation to providers so they have a plan that facilitates the beginning of the grieving process. Studies show that women who just experienced pregnancy loss submit almost unquestionably to recommendations of medical staff with regard to decisions about seeing the baby, having a funeral, burial arrangements, and so on (Lovell, 1983). The following strategies can help to inform any consultations with medical providers or hospitals wanting to respond to the needs of these patients.

CLINICAL STRATEGIES FOR COUPLES EXPERIENCING PREGNANCY LOSS

Therapy for couples experiencing pregnancy loss involves grief work—grief about the loss of hopes and dreams for a child who will not be, a loss that may be unknown to family and friends. Empathic listening with couples and families as they recount the details of their experiences is the cornerstone of this therapy. Little has been written or researched about family-oriented work with these couples. The following are strategies drawn from our own practices, and a few have been reported in the literature:

Acknowledge the Loss

Actively recognize the importance of the loss to the couple. Encourage them to view the fetus or the baby, if they desire. This also means giving patients permission to grieve. Expect these patients and their families to experience classical reactions of grief—shock and numbness, searching and yearning for the hoped-for child, disorganization and general depression in recognizing the loss, and reorientation and restructuring their lives after accepting the loss (Kirkley-Best and Kellner, 1982).

Encourage them to have a funeral, a memorial service, or some other ritual if it is desired. Help them to take the time necessary to process the event.

Normalize the Experience

Listen as the couple tries to find meaning in the loss. Help them each to construct a personal answer that eventually may bring them acceptance or comfort (DeFrain, 1991). Encourage couples for whom religion offers solace to reach out to their minister, priest, or rabbi.

Encourage the couple to communicate with their children, their parents, and other important family members and friends about what happened and include them in any rituals that mark the loss.

Help the couple understand how they and their families have dealt with previous losses, especially previous pregnancy losses. Help them determine what in these traditions they wish to claim and what they may wish to change.

Normalize "incongruent mourning" (Peppers and Knapp, 1980); many times the woman grieves the loss of the child while the man worries more about the woman. The fact that the woman carries the child creates different experiences of pregnancy and loss for a man than for a woman. Differing emotional styles can compound differences and, if unacknowledged, result in misunderstandings and conflict around loss.

Encourage Education

Encourage patients to discuss the medical details of the loss with their physician so the experience can be as fully understood as possible. This discussion can help to dispel guilt and fantasies that the loss was due to something the woman ate, did, or encountered (Eisinger, 1991). Medical information also may have implications for future pregnancies.

Suggest the couple read relevant literature (such as Borg and Lasker, 1981) and attend a support group, such as PEND (Parents

Experiencing Neonatal Death). Many people find these readings and the group experiences invaluable as they try to cope with and accept the unexpected loss.

Monitor Physical and Emotional Health

Encourage patients to take care of themselves and monitor their own physical health in the subsequent year. Intense grief may mimic or cloak other illnesses. One woman whose child died five months previously had considerable stomach distress but did not see her physician because she assumed it represented symptoms of a "broken heart." It was true that she was grieving, but it also turned out that she needed to have her gall bladder removed.

Screen for extreme and persistent grief reactions such as delusions, suicidality, flashbacks, and disproportionate responses to subsequent crises (Peppers and Knapp, 1980). Consult with the appropriate physician if medication may be needed in these extreme circumstances. Many couples have suicidal thoughts after the loss of a baby (DeFrain, 1991); these may be distinguished from those at high risk for acting on these thoughts.

Recommend Delaying a New Pregnancy

Recommend against getting pregnant or adopting too soon after a pregnancy loss. Most obstetricians recommend at least a six-month wait before attempting another pregnancy (Droegemueller et al., 1987, p. 377). Rowe, Clyman, and Green (1978) found the only predictors of a complicated grief reaction in women two years after a stillbirth were becoming pregnant within five months of the loss or having a surviving twin in addition to the stillbirth. This recommendation may be difficult for older couples who feel the pressure of the "biological clock." However, whatever time can be given to further resolution of grieving will help to prevent the "replacement child syndrome," in which a subsequent child is burdened by the previous death of a sibling and constantly compared to the idealized deceased child (Cain and Cain, 1964). Couples may need additional support if and when they do again become pregnant, to deal with predictable hypervigilance about the pregnancy and reoccurring grief reactions regarding the loss of the previous pregnancy.

Monitor Personal Responses

As therapists working with families who experience pregnancy loss, we must stay in close touch with our own experiences around loss and parenting in order to be fully available to our grieving patients. DeFrain described the experience in this way: "When one becomes involved with bereaved families as a professional, one is likely to experience over time a wide variety of feelings: feelings of being totally absorbed, shattered, challenged, frustrated, terrified, saddened, angered, awed beyond comprehension, enriched, and blessed" (1991, p. 231). These cases demand that the medical family therapist focus on self-care and examine his or her own responses to life's most challenging questions about meaning and tragedy.

Abortion

The planned termination of a pregnancy can be a stressful event in the lives of a woman and her partner, in part because of intense disagreements about this procedure in society and within families. Most studies focus on the effect of abortion on the woman only and conclude that about half of abortion patients suffer depression and other symptoms for several weeks. A small number, 5 to 10 percent of women, still report emotional symptoms eight to nine months later (Ashton, 1980; Lazarus and Stern, 1986). In one study of teenagers who presented to a clinic for a pregnancy test, however, the group who elected to abort scored higher two years later on social and psychological functioning than did either the group who had babies or the group whose pregnancy test was negative (Zabin, Hirsch, and Emerson, 1989).

Because of the powerful feelings the issue of abortion stimulates, it has been difficult for research to establish conclusively the psychological and interpersonal effects of an abortion. Family therapists may see couples or families either before or after the procedure. Because most abortions are performed in the first trimester of the pregnancy, and the sooner the better from a medical standpoint, family members feel intense pressure to resolve the issue quickly. This time pressure can increase anxiety and the potential for miscommunication among family members, making these cases challenging for any therapist. Therapists whose personal beliefs allow them to do this work can function as facilitators who help to clarify and increase communication without taking sides, so women and their partners can make the best decisions possible. Sometimes conflict in families about this issue is unresolvable:

> Mr. and Mrs. Musica presented for couples therapy in the midst of an argument about Mrs. Musica's pregnancy. The couple had three children under six years old, and Mrs. Musica wanted to continue this fourth pregnancy. Mr. Musica felt their marriage was already unstable and that this pregnancy should be terminated. Both agreed the timing of the pregnancy was stressful. However, the couple polarized around the issue of whether to abort the pregnancy. Mrs. Musica was enraged at her husband and saw his position as a symbol of his wanting to dominate and control her. Mr. Musica felt shut out of the decision-making process about the pregnancy and saw his wife's position as a symbol of her refusal to incorporate his needs into her decisions. After two sessions in close succession, Mrs. Musica refused to discuss the issue further and asserted her right to make the decision about her pregnancy independently. She had the baby, and the marriage ended within two years. After the divorce, therapy was helpful in maintaining a positive parenting relationship between the couple and all four children.

In addition to seeing couples around an abortion decision, family therapists also may see patients and their families following an abortion. As with other reproductive losses, these patients may experience unresolved grief after an abortion. And because abortion involves a choice, many women carry tremendous guilt as well. Sometimes referrals to clergy for confessionals can be helpful. Other times, informal rituals that help to work through past regrets can promote healing. One woman, married with two children, was plagued by guilt over five abortions prior to meeting her husband. She was Catholic and had a strong desire to have children, even when her male relationships were unsatisfactory. Her nightmares about the abortions stopped after she was able to go to a lengthy confessional with a trusted priest and then, with her husband's help, plant five small trees in her backyard in recognition of the pregnancies she felt she could not continue.

Most people have strong opinions about abortion, therapists included. Part of the challenge of working with patients and families who are struggling with these issues lies in clarifying the therapist's own position about abortion and communicating that clearly to patients, while still emphasizing that each situation is different and each woman and her partner have to make the decision that will be the best for them. (Example: "I am not personally opposed to abortion, but I do feel this is a very important and personal decision for each couple. I would like to help you discuss the issue so you can make the decision that is going to be best for you and your family.") Some therapists may not want to work with cases involving decision making about abortion because they believe abortion is wrong and do not wish to participate in treatment that could result in a decision to abort. These therapists may be very useful to women and couples who share their belief system and need to find alternatives to abortion. In any case, value judgments by the therapist about these situations cannot be ignored and must become part of the treatment process. Acknowledging this fact openly can help prevent the therapist from covertly influencing patients' decision making at a time when they are vulnerable and conflicted.

Infertility

Couples facing decisions about abortion often agonize about the inappropriate timing of a pregnancy. Couples struggling with infertility have a different agony, one over which they have much less control. They have decided they are ready to have children and then discover reproduction will be complicated or impossible for them to achieve. Most infertility specialists define infertility as the failure to reproduce after one year of trying (Downey and McKinney, 1990). However, Cook (1990) suggests a more experiential definition of infertility, as the failure of an individual to achieve a pregnancy within his or her own elective time frame.

In any case, infertility is a medical, psychological, and social experience requiring a redefinition by the couple of their identities as individuals and as partners. The couple moves from expecting to become pregnant to recognizing they may be unable to have biological children.

Ralph Matthews and Anne Martin Matthews (1988a, 1988b) label this experience the "transition to non-parenthood." The transition to accepting involuntary childlessness is painful and challenging for most patients. This experience differs from voluntary childlessness in that there is lack of choice, disappointment, and a sense of failure that commonly accompanies infertility.

The prerequisites for a successful pregnancy are biologically complex, involving the interrelationship of various organs and hormones. (For a concise description of the medical aspects of infertility evaluation and treatment written for psychotherapists, see Sadler and Syrop, 1987.) Psychological factors, such as anxiety and stress, may interfere with fertility in ways that are not fully understood and difficult to study because the infertility itself results in considerable stress for the patient and the family. Early studies showing a strong relationship between infertility and negative attitudes of women toward pregnancy have now been refuted (Noyes and Chapnick, 1964). Georgene Seward and colleagues (1965) found no difference on a number of emotional and attitudinal measures between fertile and nonfertile women. Most current psychosocial research and treatment for infertility avoids "blaming the victim" and focuses on the psychological consequences rather than the antecedents of infertility.

THE EXPERIENCE OF INFERTILITY

The psychosocial experience of infertility has been described by clinicians but has only recently been the subject of research. Clinically, the experience seems similar in some ways to coping with the death of a loved one and in other ways to coping with the diagnosis of a chronic illness. Like a death, patients may go through stages of mourning after the diagnosis—denial, shock, anger, bargaining, depression, and acceptance (Kübler-Ross, 1969; Myers, 1990). During treatment, they endure a chronic hope-loss cycle every twenty-eight days. Like a chronic illness, adjustments in lifestyle must be made to accommodate the diagnostic and treatment procedures. Diagnostic procedures can be invasive, embarrassing, and stressful (men may have to masturbate into a bottle to produce sperm for a sperm count, and women may have to go to their physician's office for a postcoital exam several hours after intercourse).

A sense of failure and loss of control is prominent. Many patients ask, "Why me?" Evaluation and treatment can reinforce sexual insecurities and doubts (Hertz, 1982). One infertility specialist reported that a high proportion of her patients believe their infertility is a punishment from God for some sexual or other misdeed (Menning, 1977). In addition to searching for a cause or explanation, many couples experience infertility as stressful boundary ambiguity, in that they experience the child they wish to have as psychologically present but physically absent (Burns, 1987). The cause of all this stress is invisible and so can lead to secrecy and social isolation for the couple.

Men and women report very different experiences with infertility. Forty percent of infertility problems stem from reproductive problems of women, 40 percent are from problems of men, and 20 percent are from some interaction of factors between the couple (Valentine, 1986). While these frequencies are quite balanced, the evaluation for an infertility diagnosis is much easier and less invasive for men than for women (Shapiro, 1988). The average length of time to diagnosis is less than one month for men but six months for women (Patterson, 1990). These technical and biological factors, and sex role socialization, influence the differential experiences of women and men about infertility.

For Women

Especially since the advent of new and better birth control devices, women have come to feel they have much greater control over their reproductive abilities. A larger number of women now delay childbearing for education and careers, and they and their families are anxious for them to have children quickly when they decide to do so. Most women still view childbearing as an essential part of their lives. In one study, women reported childlessness as less acceptable than did their husbands (Ulbrich, Coyle, and Llabre, 1990).

Several studies support the notion that many women experience infertility as role failure (Miall, 1985; Greil, Leitko, and Porter, 1988). These women grieve with each menstrual period and may experience reproductive failure as personal inadequacy. They can develop worries about sexual desirability, lack of sexual desire, or other sexual dysfunction or experience general withdrawal from their primary relationship. However, women are likely to be more open about their distress and more open to supportive counseling than their partners (McCartney and Wada, 1990). They are generally the ones who first suggest seeking medical advice when an infertility problem is suspected (Matthews and Matthews, 1989).

For Men

Many studies, like that of Matthews and Matthews (1989), find that men report being largely unaffected by infertility, while women report being devastated. In a study by Adrienne Kraft and colleagues (1980), one man said of his infertility, "It only upset me for about 20 minutes." Men often say the hardest part of infertility for them is their wives' pain. Many men feel they must be strong for their wives. However, as Myers (1990) stated, "There is danger in equating men's silence about reproduction with acceptance and cooperation." For some men, denial and silence may reflect strong feelings that infertility is unacceptable to them as a man and as a husband. Cella and Najavits (1986) reported a study of men treated for Hodgkin's disease with radiation and chemotherapy, who were told that their treatment leaves 80 to 90 percent of men infertile. Almost 40 percent of the men failed to bank sperm before treatment even though they were advised to do so. The overwhelming majority (93 percent) of those who failed to bank sperm said they believed they would remain fertile.

Because society often does not support men expressing their emotions or claiming ownership of their role in reproduction, some men may be out of touch or secretive about infertility, and their distress may be missed. Meanwhile women often "take care" of the infertility, regardless of who carries the medical diagnosis, and may be the partner who expresses the pain for the couple. Some women with infertile partners report they lie to friends and family, saying they themselves have the problem to protect the man and his sense of potency (Czyba and Chevret, 1979).

While some men deny or avoid their feelings about an infertility diagnosis, others find it degrading and become hopeless, brooding, or withdrawn. Like women with infertility problems, these men may experience decreased self-esteem and a sense of personal failure, and obsess about their adequacy as a man. Some studies show that men with an infertility diagnosis are at risk for erectile dysfunction (Berger, 1980) and other sexual problems. Given the complexity of the problem of infertility and men's reactions to it, medical family therapists may be most helpful if they acknowledge men's legitimate emotional stress and pain even if it is not spoken:

> Mike was a twenty-nine-year-old man with a history of having trouble keeping a job. He was playful, affectionate, and rather passive, especially next to his outgoing, aggressive, and well-organized wife, Linda. In the course of marital therapy, initiated by Linda because she was frustrated with Mike's history of not finishing school and not completing tasks at home, the couple began an infertility work-up.
>
> Characteristically, Linda pursued her diagnostic tests energetically and Mike kept forgetting to schedule the time for his appointments. Within eight months all Linda's tests came back negative, including one procedure that required outpatient surgery. Mike had one appointment that uncovered a questionable sperm count. His physician asked him to give two more samples to verify the problem. Mike never did so, in spite of Linda's anger. He forgot appointments, and when he remembered them he forgot his sperm samples. Both a male therapist and a female therapist spoke to Mike and recognized his unspoken distress. They treated him with respect and discussed how his sense of pain about being sickly as a child and not being treated as a man by his father and his wife made it very difficult for him to endure the infertility testing. Mike seemed to feel as if the tests would confirm biologically what he had feared emotionally for so long—a lack of potency as a man.
>
> Eventually, in their therapy Linda accepted the fact that her husband did not want to continue with the infertility work-up. The couple applied for adoption and adopted a beautiful baby girl. Mike seemed fulfilled and became the parent who spent the most time with their daughter, taking care of her, playing with her, and looking out for her well-being. He was happy and proud of his abilities as a father.

For Marriages

Like any crisis, infertility can bring a couple closer or result in problems. Sexual, financial, and emotional strains are all common challenges for the infertile couple. Diagnosis and treatment of infertility results in a major invasion of privacy in the most intimate area of a couple's relationship, their sex life. Several studies document the potential for infertility to damage or ruin a couple's sexual intimacy. Ronald Sabatelli, Richard Meth, and Stephen Gavazzi (1988) found close to 60 percent of women and men in an infertility support group sample reported decreased frequency of sexual intercourse and decreased sexual satisfaction after the diagnosis. Even postcoital semen analysis, a somewhat less invasive procedure, has been found to increase rates of erectile dysfunction and ejaculatory incompetence in men (Keye, 1984) and anorgasmia in women (DeVries, Degani, and Eibschita, 1984).

Sexual problems also can interfere in the assessment of infertility. In a review of eighteen studies of male sexual disturbances and fertility, Bents (1985) concluded that sexual disturbances diminish, but do not eliminate, the possibility of conception. One of the authors had two cases where the couples came for counseling while going through very extensive and expensive infertility work-ups. Careful marital histories revealed lack of sexual desire and considerable relationship disturbance such that, in both cases, the couples were having extremely infrequent sexual intercourse and were unlikely to become pregnant on those grounds alone.

Other relationship problems can occur after the diagnosis of infertility. For some couples, parenting is so basic a component of the marriage contract that infertility threatens the very concept of marriage (Kraft, Palombo, Mitchell, et al., 1980). For these people, renegotiating the contract after this diagnosis can be difficult or even impossible. Some couples implicitly or explicitly rely on childbearing to help them "become a family." For many young couples, childbearing forces them to shift their loyalties from their families of origin to each other. Infertility may then lead to marital problems related to what Burns (1987) hypothesized to be an ongoing loyalty bind between the family of origin and the spouse.

Some couples have complementary styles that allow them to increase their bond during this crisis. K. L. McEwan, C. G. Costello, and

Patrick Taylor (1987) found that women's adjustment to infertility is significantly better if she has a confiding relationship with her spouse. Other couples find their coping styles clash. These women want to talk about the stress, while their husbands want to "try and forget it." This discordance can add to the burden of the problem.

Ralph Matthews and Anne Martin Matthews (1986) found the person carrying the diagnosis may feel guilty and doubt the affection of the other partner. That person may fantasize that if the spouse had another partner, he or she would be able to conceive. Occasionally, partners do have an affair or develop substance abuse or eating problems. These symptoms are understood as disorders of control in a situation where the couple feels very out of control.

Just as men and women often report different experiences of infertility, they also report different experiences of their relationship while undergoing infertility work-ups and treatment. Patricia Ulbrich, Andrea Coyle, and Maria Llabre (1990) found that men adjust better to the experience if their wives are employed. For women, the most significant finding was that marital adjustment decreased with the length of treatment for infertility. Infertility issues can also become embroiled in the gender politics of marriage. J. Lorber (1985) reported that infertile couples more frequently divorce if the husband wants a child and the wife does not, whereas they more frequently stay married and childless if the wife wants a child and the husband does not.

Infertility can have long-term effects on couples who stay together and become parents. Linda Burns (1990), in an exploratory study of twenty couples who either eventually became pregnant or adopted, found the couples with a history of infertility reported significantly more problems in themselves, their marriages, their parenting, and their children than the couples who had not experienced infertility. Medical family therapy with infertile couples may help to prevent some of these future problems if and when these patients do become parents.

For the Extended Family

Infertility is an intergenerational crisis, for it threatens loss of the family's future. Some parents of infertile persons wonder if they somehow caused this "defect." In a small percentage of unfortunate cases this may be true. For some mothers who took DES (diethylstilbestrol) between

1941 to 1971 to prevent their own miscarriage, this drug resulted in pregnancy loss or congenital malformations in the reproductive tracts of the children. More often, the parents' feeling of responsibility for the child's infertility relates to what parents feel they owe children (Burns, 1987).

Grandchildren offer the extended family an opportunity to rebalance the family ledger (Boszormenyi-Nagy and Sparks, 1973). Children may wish to repay parents for a good childhood by giving them loving grandchildren. Other times, grandparents may give love and attention to their grandchildren that they were unable to give their own children when raising them. Involuntary childlessness prevents these rebalancing processes from occurring. Sibling relationships can also be strained when siblings are not able to share the childbearing and childrearing experiences. Involving extended family in therapy sessions with infertile couples can help to increase support for the couple by acknowledging the loss and strain that affects everyone.

For the Therapist

Infertility can be a potent topic for therapists, especially those in their reproductive years who are trying to get pregnant or whose spouses are trying to get pregnant. Pregnant therapists may choose not to begin seeing couples with infertility problems because of how negatively stimulating the pregnancy may be to patients. Long-term patients may choose to stay with a pregnant therapist if the relationship has already proven itself beneficial. One of the authors worked successfully with two ongoing infertility cases through her first pregnancy. The pregnancy, and the couples' feelings about it, were discussed openly. These discussions were frequent early on and then almost disappeared as the couples were reassured that their concerns would remain foremost in treatment.

Therapists' reproductive issues can be problematic for patients, and the reverse is also true. One of the authors worked with a couple experiencing secondary infertility* who went through three years of

---

*Secondary infertility is infertility that occurs after a couple has successfully conceived, carried, and delivered a child (or children) without difficulty and then experiences problems when trying to conceive or carry an additional child.

diagnostic testing and treatment before conceiving again. Throughout this period, the therapist knew she wanted to have a second child so the couple's struggles were especially poignant for her. This reality was acknowledged in therapy. Regular peer consultation was useful in helping the therapist to express her own concerns with colleagues and then attend to the patients' goals in therapy. Fortunately, the therapist and the couple both delivered their second children within months of each other.

Therapists who themselves have had infertility problems can offer special empathy as well as valuable information to couples with this problem. Again, the issue is to stay focused on the patients' experiences of infertility and their needs, rather than the therapist's own experience. Therapists' self-disclosure is dependent on the specifics of each particular case. Therapists who have experienced infertility and moved beyond this crisis may use their own difficult experience to develop expertise informed by both medical and emotional knowledge. While each situation requires a different approach, we have found some commonalities exist for working effectively with couples experiencing infertility.

CLINICAL STRATEGIES FOR COUPLES EXPERIENCING INFERTILITY

Encourage Communication

Discuss the "secret of infertility." Encourage the couple to discuss the problem with trusted family and friends to decrease their isolation and increase their support. This also helps to stop family pressures, such as, "When are you two going to give us some grandchildren?" At the same time, the couple may need to inform their support network as to how and how often they wish inquiries regarding infertility. Some couples experience frequent inquiries about their status as intrusive, increasing their own despair and reinforcing the importance of their infertile identity.

Listen carefully to the couple's stories to understand the specific meaning the infertility has for each person and for the relationship (Weinshel, 1990). (See Sadler and Syrop, 1987, for an outline to guide an initial interview for the psychosocial assessment of infertility.) Once the initial questions about diagnosis and prognosis have been answered, help the couple to discuss their life goals and the existential issues involved in involuntary childlessness. What is central to making their lives meaningful?

Review the family's reproductive history. Explore coping strategies used by other family members in dealing with infertility and other reproductive problems.

Encourage Education

Increase the couple's sense of agency by encouraging them to educate themselves and become experts about their infertility through discussions with their medical providers and through reading. It is often useful for the spouse who is not being assessed medically to attend the diagnostic testing procedures of his or her partner. Understanding more about the biological aspects of the problem often helps people depersonalize the problem and removes the sense of failure and blame about something over which they have no control. Work closely with the medical providers to encourage free flow of information and support the relationships between the patients and their physicians.

Separate Fertility from Potency

Openly discuss the effects of the infertility on the couple's sex life. Separate fertility from potency. Help them develop strategies to retain some control and protect this area of intimacy. For example, some couples may choose to refrain from diagnostic testing for a month or more so as to not feel pressured to have sex during that time. For couples who develop a reactive sexual dysfunction, normalize this experience. Diagnose and treat (or refer) any long-term dysfunction.

Externalize the Problem

Externalize the problem of infertility as something the couple has to join together to cope with. Clarify spousal loyalty to the marriage. Increase communication to strengthen the marital bond.

As Sandra Gonzalez, Peter Steinglass, and David Reiss (1989) recommend with chronic illness, put infertility in its place by asking, "Who were you before this took over your life?" Frame infertility as a crisis, although it may be a long one. Encourage the couple to continue

172

with hobbies and other activities they have always enjoyed rather than adapting to infertility as a way of life. Discourage the individual's "infertile self" from dominating all other roles and reinforcing other feelings of inadequacy.

Promote Grieving

Acknowledge and grieve the loss of easy reproductivity. Define the "fantasy child" for each member of the couple, then help the couple let go of that child (Burns, 1987). Encourage rituals as active markers of loss, such as a good-bye letter to the unknown child.

Encourage the couple to consider joining a support group, such as RESOLVE (5 Water St., Arlington, Mass. 12174). Monitor the success of the group. Some are invaluable, but others can be destructive if members stay immobilized and focused on their anger.

Explore Motivation

Explore each person's fantasies of life with a child and life without a child. Help them discuss how much of their desire for children is externally versus internally motivated. Explore each partner's motivation to endure the stresses of infertility treatment or the pressures of going through adoption procedures, as opposed to choosing childlessness and shifting their needs for generativity to work or other arenas.

Monitor Personal Issues

Stay in touch with the therapist's own issues about reproductivity, especially for therapists in their reproducing years. Be careful not to proselytize for or against having children; stay focused on the patients' issues.

The New Reproductive Technologies

Some couples who experience infertility turn to vicarious parenting with children of family and friends. Some turn to work and eventually come to believe childlessness has its advantages, much like the voluntary childless (Matthews and Matthews, 1986). Some focus on their desire to raise children and turn to adoption, which used to be the only pathway to parenting for couples with infertility problems. Currently, however, with the legalization of abortion, the supply of adoptable infants has dwindled. Couples who continue to want biological children and have the resources to pursue this goal now can turn to the new reproductive technologies for help. These technological, noncoital techniques include artificial insemination with the husband's sperm (AIH), artificial insemination by a donor (AID), in vitro fertilization, embryo freezing for future transfer, embryo transfer from one woman to another, donor eggs, and surrogate motherhood.

It is estimated that 55 percent of couples diagnosed with primary infertility and 22 percent diagnosed with secondary infertility seek treatment (U.S. Office of Technology Assessment, 1988). Estimates for the success rate of biotechnical interventions in the aggregate now range from 35 percent (Schwartz, 1991) to 50 percent (Cook, 1990). Precise predictions vary with the diagnosis. As a couple moves up the ladder of technological interventions to achieve a pregnancy, each new procedure represents an increased amount of physical invasiveness, increased expense, and decreased success rate. The average time a couple spends in treatment before achieving a successful pregnancy or abandoning the effort is two to three years, with a range of ten to fifteen years (Patterson, 1990).

Though poor couples are more likely to be infertile, biotechnical intervention to achieve pregnancy is an expensive, middle- to upper-income phenomenon (U.S. Office of Technology Assessment, 1988). For example, in 1990 a one-month's supply of Perganol, a drug given to women to increase the likelihood of ovulation, costs over $1,000. One in vitro procedure, with a 10 percent success rate, costs about $6,000. Some medical insurance policies cover medications; many do not. The procedures are rarely covered. Besides the obvious class issues involved in the reproductive technologies, some feminists object to their use on several grounds. First, they believe that male scientists can be cavalier in the development of unpleasant or risky procedures to increase women's fertility, while ignoring the development of treatments to improve male fertility. Some feminists advocate nontechnological solutions such as education to prevent sexually transmitted diseases that may lead to infertility, help people to adopt children of all races and ages, and decrease the social pressures that lead many to feel unfulfilled if they cannot have biological children (Corea, 1985a, 1985b; U.S. Office of Technology Assessment, 1988). Other feminists applaud the new reproductive technologies for increasing women's options for reproduction.

Although these new technologies offer much hope for those who desperately want children, they also involve complicated psychosocial and physical demands on the couple. For this reason, some infertility specialists strongly suggest that couples undergoing treatment for infertility have an ongoing relationship with a therapist (Paulson and Sauer, 1991). Sometimes couples do not realize the impact of infertility treatment on their emotional lives. One couple came for a consultation because they were embroiled in the wife's brother's attempt to gain access to his young daughter, whose mother would not allow him contact. They felt their own loss, as an aunt and uncle of this girl, and they empathized strongly with the loss of the brother in his role as father. But they were perplexed about why this situation so immobilized them, as they saw themselves as typically competent people. Toward the end of the consultation, the therapist asked this couple in their late thirties why they did not themselves have children. They revealed a stressful seven-year history of infertility treatment but had not related this experience to why they might be so emotionally involved in the brother's loss.

Medical family therapy with couples beginning to undergo infertility treatment includes helping them to carefully examine their options and exploring both party's motivations for taking on the procedures. Anne Sadler and Craig Syrop (1987) point out that not all couples seeking infertility treatment desire children. Some couples' motives may include pressures from extended family, marital discord, replacement of a loss, or desire to do what is "normal" at their stage in life. Medical family therapy must help the couple decide whether they wish to pursue having a child or whether their problem requires other treatment. When they are motivated to pursue infertility treatment, therapy then moves to a process of negotiation and renegotiation between the partners about what has been determined so far, what should be done next, and when to end treatment (Matthews and Matthews, 1989). It includes acknowledging the stresses inherent in the procedures, the ethical conflicts that emerge, and the risks that may accompany these treatments. Many of the technologies are so new that little is known about people's experiences, especially how children and parents adjust in the long term.

An important dynamic to be understood in working with these situations involves the couple's relationship with their medical provider. In the best situations, the couples and the health care team have common goals and a common "enemy" (Sadler and Syrop, 1987). However, the physician treating an infertile couple is unavoidably imbued with the power to impregnate. This physician becomes the receptacle for life-long gratitude if the procedures are successful or may be the object of intense rage if they are not (Kraft, Palombo, Mitchell, et al., 1980). Matthews and Matthews (1986) suggest that, at times, frustration at the physician may serve a latent function of unifying a disappointed couple. The cycle of idealization and embittered anger can be very stressful for the physician to endure. The relationship between the medical family therapist and the physician can offer the physician support, as well as providing information and serving as a resource for the therapist.

TREATMENTS FOR MALE INFERTILITY

Artificial Insemination

The most common treatment for male infertility is artificial insemination, either with a partner's sperm (which may have been "washed" or "pooled" to increase the chances of success) or with a donor's sperm. There are many other very arduous and uncertain treatments for men, including medication, surgery, and repeated sperm counts (American College of Obstetricians and Gynecologists, 1989; Jarow and Lipshultz, 1987).

Artificial Insemination with Donor Sperm

AID, or artificial insemination with donor sperm, poses complex issues for patients, both psychologically and interpersonally. Researchers estimate that about 500,000 people are alive at the present time because of artificial insemination with donor sperm (Dickstein, 1990).

Several controversies exist about AID. AID may be done by couples themselves, producing so-called turkey baster babies, or with medical assistance. In the latter case, physicians and sperm banks are in a powerful position in choosing the pool of donors. Most sperm banks now have catalogs so that prospective parents can pick their donors based on physical characteristics, blood type, special interests and skills, and so on. Donors give sperm for humanitarian and financial reasons. Except for being screened for AIDS and other illnesses, little is expected from them. Donating sperm is assumed to be a psychologically uncomplicated issue for men. AID allows some heterosexual couples with infertility problems to have children; it also allows single women and lesbian couples to have children. These and other controversies have led some religious traditions (such as Roman Catholic, Orthodox Judaic, and Muslim) to oppose donor insemination (U.S. Office of Technology Assessment, 1988).

Couples are sometimes hesitant about AID and may present for counseling to consider carefully the issues involved. In choosing AID the woman grieves the loss of having her partner's biological child, while the man feels the direct loss of his capacity to reproduce and may experience envy of both his wife and the donor. For couples who use medical assistance for AID, some physicians encourage the male partner to perform the insemination in the office to give them a sense of participation (Mazzola and Stangel, 1984).

Typically, the emotionally problematic issues in AID fade when the baby is born and the mother and father begin a relationship with their new child. In a follow-up study after eleven years, couples who experienced the procedure reported a high degree of satisfaction. More than 96 percent said they would select this approach again. These couples also rated their marriages as consolidated and improved (Levie, 1967).

The issue of secrecy about AID remains controversial. AID allows couples privacy about their infertility problems. They may appear to family and friends as if they jointly produced a biological child. Some psychiatrists have recommended AID children not be told of their origins (Waltzer, 1982). Others argue this is dangerous, that children have a right to know, and that family secrets can be emotionally destructive (Shapiro, 1988). Devastating scenarios can occur, such as a divorcing father revealing the AID to his child in a moment of anger. A popular movement has arisen advocating honesty to children about AID and encouraging records be kept about donors that may be opened to children later, much like adoption records (Noble, 1987). Medical family therapists may help couples discuss and resolve these issues, balancing their need for privacy with the need to acknowledge the procedure and provide the child with love, support, and information about his or her background.

Medical family therapists may be asked to evaluate or counsel single women or lesbians who request AID. Single women who request AID tend to be well-educated, financially stable, in their late thirties, and want a child before their "biological clock" runs out. Many of these women may view marriage as more complex, difficult, or undesirable to attain than parenthood. Counseling may help these women to make a realistic decision about whether they wish to continue with AID.

TREATMENTS FOR FEMALE INFERTILITY

Treatments for female infertility include medications, surgery, in vitro fertilization, and surrogacy. Choice of treatment depends on the diagnosis, although many treatments occur in the absence of a firm diagnosis. Most biotechnical interventions to achieve pregnancy are very taxing physically and emotionally (Stotland, 1990). Minimally, for example, most require some time off work for employed women.

Medication

Some women without a firm diagnosis are given medication, such as an ovulation-inducing hormone like Clomid. One in three normally ovulating women become pregnant within several months of this treatment (Lam, Baker, and Pepperell, 1988). Women diagnosed with adhesions and tubal occlusions after pelvic infection may be treated with microsurgical reconstructions of their fallopian tubes. In one study of twenty-four couples, the success rate for pregnancy after this procedure was 30 percent. For the other 70 percent studied two years later, couples reported their feelings for each other had worsened and their sex life had deteriorated. Both men and women experienced grief, and women also complained of irritability, fatigue, and depression (Lalos, Lalos, and Jacobsson, 1985). No studies have yet been done to determine whether including therapy in conjunction with the medical treatment can diminish the long-term negative effects of failed treatment.

In Vitro Fertilization

In vitro fertilization is a procedure in which a man's sperm fertilizes a woman's egg in a test tube and then is reimplanted. It is a complicated, expensive, and stressful procedure involving blood tests, ultrasound, fertility drugs, and surgery. Couples often see more than one specialist, hoping to increase their chances of success with a different doctor. The general success rate is about one in five (Leiblum, Kemmann, and Colburn, 1987). This rate is lower when sperm production is of poor quality but better when endometriosis has been diagnosed or when no specific infertility factor has been identified (Navot, Muasher, and Oehninger, 1988). In the majority of situations when this procedure is not effective, the outcome is very painful for couples because of all they have experienced as part of the procedure.

Surrogacy

Surrogacy as a treatment for female infertility has received much media attention. However, surrogacy with someone outside of one's family is rare, expensive, controversial legally and morally, and complicated psychologically and interpersonally. These cases require careful evaluation and counseling prior to any pregnancy, as well as close collaboration with both the physician and the attorneys involved.

FAMILY SOLUTIONS TO INFERTILITY

More common may be surrogacy within families. Medical family therapists with referrals from physicians practicing obstetrics may see these cases occasionally. One of the authors has seen a number of these cases, some in which brothers donate sperm to their infertile brothers, and several in which sisters or sisters-in-law offered to carry babies for their infertile sisters. No longitudinal outcome studies can yet help to guide these patients in terms of the psychosocial outcome of these situations.

Family Donors

In the AID cases, much of therapy involved careful consideration of whether to use an anonymous or a family donor. In all cases, a family donor was finally chosen because of wanting the child to have the father's family's genetic heritage. The therapy occurred over four to six months in each case and included such issues as who to ask to be a donor, who to reveal the plan to, and how to tell the child. Patients held meetings with extended family members to discuss the issues involved. The couples were careful to frame their request as a "gift" and to reinforce that the donor's functional relationship with the child would be that of uncle. Potential donors were ruled out if they or their family had any significant hesitation. Most family members reacted in a supportive and poignant way to the possibility of helping their brother have a child. In this series of cases the extended families became very supportive of the plan over time, and to date the families and children have done well. One family has had multiple children through AID with a family member as donor.

Sibling Surrogate Mothering

Surrogate mothering within families seems to be more complicated physically and emotionally. More than half of the handful of cases the authors have seen have decided not to go through with the procedure after meeting for several family therapy sessions. Concerns arose, fairly late in the process, about such things as how to handle the pregnancy with the surrogate mother's own children as well as her friends. Another couple abandoned the process after their house burned down. Somehow, for these families the surrogacy seemed like a better idea in theory than in practice. Medical family therapy allowed these extended families the opportunity to explore the many issues involved and decide against the procedure or continue with their eyes open.

The cases that completed a surrogate pregnancy all involved sisters who were quite close, where the surrogate had a stable marriage and already had children herself. One example of a successful surrogacy appeared when a national newspaper magazine asked people to write in about their nontraditional families (White, 1990). Debra White wrote a letter describing her experience with her sister as surrogate. Rise, her sister, was inseminated with Debra's husband's sperm and carried the pregnancy for her sister. The family was open and discussed the process. Debra was Rise's pregnancy coach. "Sometimes I honestly forgot I wasn't pregnant. That's how much she let me get involved," said Debra.

180

Judson, eight, reported he thinks his history is "great." "He was told his Mommy's tummy was broken, and he grew up in his aunt's tummy." Rise continues her close relationship as Judson's aunt. The extended family has been accepting of the process, but Judson has run into a few unusual reactions from outsiders. One time, for example, he came home with a note from his Sunday school teacher: "Mrs. White, when the children were asked to share a love story, your son said he grew in your sister's tummy and she gave birth to him. He sounds confused. Perhaps you'd better talk to him."

CLINICAL STRATEGIES FOR WORKING WITH COUPLES UNDERGOING INFERTILITY TREATMENT

The new reproductive technologies can introduce new ethical and emotional issues into the process of procuring a baby (Angell, 1990). Some patients may struggle with their religious beliefs when facing decisions about these procedures. The Catholic church opposes all artificial means of reproduction, Jewish law permits AIH and in vitro fertilization but not AID, whereas most nonfundamentalist Protestant religions allow these procedures (Schwartz, 1991). To many couples facing treatment for infertility there are no right or wrong answers, only difficult choices. Medical family therapy can provide a place for families to raise and discuss these options and their foreseeable consequences. The following are specific strategies for helping couples who choose to undergo infertility treatment, to be used in conjunction with the strategies previously mentioned for working with infertile couples.

Acknowledge Stress

Acknowledge the stress that always accompanies lengthy infertility treatment. Discuss difficult ethical or religious issues.

Encourage Education

Work closely with the physician to gain medical information relevant for the therapy and to support the relationship between the physician and the patients.

Encourage the couple to increase their knowledge of the medical issues. Have them read relevant literature and find out from their medical provider, "What's realistic to expect?" and "How will you know when it's time to stop?" (Patterson, 1990; Paulson and Sauer, 1991).

Encourage the couple to contact others who have undergone similar procedures. RESOLVE members may be able to supply both support and information.

Encourage the couple to develop a realistic financial plan.

Negotiate Differences

Help the couple to negotiate their differences so they can make active choices around each new test and procedure.

Acknowledge Grief

Acknowledge and help the couple grieve losses as they occur during treatment. Many couples benefit from ritualizing these losses. For example, one couple planted a flower for each fertilized egg that did not result in a viable pregnancy after an in vitro procedure.

Help the couple to decide with whom and how to discuss these procedures with family and friends. Have extended family sessions when relevant.

Set Limits

Encourage the couple to take periodic breaks from the active pursuit of pregnancy.

Help the couple decide when to stop trying, then work through the loss, and meet their needs for generativity in some other way.

Develop a Loving Story

For couples who are successful, help them develop a loving story to tell their child about how he or she came to be born. Help the parents see their child's curiosity about his or her biological or medical history as appropriate and important.

For couples who move to adoption, encourage them first to work through the loss of not being able to reproduce. Studies have found that adaptive resolution of the psychological issues around a couple's infertility is a precondition for successful adoptive parenting. Failure to do so can lead to interferences in adequate parenting (Kraft, Palombo, Mitchell, et al., 1980).

Conclusion

Many opportunities exist for medical family therapists to offer valuable services to individuals, couples, and families for whom the transition to parenthood is difficult to achieve. Collaboration with physicians and medical providers who practice obstetrics or specialize in reproductive problems enhances the therapy for families enduring these losses. A medical family therapist who is knowledgeable in the area of reproductive problems will be a valued resource to physicians and families. Medical family therapy can help patients with reproductive problems to accept what they cannot control and take charge of what they can.

CHAPTER 8

The Challenges of Chronic Illness

We must begin with the premise that chronic disease by definition cannot be cured, that indeed the quest for cure is a dangerous myth that serves patient and practitioner poorly. It distracts their attention from step-by-step behaviors that lessen suffering, even if they do not magically heal the disease. To the extent possible, the goal should be to reduce the frequency and the severity of exacerbations in the course of chronic illness. . . . The family as well as the patient must learn to accept this treatment objective. Arthur Kleinman, *The Illness Narratives*

THE DIAGNOSIS OF a chronic illness is a significant life crisis for families. The patient and family generally are unprepared for the physical changes, alternating periods of stability and crisis, and uncertainty of future functioning. Chronic illness demands new ways of coping, changes in patient and family self-definitions, and lengthy periods of adaptation. The patient with the illness realizes multiple losses, including physical health and functioning, loss of roles or responsibilities, loss of dreams, and the possibility of decreased life span. Families also experience losses, for they tend to consider themselves differently, perhaps defining themselves as a family with an ill child or adult or a family with bad luck or a family who is unlike "normal, healthy families."

Chronic illnesses are managed by patients, families, and health care systems. The long-term nature of care often results in an ongoing relationship between patient and at least one physician, characterized by William Doherty (1988) as a "chronic relationship." Families also must interact frequently with medical systems. Evan Imber-Black (1988b) noted that the uncertainties and complexities of chronic illness require that families interact with multiple helpers and that medical systems are required to work with families. Since families and health care systems share responsibility for care, they encounter many opportunities for conflicts about roles, belief systems, and expectations for optimal medical attention. Role strain for both systems can be decreased when collaborative, trusting partnerships can be facilitated. The contributions of the medical family therapist can be welcomed by both family and health care systems.

This chapter details many of the issues significant for medical family therapy with patients and families facing chronic physical illness. Some work with chronic mental illness, which is more frequently an area of expertise for family therapists, can be translated to work with physical illness. (See Robert Sherman, Paul Oresky, and Yvonne Rountree [1991] on chronically mentally ill family members.) This chapter does not review the extensive research and theoretical literature about the many different chronic illnesses but instead takes a general approach to theoretical contributions and clinical strategies that apply across many chronic illnesses.

Increasing numbers of families are coping with chronic illnesses. The National Center for Health Statistics (*National Health Interview Survey*, 1987) reported that 14 percent of all Americans are limited in their activities by a chronic medical condition. The percentage of persons whose activities are limited by their chronic disease increased to 25 percent for those aged forty-five to sixty and 45 percent for those older than sixty-five. Daniel Callahan (1991) described to an audience of health care workers how cemeteries reveal the history of modern medicine: until the nineteenth century, people of all ages arrived at the cemeteries; late twentieth-century cemeteries are primarily full of older people. Callahan suggested that the "price to be paid for medical technology and curing is increased chronic illness." The following case history exemplifies many of the concerns for the thousands of families coping with serious, chronic illness in an adult member:

Bill Ellman, age fifty-three, was a successful attorney who tried many cases of medical disability. He had diabetes since adolescence, was knowledgeable about his illness, and tried to carefully monitor his diet, insulin levels, and physical responses. Nevertheless, he had many complications, including circulatory problems leading to coronary bypass surgery, great toe amputation, and impotence. More recently, his diabetes resulted in kidney failure requiring dialysis, with the possibility of kidney transplantation.

Bill's wife, Carol Ellman, was a forty-nine-year-old clinical social worker with experience with cases of families with chronically ill children. She was in good physical health. Carol's father had a debilitating stroke when she was in her early teens, and her mother provided full care for him for the six years between his stroke and his death. Their children, Tara, age twenty-three, and Michael, age twenty-one, were in college but maintained fairly close contact with their parents.

Carol initiated therapy for herself. She felt that she had tried to cope with Bill's illness but had become increasingly overwhelmed by the continuing medical crises, frequent hospitalizations, and reminders of her parents' experiences. She worried that her husband was becoming depressed and withdrawing emotionally from her. She wanted to continue to be supportive of her husband and still find ways to cope for herself. Although primarily interested in her own therapy, Carol was willing to include her husband and children as needed.

Clinical work with families in which there is chronic illness requires therapists to evaluate their own theories about families and illness. For example, Peter Steinglass and Mary Horan (1988) identify several theories that view families as either resources or deficits:

- In the *resource model,* positive family functioning and social support are presumed to be a resource or buffer the severity of the illness.
- In the *deficit model,* exemplified by the label "psychosomatic family," family stress and interactional patterns are seen to exacerbate illness and impede optimal care.

The danger of the deficit model is that therapists, aware of Salvador Minuchin, Bernice Rosman, and Lester Baker's book *Psychosomatic Families* (1978), will attribute characteristics of enmeshment, rigidity, and poor conflict resolution to most families with chronic illness. This is a misapplication of Minuchin and colleagues' work and can lead to the extreme, blaming position that families are at fault for illness in a member.

A medical family therapist uses systems techniques to help families realize the extent to which their experiences are natural responses to a crisis and that alternative responses are possible. As in many cases, Bill Ellman's situation demonstrates the impact of multiple losses on the family. It is essential that these losses be addressed. It is also important for the therapist to help the family acknowledge their strengths, their achievements, and their positive qualities:

> A husband and wife who had been preoccupied with integrating the wife's dialysis into their schedules were surprised and pleased when the therapist helped them notice that they had effectively arranged an elaborate family party to honor their son's graduation from college. The husband commented about how good it was to see that even with all of their disappointments, they could make something nice happen in their lives. The medical family therapist and family discussed this event as evidence of therapeutic change, from the experience of isolation and lack of control to renewed feelings of agency and communion.

Understanding Families with Chronic Illness

In chapter 2, we introduced some significant theoretical and research contributions to the clinical understanding of families and chronic illness. This section explores ways of characterizing chronic illness that are useful for therapy. Large clinical and research literatures relate families and specific chronic illnesses, particularly diabetes, heart disease, and cancer. For detailed information about work with specific illnesses, we suggest Thomas Campbell's (1986) extensive review and bibliography of family and health research and William Doherty and Thomas Campbell's (1988) text. Much useful information about chronic illness is also available through discussions with referring physicians and families.

When thinking about responses to chronic illnesses, it is important to avoid the error of assuming either that all illnesses have the same effects on all families or that each illness and family need to be treated as completely unique. With that caveat, we review some theoretical contributions useful for thinking about any family in which a member is experiencing chronic illness.

DEVELOPMENTAL PHASES

Family psychiatrist John Rolland (1984, 1988) has described how the developmental phase of an illness is significant in case formulation, much like the developmental phase of a family. Rolland distinguished the crisis, chronic, and terminal phases of illness and identified family concerns and tasks for each of the phases. David Reiss and Atara Kaplan De-Nour (1989) also depicted challenges presented by illnesses at the acute, chronic, and terminal phases, noting that adaptive coping patterns for one stage may not be functional at another stage.

Crisis Phase

During the crisis phase, which often begins prior to diagnosis, when the family senses that something is wrong, the family comes together to cope with the symptoms and the medical system. At this time families temporarily reorganize to meet immediate needs, and family members begin to address the psychosocial tasks of accepting the illness, creating meaning for the illness, and dealing with uncertainty. Families tend to pull together during the acute stage of an illness (Steinglass et al., 1982).

Chronic Phase

The timing of the shift from the acute to the chronic phase varies with each illness (Reiss and Kaplan De-Nour, 1989). During the chronic phase, which may have acute exacerbations and crises, patients and families accept permanent changes, grieve for the pre-illness identity, and negotiate roles for chronic care. At this stage, families generally become more informed and active participants in caring for the ill member and attempt to balance caregiving needs with other family needs. In Rolland's (1988) words, "Families try to live a normal life in abnormal conditions." How this is accomplished is of interest to researchers and clinicians alike.

Terminal Phase

For chronic illnesses that result in death, the terminal phase occurs when the inevitability of death is clear. Families have the option of whether to deal with separation and mourning and have an opportunity to discuss unresolved concerns, help the dying person to pass on concerns and wishes, and say good-bye. The terminal phase will be discussed in detail in chapter 10 of this book.

CHARACTERISTICS: ONSET, COURSE, OUTCOME, INCAPACITATION

As mentioned briefly in chapter 2, John Rolland (1984) has provided a typology of illness that helps to differentiate family responses based on characteristics of the illness. Variables in the typology include onset, course, outcome, and degree of incapacitation (table 8.1 depicts these variables with exemplifying diseases):

- *Onset* of illness can be either acute, like a cerebral vascular accident or stroke, or gradual, such as cardiac disease.
- The *course* of chronic disease can be progressive, constant, or relapsing-episodic. Alzheimer's disease can be considered progressive, a spinal cord injury is constant, and asthma is an example of a relapsing illness.
- *Outcome* refers to the expectation of whether the disease will shorten the life span. Disease outcome can be classified as fatal, such as metastatic cancer; possibly fatal, such as cardiovascular disease; or nonfatal, such as arthritis.
- *Incapacitation* reflects degree of disability and in Rolland's typology, an illness is categorized as either incapacitating, such as Parkinson's, or nonincapacitating, such as hypertension.

This typology may be used for research classifications but is also a useful tool for clinicians. Diseases that are progressive, fatal, and incapacitating, such as severe lung cancer, will have different implications for patients and families than will diseases that are constant, not fatal or incapacitating, such as a mild myocardial infarction (heart attack). And diseases that are quite different biomedically from one another may have similar psychosocial effects on families.

TABLE 8.1

Categorization of Chronic Illness by Psychosocial Type

	Incapacitating		Nonincapacitating	
	Acute	Gradual	Acute	Gradual
Fatal:				
Progressive		Lung cancer with CNS metastases AIDS Bone marrow failure Amyotrophic lateral sclerosis	Acute leukemia Pancreatic cancer Metastatic breast cancer Malignant melanoma Lung cancer Liver cancer, etc.	Cystic fibrosis
Relapsing			Cancers in remission	
Shortened life span, possibly fatal:				
Progressive		Emphysema Alzheimer's disease Multi-infarct dementia Multiple sclerosis (late) Chronic alcoholism Huntington's chorea Scleroderma		Juvenile diabetes Malignant hypertension Insulin-dependent adult-onset diabetes
Relapsing	Angina	Early mutiple sclerosis Episodic alcoholism	Sickle cell disease Hemophilia	Systemic lupus erythematosus
Constant	Stroke Moderate/severe myocardial infarction	PKU and other inborn errors of metabolism	Mild myocardial infarction Cardiac arrhythmia	Hemodialysis-treated renal failure Hodgkin's disease

Nonfatal:

Progressive		Parkinson's disease Rheumatoid arthritis Osteoarthritis		Noninsulin-dependent adult-onset diabetes
Relapsing	Lumbosacral disc disease		Kidney stones Gout Migraine Seasonal allergy Asthma Epilepsy	Peptic ulcer Ulcerative colitis Chronic bronchitis Other inflammatory bowel diseases Psoriasis
Constant	Congenital malformations Spinal cord injury Acute blindness Acute deafness Survived severe trauma and burns Posthypoxic syndrome	Nonprogressive mental retardation Cerebral palsy	Benign arrhythmia Congenital heart disease	Malabsorption syndromes Hyper-/Hypothyroidism Pernicious anemia Controlled hypertension Controlled glaucoma

Source: J. Rolland (1984), Toward a psychosocial typology of chronic and life-threatening illness. *Family Systems Medicine, 2,* 245–262. Used by permission.

In the Ellman family, Bill's diabetes had a gradual onset. It became progressively worse, resulting in increasing incapacitation and an expectation of decreased life span. Each hospitalization for a small amputation or heart arrhythmia or for surgery for kidney dialysis was a crisis requiring acute family response during the ongoing period of chronic illness. The progressive nature of the illness meant that each new crisis resulted in somewhat more disability and a slightly altered quality of family life.

FAMILY LIFE CYCLES

Chronic illness occurs at all stages in the family life cycle. To further differentiate family responses, John Rolland (1988) suggested that clinicians consider the interface between the illness and the life cycles of the individual and family. Rolland's work was based on Lee Combrinck-Graham's (1985) description of three generations of a family oscillating over time between periods of family closeness and family disengagement. Figure 8.1, Combrinck-Graham's spiral model, shows how during the periods of closeness, centripetal forces from communities and families pull the generations in toward one another. During the developmental periods of separation, families are described as if centrifugal forces are pulling the members and generations from one another.

Consider the family impact of a fifty-year-old woman's diagnosis of Alzheimer's disease: that impact is different if her children have young children of their own (centripetal period) than if her children are just leaving home themselves (centrifugal period). Although young parents may feel pressed for time, they may have a more scheduled and predictable life and be more available as caregivers than young adults who are attempting to leave home.

Rolland suggested that chronic disease generally exerts a centripetal pull on families. If an illness begins during a centrifugal period, such as when young adults are leaving home, the illness can detract from the family task of launching; if the illness onset coincides with a centripetal period, such as childrearing, it may prolong that period. Peggy Penn (1983) described a similar phenomenon—of families becoming static as a response to the illness, when "evolutionary time seems to stop, and the system becomes dominated by the recovery time of the patient" (p.

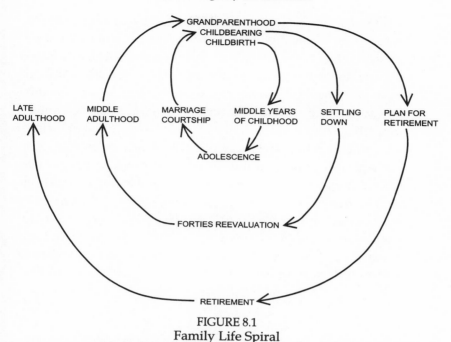

FIGURE 8.1
Family Life Spiral
Source: L. Combrinck-Graham (1985), A developmental model for family systems.
Family Process, 24, 139–150. Reprinted with permission.

23). Penn described a particular form of "binding interaction" that helps the family maintain the existing family form and avoid life cycle changes that ordinarily would unfold. The family coalitions, for example, that were appropriate for an earlier period of family development become fixed or frozen and inhibit further development and change.

Sandra Gonzalez, Peter Steinglass, and David Reiss (1987), who have studied extensively families with chronic illness, also concur that normative family needs generally are subordinated to the needs of the illness or the ill family member. Other needs of family members can become neglected, which results in frustration, resentment, and poor communication. Medical family therapists need to attend to the fit between stage of illness and stage of family development, and discuss these relationships with families:

> In the Ellman family, Bill had diabetes throughout his child-rearing years, but the crises of kidney failure, amputation, and heart disease

increased at the time that the children were leaving home for college. The parents tried to encourage the children to leave and attend to their own lives, but all family members had very mixed feelings about this issue. At the same time, Bill and Carol felt isolated by the illness crises and were reluctant to increase their interactions with friends who might have been able to provide support.

Although the parents did not expect their children to come home for every hospitalization, they sometimes found themselves feeling abandoned and resentful. Similarly, the young adult children wanted to show their support for both parents but sometimes resented feeling that they should not enjoy their own lives fully. Discussion about the fit between their lives and the "life of the illness" helped members to realize the predictability and appropriateness of their mixed emotions.

FAMILY CHARACTERISTICS THAT AFFECT RESPONSE TO ILLNESS

Overprotection

Family therapists attend to the family patterns that seem to enhance or maintain different patterns of behavior. Most families coping with the severe stress of chronic illness develop "within-family emotional coalitions and exclusions" in response to illness care (Gonzalez, Steinglass, and Reiss, 1987). Many therapists describe these coalitions as *family overprotection*, a negative characteristic that can lead to less personal autonomy and more illness or disability in the patient.

Yet research supports the common-sense view that some degree of protectiveness is necessary to care for ill family members (Gillis, 1984). From research with couples in which husbands had heart attacks, Veronica Fiske, James Coyne, and David Smith (1991) found that overprotectiveness was not related to physiologic or psychologic outcomes but that a husband's perception of a wife's attitudes as hostile or critical were negatively related to patient efficacy and psychological adjustment. David Reiss, Sandra Gonzalez, and Norman Kramer (1986) examined the variable of coordination, which reflects the family's belief that they must face uncertain situations as a group and may be similar to protectiveness. In their research, highly coordinated families provided effective responses to an acute illness situation but were less effective in meeting the needs of other family members when care became chronic. Thus what appears to be overprotection may be desirable at early or crisis stages of illness but may be less functional in chronic situations or at different family developmental periods.

Tolerance for Ambiguity

Other family theorists believe that tolerance for uncertainty or ambiguity is a salient characteristic for successful adaptation to chronic illness (Boss, Carron, and Horbal, 1988; Kleinman, 1988). Boss and her colleagues have suggested that it is the uncertainty about the course of the illness that is more draining to caregivers than the actual care of patients with Alzheimer's. Ability to tolerate uncertainty may be similar to the adaptability dimension of David Olson, Douglas Sprenkle, and Candyce Russell's circumplex model of family functioning (1979). These researchers predict that moderate ranges of adaptability are the most functional for coping with stressful situations.

Families need to be flexible enough to accept uncertainty but organized enough to be effective in obtaining information and managing their environment. Yet Sandra Gonzalez, Peter Steinglass, and David Reiss (1987) state that family patterns formulated in response to illness demands are often adhered to rigidly: "It is as if the family believes that any adjustments to the precarious structure of its coping with the illness will bring the whole house down" (p. 2). Thus therapists should attend to the patterns of response to illness and the family members' willingness to tolerate uncertainty and consider changes in their interactions.

The apparent rigidity of family interaction may be maintained, in part, by the family's isolation in coping with the illness (Gonzalez et al., 1989). Families generally do not talk with one another about their illness concerns (Gonzalez, Steinglass, and Reiss, 1987). Even when families are isolated from other families, it is almost a therapeutic given that family members do better when they can talk with one another about their needs and desires (Baker, 1987).

When they do talk together, however, members differ in their comfort level. As mentioned in chapter 4, Dakof and Liddle (1990), in studying cancer patients, found that agreement about how much to communicate was more important for satisfaction than was the amount of spousal discussion about the illness. For example, couples may choose to discuss their concerns about illness very infrequently, but if both feel satisfied with their communication, they can be satisfied with their response to the illness. In many families such as the Ellmans, however, members disagree about how much to discuss the illness. Carol Ellman felt that Bill did not share his feelings with her as much as she wanted. Bill felt that Carol was often pushing him and urging him to focus on the illness more than he wanted to. Thus therapists should be cautious about uniformly encouraging more communication among family members and attend to the individual family members' desires for kinds and amounts of communication.

Gender Differences

This last example highlights a within-family difference that may be related to gender. Men and women often differ in their interest in intimate communication, and in our clinical experience, expectations about illness communications may also differ. Women often want more discussion of feelings about medical problems than do men. Expectations about provision of care may also differ for men and women with traditional gender roles. In couples caring for a spouse with Alzheimer's disease, Pauline Boss, Wayne Carron, and Joan Horbal (1988) found that women caregivers were less comfortable than men about focusing on the necessary self-care required for successful, long-term caregiving.

Issues around Referral

Family therapists usually are curious about how families decide to come for therapy, and it is particularly informative to consider issues about referral when working with families with chronic illness. Although most families concur that family stress is increased when a member has a chronic illness, few families like to feel that they are unable to cope with these stresses and are in need of a therapist. They already know that the patient is "sick"; they don't want to be told that he, she, or all of them are "crazy," too.

In their work on multiple family educational groups for families with chronically ill members, Gonzalez, Steinglass, and Reiss (1987) described some general family responses that negatively affected family interest in support groups or therapy:

- Family members are often well aware of their feelings of disappointment, anger, guilt, and resentment but experience their feelings as unacceptable because of the patient's medical condition.
- Most families coping with chronic illness report having negative experiences with at least one part of the medical delivery system and may be reluctant to make room for more illness-related activities.
- Families may often feel criticized by the offer of help, particularly if the help is of a psychological nature.

These responses make such families difficult to refer for medical family therapy. When they do come, they usually arrive at the office of the medical family therapist with feelings of hopelessness and failure. Early interactions with the families can either support these fears or provide measures of hope.

Physicians, not families, often initiate referrals of families with chronic illness to a medical family therapist. When these referrals are made, it is crucial to determine how the referral was discussed and what possible competing agendas may exist. For example, one physician felt that couples therapy would provide support to the spouse of a man with Parkinson's disease and enhance the marital relationship. The wife, however, perceived the referral as evidence that she was not fulfilling her caregiving functions adequately and the physician had tired of her and wanted someone else to deal with her. After rescheduling two initial appointments, the wife reluctantly expressed her concerns to the therapist. Only after a brief joint session with physician, couple, and therapist did the wife feel supported by the physician and interested in receiving more support through therapy. This joint session also provided an opportunity for physician and therapist to discuss directly issues in the referral process.

When physicians and families agree about the direction for therapy, the medical family therapist also must agree with the contract.

Families with chronic illness want help with managing their lives and caring for the ill member. They may not be interested in marital therapy. Medical family therapists may ask about intergenerational alliances or marital communication but in ways that maintain the focus on the family's goals. Of course, therapy contracts may change over time, as the following example demonstrates:

> A young family in which the wife had severe rheumatoid arthritis was seen for brief periods over four years. Initially, the couple was referred to consider how the illness affected them as parents. They wanted help with explaining the disability to the children and with managing daily routines when the mother's disease was severe. After a few sessions, the husband and wife were pleased with their gains in confidence as parents. Although noticing stress in the marital relationship, the therapist supported their decision and arranged a soft termination. She described how illness affects many areas of family life, including marriage, and indicated her willingness to meet with them in the future if they desired. Two years later, the couple returned to discuss the ways in which the illness had affected their marital and sexual relationship. Both partners agreed that they would not have been willing to consider these issues during the earlier treatment sessions.

William Doherty (1988) cautions that expectations for cure by therapist, physician, and family may be too high. Most chronic illnesses, by definition, will not be cured. After traditional biomedical treatment has "failed to cure," families and therapists may be seduced into thinking that therapy to enhance interactional patterns may be the magic ticket that will decrease symptoms or improve prognosis. Medical family therapy ought not to be a last resort that ends in disappointment. The therapist who is comfortable with uncertainty and appropriately humble can help to negotiate expectations about the possible outcomes of therapy.

As in all medical family therapy, good collaborative relationships with referring physicians are essential, particularly given the long-term nature of chronic illness. Evan Imber-Black (1988b) described how splits in the family over patient care or responsibility can be replicated in splits among the helpers. Family members, burdened with responsibility and worry, can inadvertently search for allies in physicians and therapists. This process also works in reverse, however, when therapist and physician disagree about care, and each subtly influences family members to support their divergent positions. Thus the family therapy standards of multipartial alliances, awareness of triangles, and communication with colleagues are fundamental throughout the referral and treatment period.

Strategies for Managing Chronic Illness

Sandra Gonzalez, Peter Steinglass, and David Reiss (1987), researchers and clinicians interested in families coping with chronic illness, described multifamily educational groups for families with chronic illness. A central organizing theme of their work is that chronic illness threatens to take over the family's identity and interfere with the family's development. The aim of their research and intervention groups is to learn how families can accommodate the illness and still keep the family as a unit on an appropriate developmental course. This can be a principal goal for medical family therapists, as well.

The general clinical strategies useful for managing illness and maintaining other family goals were described in chapter 4 of this volume. Without repeating that discussion, we highlight the strategies that are most important for work with chronic illness—respecting defenses and removing blame, maintaining communication, and increasing agency (see table 8.2). Other strategies suited for chronic illness issues include reinforcing family identity, eliciting family illness history and meaning, providing psychoeducation and support, and maintaining an empathic presence with the family.

RESPECTING DEFENSES, REMOVING BLAME, AND
ACCEPTING UNACCEPTABLE FEELINGS

Families with chronic illness want to know why the illness occurred and who or what is at fault. Commonly associated with this search for blame are feelings of defensiveness and guilt. Thus families often have spent much time trying to understand what has occurred and

TABLE 8.2

Strategies for Managing Chronic Illness

---

1. Respect defenses, remove blame, and accept unacceptable feelings.

2. Maintain communication.

3. Reinforce family identity.

4. Elicit the family illness history and meaning.

5. Provide psychoeducation and support.

6. Increase the family's sense of agency.

7. Maintain an empathic presence with the family.

---

may have blamed each other, bad genes, environmental events, or the medical system. Family members without illness often experience guilt about being healthy and conflict about feelings of resentment toward the ill person. In order to interrupt vicious cycles of guilt and blame, the therapist can help the family put "illness in its place" and consider how the illness threatens family identity and development (Gonzalez, Steinglass, and Reiss, 1987).

It can be helpful to think of the illness as an intrusive and demanding part of family life. Gonzalez, Steinglass, and Reiss (1987) vividly describe how intrusive the illness can be. They suggest that we imagine a family ready to start on a long car trip: "The illness comes along crowding the family with extra baggage, demanding to stop every 5 miles for snacks or to use the bathroom, and threatening to need emergency treatment at any moment" (p. 20). With this experience, it is not surprising that families become discouraged and curtail activities.

Therapists can inadvertently create blame by the nature of therapeutic conversation. It is not generally helpful, for example, to ask questions about the "function of the medical symptom," a point that Chloe Madanes (1980) emphasizes in the area of nonphysical symptoms. Even when family dynamics clearly are contributing to unhealthy responses, change is most likely to occur when the patient and the family do not feel blamed. If, for example, a family continues to hover over the father in the chronic phase when he should be recuperating from his stroke, the behavior can be considered from a developmental perspective. In this case, it may have been functional early in the recovery

200

period for the family to pick up many of the father's responsibilities. In the chronic phase, however, that behavior should change as the father increases functioning within his existing limitations. The therapist can note that some behaviors may be considered functional during the acute phase of illness but less helpful throughout the chronic phase. Focusing on the developmental phases of an illness and the tasks for that phase helps limit blame and increases the likelihood of helpful family responses.

MAINTAINING COMMUNICATION

There is never only one illness story. Each family member has a unique story of the illness and a unique view about the meaning of the symptoms and the impact of the illness on the family. Each member's view may change over time, resulting in a complex family story. When the different views are elicited, the therapist can help families realize that multiple perceptions are to be expected and that many possible responses are acceptable. It is helpful for children, for example, to understand that their experience of their father as sometimes discouraged and sometimes hopeful is accurate and normal for someone facing the challenges of a new illness.

Encouraging individual members to hear and appreciate the perceptions of others can have multiple benefits. When an adolescent acknowledges his fear that his father's stroke was caused by an argument he had with his father prior to the stroke, family members can reassure one another and diminish blame. Listening to each other promotes empathy within the family. In the family in which the wife had rheumatoid arthritis, the husband fell and broke his arm during the course of marital therapy. He used his experience to better understand his wife's frustrations and limitations. When he explained how difficult it was not to be able to do things he usually took for granted, she began to believe that he could empathize with her pain and disappointments.

Encouraging discussion about family members' adaptations to a chronic illness highlights individual differences about dealing with the illness. Family members sometimes want to talk about their concerns and at other times want to ignore the effects of the illness—and family members may be "out of synch" with one another in these regards. Lisa Baker (1987) described how this "rhythm of adaptation" can be considered an asset: if different family members respond at different times, the patient and other members are allowed necessary respite. When the family understands expectable individual differences, members are not misunderstood as withdrawing or inconsiderate.

Maintaining communication assists families throughout the inevitable periods of uncertainty. Even when the illness can be characterized as a constant, predictable event, changing life events require at least minor alterations in coping. Medical data, obtained from physicians, can be supplemented with information from the therapist about expectable phases of psychosocial adaptation. Anticipatory discussions can help families discuss how they would like to manage an illness crisis before it occurs. Communication can occur around highly emotional topics, such as living wills, and around predictable aspects of chronic illness management, as illustrated in the following case:

A family session was held with Michael, a twenty-three-year-old with Crohn's disease and his visiting parents, after an emergency hospitalization and surgery. The family understood that Crohn's disease affects the digestive and excretory systems and that exacerbations can be related to diet and other life changes. The parents were respectful of their son's autonomy, pleased that he had moved to a new city and found an interesting job, and yet worried that the stress of living alone contributed to his unstable condition. Their respect for each other was apparent, but so was the fearfulness in their interactions with one another. Once the therapist conveyed appreciation of the parents' respect for their son's autonomy, she also noted that it seemed as though they walked on eggshells around one another. The therapist suggested that sometimes the parents probably wanted to ask their son whether he ate well but worried about whether it was developmentally appropriate.

Visibly relieved to overtly discuss their problems with communication, the parents and son agreed that the parents could raise their concerns and that the son could say when he was not comfortable talking about an issue. The therapist noted how the usual life cycle stress of launching adult children was complicated by illness, an explanation that was both comforting and freeing for the family.

REINFORCING FAMILY IDENTITY

Families with a chronically ill member often feel that they are defined more by an illness than by other family goals and markers of identity. Gonzalez, Steinglass, and Reiss (1987) suggest that families can be assisted by focusing on who they are and what they want out of life apart from the illness. When family routines, rituals, plans, and priorities often have been put aside, medical family therapy can help families redefine themselves by focusing on how they defined themselves prior to the illness or how they would prefer to define themselves now. Often this is a very difficult task for families, and the therapist may need to ask what members would like to be doing if the illness did not exist. This can be threatening to the family if the existence of the illness is confused with the existence of the patient. Thus it needs to be clear that family identity and goals include the patient but may not include the illness:

In the family in which the wife had rheumatoid arthritis, the parents were asked to describe an illness-related event that had kept them from a planned activity. Only a few days before the therapy session, they had not attended an outdoor family reunion because the wife's arthritis was so painful that she could not sit up for long. Questions about why the disruption of this event was significant led the parents to realize that they were letting the illness keep them from their goals of enjoying an active social life as they reared their children. With an overt family identity and goal in mind, the couple could concentrate on ways that they could better limit the intrusion of the illness.

ELICITING FAMILY ILLNESS HISTORY AND MEANING

Lyman Wynne, Cleveland Shields, and Mark Sirkin (1992) describe how construction of meaning about illness is a transactional relationship. It is a process requiring a continuing series of negotiations about what constitutes illness and what roles are appropriately limited by the illness.

Family meaning is influenced by illness interpretations that may have developed across generations. Culture and personal experience combine to create family beliefs and expectations about causality of illness, appropriate responses, and patterns of family adaptation. These family responses and beliefs become intricately woven into the fabric of family life, and each generation has new opportunities to replicate or alter the significant historical patterns (Boszormenyi-Nagy and Spark, 1973). The therapeutic power of chronicling the transgenerational meaning of illness is beautifully illustrated by David Seaburn, Alan Lorenz, and Diane Kaplan (1992).

Patterns of response to illness are often influenced by family history. Susan McDaniel, Thomas Campbell, and David Seaburn (1990) suggest that beliefs and expectations about illness can be obtained with an illness-oriented genogram. In a brief time, families can articulate their experiences with illness by identifying who had which diseases, how caregiving was provided, and what effects ensued.*

Carol Ellman was aware of the frightening similarities between her mother's position as caregiver of her father and her own struggle as support for her husband. This knowledge made her try to do things differently than her mother had done—continuing with her work outside of the home, for example. In therapy, she realized that her conscious attempts to maintain a full life did not protect her from the similar feelings of disappointment and resentment that she had seen in her mother.

Carol became interested in how attempts to prevent repetition of family patterns had unanticipated outcomes. Carol tried to protect her daughter from assuming the strong caregiving function with her father that Carol had assumed with her own father. Yet Carol also sometimes felt critical of Tara and found her selfish, since Tara did not provide the same support to her mother that Carol remembered providing to her own mother. Carol and Tara were able to discuss how the balance between caregiving and support was handled in the previous and present generations, and each began to feel more comfortable with their relationship.

*We also suggest that family therapists who work with medical problems complete their own illness-oriented genograms and discuss them with colleagues.

PROVIDING PSYCHOEDUCATION AND SUPPORT

Families with chronic illness often feel very isolated, both from potential resources and from those who also may be coping with chronic illnesses. We have discussed the importance of encouraging community and helping families identify others for possible assistance and social interaction. Families may also be isolated from knowing that their concerns are shared by others. Medical family therapists may make it easier for family members to discuss their unacceptable feelings by providing stories about other anonymous families, as in the following case:

> The spouse of a man with Parkinson's disease had difficulty describing her disappointment about his deteriorating condition. The therapist described her experience with other wives who loved their husbands, wanted to care for them, and still felt frustrated that they could no longer take a simple walk together. The wife agreed that she also felt that way but felt guilty speaking about it, since her husband's situation was so much worse than hers. Once the unacceptable feelings were acknowledged as legitimate and acceptable by the therapist, they could be discussed and considered within the family.

Families coping with chronic illness benefit from receiving information about the illness and possible coping strategies. Robert Sherman, Paul Oresky, and Yvonne Rountree (1991) note that family therapists are often reluctant to take the role of teacher but that chronic illness care is facilitated when families have opportunities to learn about a disease and possible coping strategies. Sherman and his colleagues suggest that therapists structure some initial sessions as psychoeducational sessions, in which discussion is focused on the illness rather than family patterns around the illness. The therapist can share information about how families cope and can encourage families to read and ask questions of other families. Maurer and Strasberg's *Building a New Dream* (1989) is an excellent book written for families to provide general information about living with chronic illness. It includes resources for additional material, including support groups for families and persons with particular illnesses.

In many large cities or hospitals, support groups are available for patients and families with specific diseases. Many illnesses have family associations with national or regional meetings for information, support, and advocacy. The groups often provide helpful opportunities for learning about illness management and obtaining support. Some patients and families, however, become discouraged by a particular group's focus on disabilities and loss or by participating in a group in which members are in more advanced stages of an illness. Thus therapists should monitor a family's experiences and satisfaction with groups.

Exciting clinical interventions are suggested by Gonzalez, Steinglass, and Reiss's (1987) multifamily groups—structured, psychoeducational discussion groups. Groups are intentionally composed of patients with different chronic illnesses and their families, so that discussion remains on general issues in chronic illness instead of focusing on details of particular disease management. Patients talk with each other about their experiences while their family members listen, and family members talk while patients listen. These researchers have created a detailed protocol pamphlet for therapists or groups interested in initiating similar programs, and other centers for study of chronic illness are beginning to replicate this work.

INCREASING THE FAMILY'S SENSE OF AGENCY

When family members do not feel completely entrapped by illness, they have greater enthusiasm for constructing more enriched lives. Helping families see alternative ways of coping is the spark that draws us to family therapy. Because this is an area of expertise for family therapists, this section only briefly identifies some of the clinical considerations that are useful for helping patients and families expand options and increase agency.

Although many areas of illness and care cannot be changed, therapists can help families identify the areas that can be controlled and make mutually acceptable decisions. Therapists can also help families to continue to feel good about the decisions, particularly when families feel competing pressures from others. For instance, families can determine how much they will be responsible for physical care, both in the hospital or at home, as exemplified by the Ellmans:

In the Ellman family, the couple decided to have visiting nurses provide most of the care for the healing of a wound after amputation. Although Carol was less involved with routine care than other spouses might be, she felt more empowered because she and her husband had made the decision that seemed the best for them.

A medical family therapist can work to remind the family of how well, in fact, they are functioning. Families are not usually told that they are doing well—that they are meeting the ill person's needs, that they are adjusting to the social, economic, and physical changes, and that other family responsibilities are getting done. With support for the work that is going well, families will have renewed enthusiasm for attempting further changes. Sometimes, as in the following case, humor can be used effectively to demonstrate competence and control:

In one family, the wife felt that she could no longer tolerate her husband's depression after he had physically recovered from his heart attack. She felt out of control and described how she "lost it totally" in a fight: she took her husband's shirts out of the closet and threw them out of the window. The therapist asked if she had taken scissors to them or ripped them up before she had thrown them out. The wife laughed and realized that even when she felt that she had no control, she had arranged her outburst so that the couple could easily retrieve the undamaged clothing.

The therapist also provides needed support for families who face multiple losses and changes in their lives over which they have little control. As families try to focus on coping, they may be reluctant to discuss their concomitant feelings of loss. The therapist may need to initiate questions about loss and discuss the continuing balance that occurs between grieving losses and creative coping.

Coping strategies that are valued by different family members should be encouraged. Some may feel supported by talking with friends or clergy; others may prefer being involved with individual activities that distract them from illness. Therapists who use their expertise wisely can enhance the competence of families. In the family in which the wife had rheumatoid arthritis, the parents asked the therapist to include the children and assess how they were coping. In a follow-up session, the mother stated, "I wanted someone who was a professional—who could say that they are doing well and could say that we were doing well."

Families can try new behaviors to allow them to achieve a better balance between providing for the ill family member and meeting the needs of other family members. What is best for the patient may not always be best for all family members (Reiss, Gonzalez, and Kramer, 1986; Steinglass et al., 1982). It may enable healthy family members to remain supportive if they have permission from the ill person to participate in some activities alone. Therapeutic discussions can encourage family members to negotiate activities and find ways to compromise on activities. Creative coping is demonstrated in the following example:

When Bill and Carol Ellman felt that Bill's dialysis needs prohibited them from taking vacations away from home, Carol felt discouraged and resentful. They compromised and joined a country club, which enabled Carol to take afternoon swims and socialize and allowed the couple to dine occasionally and participate in organized social activities. Bill was concerned about the financial expense but realized that the membership would eliminate travel expenses and an important source of support would be opened for Carol and for them as a couple. Carol was enthusiastic about their decision, which became an adventure for both of them.

Families can be assisted in increasing their tolerance for uncertainty and their ability to build flexibility into their plans. Discussion can help members consider alternatives, for example, when the mother's arthritis flares up on the day that the family planned to attend a picnic. Is it necessary for all members to stay home or for just the patient to stay home? Or could the family go to the picnic and place an air mattress under a tree so that the mother could lie comfortably in the shade and still be a part of conversations and activity? Using therapeutic sessions to discuss possibilities and encourage activity provides a template for families to continue this freeing and exciting work on their own.

MAINTAINING AN EMPATHIC PRESENCE WITH THE FAMILY

Like patients and families with chronic illness, medical family therapists must learn to tolerate uncertainty and work with situations that are not easily controlled. Therapists may feel most comfortable in the beginning stages of therapy when visible changes occur in family communication and interaction patterns. Some families are satisfied with these changes and soon cease therapy. Other families elect to continue, perhaps less frequently, with the therapist continuing to be a significant source of emotional support.

It is essential that therapists not withdraw from families when cure or change is unlikely. William Doherty and Thomas Campbell (1988) included a beautifully written letter from a grateful patient (Craig Peters, pp. 89–91) who thanked his physician for the ways that he stayed with him throughout his illness, even when cure was no longer available. In the letter, Mr. Peters described how the provider did not run from the intensity of the emotional needs and feelings of the patient. As a means of shifting our attention from change to care, the medical anthropologist Arthur Kleinman (1988) asks "that the uniqueness of illness as human experience, in all its many social and personal manifestations, becomes the center of the healer's gaze" (p. 228).

Learning from Chronic Illness

Coping with chronic illness is tiring work. Families can become isolated, and families and providers can easily become exhausted by daily care, the burden of responsibility, and feelings of disappointment and loss. Yet there are benefits for those who persist. Patients with chronic illness often appreciate aspects of life that healthy people take for granted. When someone can only intermittently walk without pain, the days of painless walking become special days for that person and those around him or her. Participating in new or favorite activities, even with physical disabilities, can be exciting and significant events. Families also share this recognition and may develop a thoughtful perspective about what is important in life. As providers, we benefit from learning from those who live with chronic illness.

We do not intend to imply that learning to appreciate health and life in some way offsets the suffering of those with chronic illness. The disappointment and loss experienced by patients and their families are significant. Yet when families and providers support each other, the emotional and physical needs are shared by more, and each part of the system is less likely to become overwhelmed. With more participants as problem solvers, it may be easier to find meaning, to define new dreams, and to consider new possibilities for action and relating.

CHAPTER 9

Childhood Chronic Illness

C HRONIC ILLNESS IS A STRIKINGLY common feature of child-hood. An estimated 10 to 15 percent of all children have a chronic medical disorder, with about 1 percent of all children having a severe disorder. These percentages translate into about 7.5 million children with a chronic illness and about 1 million with a severe chronic illness (Hobbs, Perrin, and Ireys, 1985; Pless and Perrin, 1985). Since these children and their families are apt to feel stressed and burdened by the medical condition, we suspect that the prevalence of childhood chronic illness is even higher in the practices of child and family therapists. A therapist who has developed a biopsychosocial perspective or a systems perspective can make a significant contribution to these families.

As Joan Patterson (1988) pointed out, there is much more diversity in chronic illnesses among children than among adults. That is, the majority of adult chronic illnesses come in the form of three disease categories—cardiovascular disease (especially hypertension and heart disease), diabetes, and cancer. But childhood chronic illnesses are much more diverse in prevalence, making each illness much rarer than the "big three" adult illnesses. Table 9.1 lists some of the most prevalent of these childhood chronic illnesses. Note that asthma ranks highest, with a prevalence of about 1 percent of the childhood population, followed by congenital heart disease, seizure disorders, and cerebral palsy. One implication of this diversity of childhood chronic illnesses is that medical family therapists have to do a great deal of research to learn about the medical aspects of cases they treat.

This chapter describes some of the unique features of therapy with families who have a chronically ill child and builds on this book's

TABLE 9.1

Estimated Prevalence of Select Chronic Illnesses in Children Ages Birth to Twenty Years in the United States, 1980

Chronic illness	Prevalence estimate per 1,000
Asthma (moderate to severe)	10.00
Congenital heart disease	7.00
Seizure disorder	3.50
Cerebral palsy	2.50
Arthritis	2.20
Central nervous system injury (paralysis)	2.10
Diabetes mellitus	1.80
Cleft lip/palate	1.50
Down's syndrome	1.10
Blindness	.60
Spina bifida	.40
Sickle cell anemia	.28
Cystic fibrosis	.20
Hemophilia	.15
Leukemia	.11
Deafness	.10
Chronic renal failure	.08
Muscular dystrophy	.06

Source: J. Patterson (1988). Chronic illness in children and the impact on families. In C. S. Chilman, E. W. Nunnally, and F. M. Cox (eds.), *Chronic illness and disability.* Families in Trouble Series, Vol. 2. (Newbury Park, CA: Sage). Reprinted by permission.

previous chapters on treatment, collaboration, and chronic illness in adults. Because much of this earlier material applies to children's illnesses, we focus here on special issues for children's illnesses. We also note that severe childhood chronic illness is emotionally challenging for therapists and other professionals. Working with these families triggers personal fears for our own children or child relatives, our desire to protect children, our sense of unfairness that young ones should suffer and die, and our anger at parents, physicians, and other adults whom we may see as not providing the best care for sick children. Immediate compassion and identification provide therapists with a strong incentive to help these children, but we must also monitor our tendency toward overinvolvement and scapegoating parents or other health professionals.

Special Issues for Families with a Chronically Ill Child

Although all families are stressed by a chronic illness or disability, several specific issues are especially pertinent in the case of childhood illnesses:

PARENTAL GUILT

Since they see themselves as their children's protectors in life, parents often feel personally responsible in some way for their child's illness. This guilt may be demoralizing for parents and may show itself in anger against other family members or against health professionals for their failure to cure the child. One father realized that the rage he was feeling stemmed from his inability to forgive himself for letting his daughter contract leukemia.

GRIEF OVER LOSING "NORMAL" CHILDHOODS AND IMAGINED FUTURES

When family members realize that the illness or disability is chronic—which means, here to stay—they mourn having to relinquish their dream of having a healthy child. When this grief begins at the child's birth, as in the cases of many genetic and birth trauma disorders, it can complicate the process of bonding with the child.

When family members realize that the illness will limit the child's life expectancy or the child's quality of life as an adult, there is an additional grieving and anger over being cheated out of future hopes and plans. Although this reaction is common in adult illness as well, there is a particular poignancy to the loss of many decades of healthy living in the case of childhood illness or disability. One older mother of a child diagnosed with a fatal form of muscular dystrophy said that an unexpected grief came over her when she realized she would never have grandchildren.

FEAR OF "CONTAGION"

Because of fear and ignorance, other parents, even relatives, may avoid the child and the family out of fear that the child's severe illness— such as cancer, seizure disorders, or AIDS—will somehow contaminate their child. One family experienced a decade-long rift during the polio epidemic of the 1950s, when the aunt and uncle of a child with polio declined to visit the child in the hospital out of fear that they would bring the disease home to their own children.

DEVELOPMENTAL ISSUES

Depending on the child's developmental position, the timing of the onset and exacerbations of a chronic illness can have serious long-term implications. The illness, or how it is handled by the family, can "freeze" a child developmentally. A young adult one of the authors worked with never grew up psychosocially once her Crohn's disease began in her early adolescence.

Just as for individual development, expected family transitions can be delayed or stopped by a childhood illness. Transitions that occur normally for other families, such as children leaving home, can become excruciating decisions for parents, say, of a Down's syndrome child.

VULNERABILITY TO HEALTH PROFESSIONALS

Parents experience a unique vulnerability to perceived criticism or lack of support from health professionals who have the task of keeping the child alive and as healthy as possible. This vulnerability occurs particularly in chronic disorders such as cystic fibrosis and diabetes, in which parental actions and supervision frequently show measurable results in the child's condition. When parents are sometimes held accountable for poor outcomes, they feel as if they are being told they are bad parents.

Tanya is a seven-year-old child with serious asthma. She and her older sisters, ages eleven and thirteen, were adopted by their parents four years ago. Tanya takes medication regularly for her asthma and uses an inhaler for acute flare-ups. On a number of occasions, the parents have taken her to the emergency room with medical crises. Tanya's asthma episodes stem primarily from allergic reactions but also can be precipitated by stress, particularly when separating from her parents when she goes to school or when she is left with a baby sitter. The parents explained to the therapist that Tanya had been found abandoned in Peru at age two. Part of the parents' stress stems from lack of support from their extended families, who view Tanya as "damaged goods" foisted on the family by the adoption agency. Because Tanya looks healthy most of the time, these family members believe that the parents are overprotective and too worried about her condition. Tanya's allergist and pulmonologist become involved mainly when there is an emergency, at which time the parents feel as if they have failed to do their job. The parents argue with each other about what risks are acceptable, such as allowing her to go to a birthday party at a good friend's house, where she may have an asthmatic reaction to the house cat.

This case illustrates several of the special issues for families with a chronically ill child. Because their daughter's asthma is environmentally induced—and they are supposed to control the environment!—the parents often feel guilty when she has an attack. They worry about her future when they are not there to protect her and also about whether she will be able to have an independent future. Although relatives do not fear contagion, they do not understand the child's problems and view the parents as overprotective. And the parents are vulnerable to criticism from some health professionals who are more concerned with asthma control than with whether Tanya is able to attend social events.

Family Dynamics That Influence Children's Health

One of the most fascinating areas of research on childhood chronic illness is the small but growing body of work on how family interactions affect biological activity in children. Noting that many research studies have associated marital conflict with behavioral adjustment problems in children, John Gottman and Lynn Katz (1989) decided to investigate the effect of marital discord on four- to five-year-old children's physiological health, physiological arousal, stress-related hormones, and peer relationships. Using complex laboratory procedures to assess marital and family interaction, along with a variety of physiological measures, the researchers found that children of maritally distressed couples have higher levels of chronic stress (as indexed by high levels of stressed-related hormones in their urine), higher levels of illness (as reported by mothers), and higher levels of physiological arousal (as measured during the laboratory interaction tasks). In other words, health-related physiological processes in children were shown to be linked to the quality of parental relationship.

In this study, which used state-of-the-art assessment tools, Gottman and Katz (1989) continued a research tradition begun eleven years before by Salvador Minuchin, Bernice Rosman, and Lester Baker (1978). Their book, *Psychosomatic Families,* proposed a family systems theory of psychosomatic illness, along with results of an experimental research study showing a linkage between triangling behavior of the parents toward the diabetic child and the child's blood levels of free fatty acids, which are thought to be related to stress. The original psychosomatic family model proposed that the following patterns of family interaction influence, and are influenced by, childhood chronic illness:

- Enmeshment, which means overinvolvement and hyperresponsivity;
- Overprotection, which means excessive nurturing and restricted autonomy;
- Rigidity, which means the tendency to maintain fixed patterns that are not working;
- Poor conflict resolution or conflict avoidance; and
- Triangulation, in which the focus on the child's illness detours marital or family conflict.

The psychosomatic family model, which stimulated considerable interest in the family dynamics of childhood chronic illness, has come under criticism for blaming parents for children's illnesses, for employing an outdated term *(psychosomatic)* that perpetuates the mind-body dichotomy, and for having an insufficient empirical base (Coyne and Anderson, 1988; but also see the rejoinder by Bernice Rosman and Lester Baker, 1988). Some family therapists' only familiarity with the psychosocial aspects of childhood illness is the psychosomatic family model—and they generally have only a superficial understanding of this model. These therapists tend to misuse the model by taking a judgmental and blaming stance toward parents, neglecting the biological dimension of diseases such as diabetes and asthma, and taking a conceptually simplistic view that family dynamics "cause" certain childhood diseases. Worse still, some even take the clinical stance that the family's "need" for the child to be ill somehow creates the original illness. Without the biopsychosocial framework that Minuchin and colleagues (1978) intended, the psychosomatic family model can be dangerous.

Beatrice Wood and her colleagues have updated the original psychosomatic family model with greater theoretical sophistication and more accurate research methods (Wood et al., 1989). These researchers examined how family processes interacted with three different childhood abdominal illnesses—Crohn's disease, ulcerative colitis, and functional recurrent abdominal pain syndrome. Families were rated during standard, videotaped family interaction tasks, during lunch, and during an interview. The authors used laboratory scores of disease activity as outcome measures—for example, platelet counts and levels of hematocrit and albumin. They found that disease activity was associated with triangulation, marital dysfunction, and a total psychosomatic family score. Two important findings had implications for the psychosomatic family model: that the three diseases differed in how family patterns related to disease activities, with Crohn's disease being associated with the highest psychosomatic family levels; and that marital dysfunction and triangulation were more powerful factors than enmeshment, overprotection, rigidity, conflict avoidance, and poor conflict resolution.

In a subsequent theoretical paper, Beatrice Wood (1991) extended the psychosomatic family model into a broader framework she calls a "developmental biopsychosocial" framework. This model is designed to transcend the mind-body dualism of the original term *psychosomatic*, make the model less pathology-oriented, and include relevant factors such as individual psychological and developmental issues, other social contexts such as schools, and the psychosocial aspects of the illness. All of these factors interact to influence the well being of the child and the family.

There is mounting evidence for a linkage between certain family interaction processes and children's physical well-being as well as psychological well-being. The original psychosomatic family model stimulated much useful clinical work and some subsequent research and theoretical development in this area but has been surpassed by more sophisticated theoretical and empirical work. Scholars such as Gottman and Wood have demonstrated complex levels of subtlety in the connections between family relationships and children's health.

How the Child's Chronic Illness Affects the Family

As described earlier, empirical work and theoretical work are converging in the formulation of models for understanding how family processes influence physiological processes in children. In serious illnesses, of course, the arrow of influence goes in the other direction as well—how the child's health affects the family. The following quote from Nicholas Hobbs, James Perrin, and Henry Ireys's book *Chronically Ill Children and Their Families* (1985, p. 80) summarizes the multiple, simultaneous challenges these families face:

Families with a chronically ill child confront challenges and bear burdens unknown to other families. The shock of the initial diagnosis and the urgent and compelling need for knowledge; the exhausting nature of constant care unpredictably punctuated by crises; the many and persistent financial concerns; the continued witnessing of a child's pain; tensions with one's spouse that can be aggravated by the fatiguing chronicity of care; the worries about the well being of other children; and the multitude of questions involving the fair distribution within the family of time, money, and concern—these are challenges that parents of chronically ill children must face.

Joan Patterson (1988) has organized this information on the effects of childhood chronic illness on the family under the heading of the Family Adaptation and Adjustment Response Model (the FAAR model was developed by Patterson and Hamilton McCubbin). In this model, families are viewed as balancing their demands and capabilities within a set of beliefs or meanings. Childhood chronic illness can tip the balance toward the side of the demands—physical, emotional, social, financial—and leave the family's resource capabilities depleted and inadequate. The family then goes into crisis and must find a way to rebalance itself.

The medical family therapist is apt to become involved with the family at times when it is out of balance, and the therapy may be a factor in increasing the family's capabilities to manage both the illness and other life demands. Sometimes the family seeks therapy not because it is not handling the ill child well but because the marital relationship or siblings are suffering. Because childhood chronic illness can unbalance families in many areas, a therapist's working with subsystems in the family can be invaluable.

In their excellent book on families of children with developmental disabilities, Milton Seligman and Rosalyn Benjamin Darling (1989) describe the burdens of caring for a developmentally disabled child. Parents of retarded children deal with numerous stressors that tax their resources, including the social stigma of mental retardation. Seligman and Darling describe how siblings often suffer invisibly: they lack information, worry about their brother or sister, are moved into caregiving roles, and have no one to talk to about their anger and also their guilt over being "normal." As with any childhood health problem, the more severe and disabling the disorder, the more stress on the family system. Medical family therapists are apt to be called when someone, or some relationship, breaks down under the strain.

The clinical illustration of Tanya and her family illustrates how family dynamics and the child's asthma are mutually influential:

> Vigilance was a central dynamic in Tanya's family: the parents were vigilant about her asthma symptoms and her anxiety, and she was vigilant about signs of separation from her parents. In addition, Tanya took on the stress of other family members when conflict arose, sometimes translating this stress into problems with her breathing. When this happened, her parents would drop what they were doing to give Tanya her medicine or sometimes take her to the emergency room. When a previous therapist suggested that the parents needed to go out and take time for themselves for the good of their marriage, Tanya had an anxiety attack after they left, which led to an asthma attack. For the parents, separation from their daughter seemed like a life and death issue. They decided to engage in home-based schooling for her, with the mother doing the teaching. This, in turn, compromised Tanya's ability to take social risks, make new friends, and engage with new adults. Thus, the child's predisposition to asthma, combined with her personal history of abandonment and the enmeshed, overprotective family dynamics, created a very troublesome medical and psychosocial situation.

Special Assessment Issues in Childhood Chronic Illness

This discussion on assessment and the following one on treatment expand on the discussion of general assessment and treatment issues in chapters 4 and 8 of this book. They highlight several important aspects of working with families when the chronically ill or disabled family member is a child (see table 9.2).

TABLE 9.2
Special Assessment Issues in Childhood Chronic Illness

1. What beliefs and meanings do family members bring to the child's health problems?
2. Has the child's illness become part of dysfunctional triangles in the family?
3. How are other relationships being attended to?
4. How are the siblings functioning?
5. What part of the problem is developmental and what part is illness-related?
6. How are the parents relating to health professionals?
7. How supportive is the family's social network?

FAMILY BELIEFS

Family members bring beliefs and meanings to the child's health problem. Most important, children may not be developmentally able to understand their illness in the way that their parents and health professionals do. For example, children with cystic fibrosis may not believe the disease is present when they feel no discomfort or may see no connection between managing their illness and the back pounding (for drainage of fluid from the lungs) they resent receiving from their parents several times a day. The health beliefs of parents, grandparents, and other relatives and close friends may also be important factors for the family. Similarly, the splits and controversies in beliefs among family members are important to assess. When a child's health and survival are at stake, adults' convictions can run very strong.

DYSFUNCTIONAL TRIANGLES

Sometimes the child's illness becomes part of dysfunctional triangles in the family. Family therapists are generally well equipped to assess triangulation and detouring of parental conflict onto a child. A chronic illness or disability provides a fertile ground for these family dynamics to blossom. These triangles may take the form of *detouring*, in which parents retain their unity by focusing on the child, or *cross-generational*

221

coalitions, in which one parent forms an alliance with the child against the other parent:

> In Tanya's family, the parents played out their conflict through arguments about being "hard" or "soft" on Tanya's accommodations to her asthma. This conflict culminated in a argument about whether she should attend a friend's birthday party despite the risk that an asthma attack would be triggered by the friend's cat. The father "won" the struggle, and Tanya went to the party; the mother "won" the aftermath, however, because Tanya had an acute attack, the mother stayed up with her all night, and the doctor agreed with her opinion in the morning. These conflicts stemmed both from relational issues in the parents' marriage and from different health beliefs about how to manage the asthma in light of Tanya's other developmental needs. In other words, the parents differed on how big a place to make for the illness in Tanya's life and the family's life. The father wanted "business as usual" as much as possible, within the bounds of acceptable risks, whereas the mother's focus was on preventing asthma flare-ups.

OTHER RELATIONSHIPS

The most common family interaction difficulties in childhood chronic illness begin when one parent (usually the mother) becomes the main caregiver for the child. As the father or other adults become more disengaged over time from the mother-child dyad, other relationships in the family—marital, father-child, parents-to-other child, extended family, friendship—begin to erode. Pressure builds on the mother-child relationship. Others begin to accuse her of being overprotective; she accuses them of not understanding and not supporting. Eventually, when the relationships are far enough out of balance, someone or some relationship breaks down.

SIBLINGS

Siblings are often the neglected figures in families of chronically ill children. Milton Seligman (1988) described how siblings are often kept out of the information loop in the family, how they may assume caregiving responsibilities, how they fear "catching" the illness or disability, and how they often feel anger and guilt over their sibling's condition. If, as the saying goes, "the squeaky wheel gets the grease," healthy siblings may have trouble competing for parental attention. Sometimes they develop their own "squeak" in the form of behavioral problems as a way to persuade their parents to attend to their concerns. Parents, however, are apt to see this misbehavior as a betrayal by a child who has "no reason" to be uncooperative, given the already major strain the family is under. In these cases, the family may present to the therapist with the sibling as the identified patient, not the chronically ill child.

DEVELOPMENTAL AND ILLNESS-RELATED PROBLEMS

A problem may have both developmental and illness-related components. A noncompliant adolescent diabetic may use the illness behavior to engage in typical adolescent resistance to parents. Children with chronic illnesses are naturally going to challenge their limitations and their medical regimen from time to time. Similarly, an ill child may experience a flare-up at a family developmental transition such as the birth of a new sibling. Therapists should not necessarily assume that the child's problematic behavior is stemming from problematic family dynamics related to the illness. Sometimes the illness is just the playing field for a normal, but irksome, family struggle.

PARENTS AND HEALTH PROFESSIONALS

When a family has a member with a chronic illness, the family also has a "chronic" relationship with health professionals: both are part of the family's life more or less forever. As mentioned before, parents feel particularly vulnerable to—and may resent—nonsupportive behavior from health professionals. Negative escalation is common in two scenarios, and each leads to frustrated staff and angry and resistive parents: when the diagnosis is uncertain or the treatment not working well, parents are apt to be angry with the health team for not helping enough; when the health team is showering the child with supportive and technically competent care, the parents may feel supplanted as nurturers and protectors of their child. The situation becomes even more difficult when parents triangle staff into family conflicts. Helping families with these disabled relationships with professionals is one of the hallmarks of a competent medical family therapist.

THE FAMILY SOCIAL NETWORK

Ultimately, children are raised not just by their parents but by an extended support network of family, friends, neighborhood, school, church, and community. Raising a chronically ill or disabled child is so difficult for most parents that their support network must be active and committed. Particularly important resources are other parents with ill or disabled children, since they really understand chronic illness. It is important to assess how well the family accesses their support network. How do they ask for help? How do they accept help? Can they relate to others outside of the illness context—that is, can they engage in mutual exchange of support with others when the child's illness is not a main focus?

Tanya's family illustrates many of the special assessment issues that arise in working with families coping with chronic childhood illness:

As the parents' marriage increasingly centered around Tanya and their other two children, disagreements over health beliefs became even more troublesome, since little else remained of their marital relationship. The oldest sister, age thirteen, was left with the caretaker role when both parents had to be absent from the home. She felt helpless whenever Tanya had a separation anxiety attack and then resented her parents for leaving her in charge. The eleven-year-old sister resented the amount of attention Tanya received and engaged in numerous small rebellions against her parents. This sister formed an alliance with her father over the issue of how overprotective the mother was toward Tanya. The mother, in turn, felt out of control of her eleven-year-old daughter. Health care professionals unwittingly became triangled into this family's coalitions when they dealt only with the mother, who the father believed distorted what the doctors said about Tanya. Finally, Tanya's family was isolated from its families of origin, who were unsympathetic to the adoption in the first place, and from the major community institution for children—the school—because Tanya was taught by her mother at home.

The family did have some important strengths, however. Church provided the family with a sense of community, and the family showed a good deal of resilience in maintaining caring, committed relationships despite their problems. Although generally anxious-appearing, Tanya had an attractive personality and a great ability to empathize with other children.

Special Treatment Issues in Childhood Chronic Illness

This chapter does not promote a single model for doing therapy when childhood chronic illness presents in the family. Therapists can successfully use a wide range of clinical models and techniques, but they should keep in mind—and address in a manner that suits their mode of therapy—the following special issues.

ACCEPTING THE CHILD'S ILLNESS

In families who adapt poorly to a child's illness or disability, patterns of denial and unresolved grief often prevent the family from adjusting to accommodate the new reality. They do not make a place for the illness in their life, and inevitably they do not accept the health professionals who also have entered their lives. The therapist has to work with these issues of denial and grief as a prelude to helping the family change its behavioral patterns. It is not uncommon for one parent to accept the illness and begin to make a place for it, while the other parent or grandparents experience such adjustments as a betrayal. Often health professionals see as underresponsible a family that has not been able to cognitively understand or emotionally accept the reality of the child's serious medical problem.

Accepting the realities and limitations of a progressive illness requires continual reevaluation, and each cycle of reevaluation carries its own possibilities for blocked grief, denial, and parental splits. When a single parent of a child with Duchesne's disease (a progressive, fatal form of muscular dystrophy) told her mother that it was time for a wheelchair for her son, the grandmother was appalled that her daughter was "giving up" on the child in this way. The therapist had to help the family make a place for the wheelchair as a metaphor for accepting the presence and power of the illness in their lives.

PUTTING THE CHILD'S ILLNESS IN ITS PLACE

The next challenge for a family that has adjusted to a childhood chronic illness or disability is maintaining the integrity of its relationships, rituals, and world view in the face of the demands of the illness. Illness is inherently unbalancing for families, and the worse the illness or disability, the more unbalancing it is. Unbalancing can occur when the child is not given appropriate developmental responsibility and challenge; in such cases, the child has disappeared behind the illness. Unbalancing can occur in a two-parent family when the parents' relationship is subsumed by discussion and worry about the child, and in a one-parent family when the parent has too few outside enjoyments and interests. A sibling may be left out of the family emotional hearth or given responsibilities that curtail normal childhood experiences. Just as families who do not make a place for the child's illness develop underresponsible patterns, families who fail to put the illness in its place develop overresponsible patterns of handling their child's problems.

We have found it helpful to speak with families about protecting themselves from the illness, even using metaphors such as assigning a room in the house to the illness—an upstairs spare bedroom, perhaps, but not the kitchen or living room, where the family has its most intimate transactions. The therapist then can work concretely to help family members plan activities that are not based on caring for the illness. Another technique for putting the illness in its place is to emphasize the normal developmental aspects of a child's presenting problems—such as age-appropriate rebelliousness or nonresponsibility—and thereby treat the child as a child and not as an illness.

PROMOTING OPEN COMMUNICATION

As Milton Seligman (1988) has observed, open communication about the illness or disability is one of the first casualties of a child health problem. Parents are afraid to upset the ill child or the siblings. Children likewise are afraid to upset parents and each other. The child's condition becomes a taboo subject, spoken about only with code words such as "fine," "doing well," or "wait and see." One of the principal tasks of a medical family therapist is to facilitate communion in the form of an open discussion among family members about their beliefs, expectations, fears, and hopes about the illness. It is often helpful to involve the relevant health professionals in this discussion. The therapist's presence and support can help the family break down the walls of silence that distance and confuse family members.

HELPING FAMILIES NEGOTIATE WITH HEALTH PROFESSIONALS AND SCHOOLS

For some parents, interactions with health professionals are one of the most painful aspects of a childhood chronic illness. The medical family therapist should carefully analyze the family's past and present interactions with professionals, looking especially for critical incidents that shaped the family's beliefs and expectations. For example, families with a child with muscular dystrophy have said that the callous way in which they felt that the physician told them about the diagnosis predisposed them to dislike the physician afterwards. One family was even asked for an autopsy permission by a resident who approached them immediately after the attending physician gave them the diagnosis.

Parents with disabled or chronically ill children must grapple with the educational system as well as the health care system. They must conduct difficult negotiations with school personnel about whether to mainstream their child or provide out-of-classroom school services and in-home educational services. These discussions often are complicated by a lack of coordination and communication between school and health care professionals (Doherty and Peskay, in press).

The challenge for the medical family therapist is to listen and support parents without scapegoating or triangulating against the health care team or the school team. The therapist needs to understand the workings of the health care system and the culture of medical care. Families can be coached to empower themselves without being disrespectful to health professionals: they can learn to ask questions, make legitimate demands, seek consultations and second opinions, check the accuracy of medications and medical communications, and, if necessary, terminate certain professional relationships and seek new ones. The same skills apply to dealing with school systems, although families may be more limited in their options to leave the public school system and go elsewhere.

The following critical incident in Tanya's case illustrates how the medical family therapist worked with her family and their interactions with the health care system and the school system:

Tanya was scheduled for surgery for a chronic knee problem, a congenital condition that sometimes led to injuries but otherwise did not affect family life as much as her asthma did. She and her parents were very concerned about repeating the painful experience of her previous surgery, when medical students and surgery residents took forty-five minutes to start an intravenous line in her arm. She felt like sliced meat—an experience that was worse for her than the surgery and the recovery afterwards. The parents felt helpless to do anything about the situation, since they knew that her veins were difficult for the doctors to work with.

The medical family therapist pointed out that anesthesiology residents are generally expert IV starters; they do it routinely, sometimes in emergency situations, and commonly are called in by other physicians to start an IV line for difficult cases. The therapist coached the parents to request, and to insist if necessary, that the most senior anesthesiology resident start the IV. The surgeon made no objection, and the resident started the line on the first try. Tanya was thrilled, and the parents felt empowered to choose options within the health care system.

Working together as a couple with their daughter's surgery and its aftermath (where the parents caught a medication mistake) proved to be a positive experience for the parents. As for the problem with their daughter's asthma, the therapist acknowledged the difficulty of balancing their need to protect Tanya with their desire to let her decide to take risks. Part of the parents' disagreement, the therapist noted, came from having different information, since the mother and Tanya generally visited the pulmonologist alone. The parents agreed to both be available for discussions with doctors in person or on the phone and to make joint decisions only after they both heard the medical information and advice directly from the physician.

The medical family therapist did other balancing moves with these parents, including holding Tanya responsible for taking her medication and encouraging her to attend public school. At the therapist's suggestion, the parents met with Tanya's teacher and principal to explain their daughter's medical condition and separation fears. The mother walked Tanya to and from school for several months until Tanya was ready to walk on her own. The therapist then turned to address the sibling issues—helping to clarify the limits of the oldest sister's responsibilities, addressing openly the eleven-year-old's resentment of her younger sister for receiving more attention than the other siblings, and reestablishing the parental boundary with the eleven-year-old.

After progress was made on these medically related and childrearing issues, the couple wanted to work more strongly on the marital relationship and family-of-origin relationships—with periodic returns to medical issues as they reemerged. Both parents went on to make important strides in their strained relationships with their parents and siblings, which lessened the pressure of their isolated relationship.

Issues in Collaboration

A special issue for therapists who collaborate with physicians and other health professionals around problems of childhood chronic illness is the exceptional level of vulnerability and protectiveness that professionals experience in the face of seriously ill children and their sometimes dysfunctional families. When these cases are discussed, it is not uncommon for physicians and nurses to show emotional distress about the child's condition. Sometimes the most helpful collaborative activity is for the therapist to listen and offer emotional support (see chapter 3 for a general discussion of collaboration). Of course, the therapist also may need support when children are sick and dying. These feelings of distress seem especially intense for professionals who are parents themselves.

Connected with the pain and grief are feelings of anger and resentment toward parents who do not do "right" by their children. When difficult medical and family cases are discussed, someone on the health care team may call for removal of the child from the home—a suggestion that can stem from emotional overinvolvement, burnout, frustration with the parents, and lack of understanding of complex human behavior and family dynamics. The challenge for the medical family therapist is to support the feelings and legitimate concerns of the health professionals while preventing the parents from being scapegoated and coerced. Systems trained therapists avoid replicating this problem by scapegoating the health care team on behalf of the family. As in the case of Tanya's family, the therapist also reaches out to schools and other systems that interact with the child and the family. Even in "disaster" cases, where the family-professional split is so wide that the family is unamenable to help, the therapist can help the health care team to learn from the case and try to work differently with similar cases in the future. Over time with these difficult cases, the health team can learn to ask the core question that denotes a systems perspective: "Are we helping to maintain this problem in some way?"

Conclusion

Working with chronically ill children and their families is central to the mission of medical family therapy in the health care system. It is where Salvador Minuchin and his colleagues started in the mid-1970s, following an informal request for help from the head of diabetology at Children's Hospital in Philadelphia. What we have learned since the mid-1970s is that children's health is biologically as well as psychosocially part of their family relationships. Children's bodies, like all of our bodies, are tuned to the resonance of family rhythms, and when something goes wrong with children's bodies, the reverberations penetrate deep into the consciousness of families and health professionals alike. We owe our children, especially poor children, better than we are giving them in health care—better prenatal care, better access to preventive care and treatment, and a more healthful environment. We also owe them more help for the families who influence their lives so profoundly and who struggle, often without adequate support and guidance from professionals, to cope with the unanticipated shock and burden of a chronically ill child.

CHAPTER 10

Caring for Dying Patients and Grieving Families

Life ends in death but all is not gone
The joy, the pain, the softness, the blueness.
Welling love, fear of departure.
My own mortality is safer to me
Deep in our hearts is our first born son.

Nancy Ann Dahl

EACH OF US has powerful memories and associations about death, grief, and loss. We are influenced by our family experiences and beliefs, our ethnic and cultural traditions, and our professional belief systems. An initial response to Nancy Ann Dahl's verse might reflect each of these three perspectives. First, we might feel sadness about this woman's loss, reminded perhaps of the actual or feared loss of one of our own family members. Second, we might think of how her cultural beliefs about death comfort her and how she integrates the memory of her son into her life to help lessen fear of her own death. Finally, as family therapists, we might applaud her ability to write about her experiences, believing that this represents acknowledged and healthy grief.

A Cultural Reticence about Death

Families also have complicated beliefs about death and loss. Personal history, unique ethnic experiences, and larger societal expectations influence the discussions and rituals that surround death and terminal

231

illness. Family therapists have recently directed more attention to the significance of family loss. Froma Walsh and Monica McGoldrick (1991), in their edited book about loss and families, note as remarkable that not a single previous book in the field of family therapy dealt with loss from death. Perhaps family therapy is developmentally more prepared to consider loss now that the field has been shaken by the deaths of pioneers Virginia Satir, Murray Bowen, and Harold Goolishian.

Medical family therapy requires that therapists attend to issues of loss, death, mourning, and grief. Illnesses and disabilities confront families and providers with issues of mortality. Therapists make decisions either to ignore the issues of loss or to use the opportunity to encourage families and providers to come together, face realities, and assist one another with their pain. This chapter focuses on how therapists may better realize these opportunities by discussing the meanings and impacts of loss on families and considering clinical issues useful for helping families cope with terminal illness and death. Unanticipated deaths, traumatic losses, and unresolved grief responses are events that may lead families to a family therapist. It is important that all family therapists become better prepared to assist families at these critical times, and to recognize the relationship between loss and many of the symptoms brought to physicians and to therapy (Paul, 1967). A medical family therapist also may be sought to help families who anticipate the death of a terminally ill member. We focus on anticipated loss in this chapter, discussing patients with cancer and AIDS to illustrate the medical family therapy approach to illnesses that may be terminal.

Our cultural reluctance about dealing with death is mirrored in our use of language. Phrases like *passed away, gone on,* and *no longer with us* help us avoid the uncomfortable acknowledgment of death. Psychiatrist Elisabeth Kübler-Ross (1969), through writings and workshops, has been the most visible agent for change in revising these cultural patterns of avoidance. She has encouraged health care providers and general audiences to face their discomfort, discuss death with those who are dying and surviving, and use language that reflects the reality of death. Kübler-Ross (1975, p. xvi) describes a social worker's recognition of the avoidance:

> One of the main reasons why many of us avoid any talk of death is the awful and unbearable feeling that there is nothing we can say or

do to comfort the patient. I had a similar problem in working with many aged and infirm clients in the past years. I always felt that old age and sickness was so devastating, that although I wanted to communicate hope to them, I only communicated despair. It seemed to me that the problem of illness and death was so insolvable and therefore these people could not be helped.

Those in the medical system are influenced by the larger social community as well as the professional cultural beliefs about medical treatment and cure. A physician, Laurens White (1969, p. 828), regrets that many physicians conspire to avoid discussion of death: "Another and greater failure in taking care of the dying patient is our reluctance to talk about dying. . . . Our failure to think about what death means to others or what death means to us may paralyze us in some of the things we do."

White notes that when cure is the physician's goal, death of patients becomes a painful, disappointing personal failure. Many medical providers react to death of others with at least two responses: as members of the larger social community, death represents the unwanted recognition of one's own mortality; however, death of a patient also carries a sense of professional failure, even when the death could not be prevented. Thus it is understandable, if not desirable, that medical providers often hide behind life-sustaining technology rather than face the emotions of impending loss. Even without benefit of the technical armaments, family therapists, too, may often have hidden from these painful reactions.

Learning to Talk about Death

Many patients and their family members, however uncomfortable, want to talk about death (Bowen, 1991; Paul 1967; White 1969). In addition to assisting the patient and family, direct discussions about death also offer much to providers (Kübler-Ross, 1969). "If there is a single dimension of illness that can teach us something valuable for our own lives, then it must be how to confront and respond to the fact that we all die, each of us" (Kleinman, 1988, p. 157). Despite this recognition of cultural and professional reticence about dealing with death, for families during terminal illness the anticipation of death is a component of the illness.

Families have varying responses to terminal illness, partly due to characteristics of the illness (see chapter 8) but also due to the unique metaphors and meanings associated with each disease. When a family member is diagnosed with an illness such as cancer or AIDS, the meaning of the illness is filtered through families' explanatory models (Kleinman, 1988). Explanatory models include beliefs about origin or blame for the illness, expected consequences and prognosis, and appropriate treatment options. Individual explanatory models are based on cultural meanings of illness as well as unique beliefs and experiences.

Illnesses also have cultural and historical metaphors associated with them that may be attributed to those diagnosed with the disease. In her brief and fascinating book *Illness as Metaphor* (1978), Susan Sontag compares the historical and literary images of tuberculosis and cancer. She argues that tuberculosis, partly because of its use by romantic novelists such as Hugo, has the image of a gentle disease, affecting the good but poor people who remain healthy-looking until they die from "consumption." Cancer, by contrast, evokes an image of an evil disease that invades the bad, rich people, making them look terrible and distorted. "In TB, you are eating yourself up, being refined, getting down to the core, the real you. In cancer, non-intelligent ('primitive,' 'embryonic,' 'atavistic') cells are multiplying, and you are being replaced by the non-you" (p. 67). These images of cancer, particularly, have become a part of our cultural consciousness, such that cancer has become a name for any undesired growth or movement, including political movements or ideas.

AIDS also has acquired very strong cultural and emotional meanings. Like cancer, the opportunistic infections that arise within the impaired immune systems of persons with AIDS are described as attacking, goal-oriented, invading diseases. Unlike most forms of cancer and almost any other disease, AIDS has associated images of personal culpability, if not punishment. The power of these covert meanings becomes apparent in the family and societal responses to persons diagnosed with these illnesses. In order to provide more than superficial support, medical family therapists must consider the cultural meanings of illnesses, unique family explanatory models, and hesitancies about dealing with death when working with families with terminal illness.

Cancer and AIDS: Caring during Terminal Illness

Cancer and AIDS are examples of chronic illnesses that often become terminal illnesses and lead to death. Although the survival rates for patients with cancer are improving, hundreds of thousands of Americans continue to die yearly from one of the many forms of cancer. In the United States, cancer deaths have increased since 1980, when 416,000 people died from cancer, accounting for 20.9 percent of all deaths (U.S. Bureau of the Census, 1990). In 1988, more than 488,000 people died from cancer, accounting for 22 percent of all deaths that year. With only one exception, cancer is either the leading or second highest cause of death for all age groups in the United States. The exception is young males, aged fifteen to thirty-four, for whom the number of cancer deaths ranks behind deaths due to accidents, suicide, homicide, and AIDS (*CA: A Cancer Journal for Clinicians*, 1991).

Cancer is a general category for various kinds of cell growths affecting many organ systems. The most common sites for cancer are the lungs, colon or rectum, and breast or prostate (American Cancer Society, 1987). Cancer disease is described by five general stages, ranging from stage 0, a precancerous condition evidenced by abnormal cells that have not multiplied, to stage 5, in which cancer in one organ has invaded distant parts of the body. The primary forms of cancer treatment include combinations of surgery, radiation, and chemotherapy, with treatment dependent on stage, site, and type of cancer. Each form of treatment has negative reactions, including disfigurement, nausea, vomiting and diarrhea in response to chemotherapy, pain, or destruction of white blood cells. Treatments may either eradicate the cancer, slow its growth, or be ineffective. Thus patients with cancer and their families may experience years of living with the often emotionally exhausting course of treatment, remission, recurrences, and sometimes death. Therapists and families need to become informed about the prognosis and treatment options for each unique experience.*

AIDS affects fewer people than does cancer but is rapidly increasing and is almost always terminal over a number of years. Epidemiologists at the Centers for Disease Control in Atlanta have carefully moni-

---

*Much is written for families about cancer. A general chapter useful for therapists is "Caregiving in Cancer" in Biegel, Sales, and Schulz (1991).

tored transmission and disease progression of AIDS, providing more accurate statistics for AIDS than for almost any other disease. By the end of 1991, 195,718 people had been diagnosed with AIDS, and more than 60 percent of those had died from the disease* (Centers for Disease Control, 1991b).

Until 1991, diagnosis of AIDS required the presence of HIV infection and one of the serious opportunistic infections like pneumocystis carini pneumonia or Kaposi's sarcoma. The nationally mandated reporting of cases of AIDS identified only those in the late-stage of HIV infection. As of April 1992, the Centers for Disease Control started using a new AIDS case definition to better identify those exhibiting the severe end of HIV infection. New case definition is based on a measure of immune functioning, the T-cell lymphocyte count, with AIDS defined when the CD4 (helper T-cell) count is below 200 per cubic millimeter of blood; normal T-cell count is around 1,000. The Centers for Disease Control estimate that the new definition will increase the number of people defined as having AIDS by as much as 40 percent. Increasing the number of persons defined as having AIDS who have not developed opportunistic infections also decreases the fatality rate. Thus therapists will be meeting more persons who appear to live longer after their diagnosis with AIDS.

In the mid-1980s, people with AIDS were expected to die within two or three years after diagnosis. In G. Solomon, L. Temoshok, and J. Zich's (1987) research on physical and psychological variables related to long-term survival, long-term survivors of AIDS were defined as living at least three years after their diagnosis. Based on existing research at that time, it was expected that five-year survival was only 15 percent. The drug zidovudine (AZT), which appears to increase life expectancy for people with AIDS, became generally available in the fall of 1986. With AZT, other experimental drugs, earlier identification of HIV infection, and dietary and behavior changes to reduce stress and illness susceptibility, increasing numbers of people are living longer with a diagnosis of AIDS.

Cancer and AIDS, then, have similar psychosocial properties. They usually have acute onset, although symptoms may precede a confirming diagnosis. The course of these illnesses is generally progressive but may

*Case fatality rates for AIDS are 64.5 percent for adults, and 53.5 percent for children.

be considered relapsing, with intermittent periods of illness and well-ness. For a period of time, both diseases may be considered chronic diseases. In cancer, persons may feel well although the illness spreads, or feel exhausted and ill from radiation or chemotherapy treatments that may halt the spread of the disease. With AIDS, persons may feel well until they experience acute opportunistic infections that increasingly damage the immune system and eventually cause death.

THE SPECIAL STIGMA OF AIDS

Although cancer and AIDS have many similar properties, family therapy treatment must identify the different contexts of these illnesses, including the family's social and demographic characteristics and their attitudes about the illness. Cancer affects families of all racial, ethnic, and socioeconomic groups; AIDS disproportionately affects families that are African-American, hispanic, and poor. Although transmission of HIV by heterosexual contact continues to increase, persons with AIDS often are presumed to be homosexual or IV drug users. When people who are homosexual or IV drug users are diagnosed with AIDS, their families often learn both of the AIDS and of the behavior that had been kept hidden at the same time. These families can adopt cultural perceptions that make them less accepting of their family member with AIDS, and, in fact, both inside and outside the family, people with AIDS can be subtly or overtly blamed for their illness. Often these perceptions about people with AIDS affect a family's initial response to learning about the diagnosis, as in the following illustration:

Michael, a twenty-two-year-old college student, was hospitalized for an illness that later was diagnosed as pneumocystis pneumonia. He was involved in a long-term gay relationship with another college student but kept his sexual orientation secret from his middle-class Jamaican-born parents and siblings. He never suspected that he had the HIV virus, but hospital laboratory tests confirmed that he had AIDS. While in the hospital, Michael met with a medical family therapist recommended by his physician. Three days after the tests, when Michael accepted his diagnosis, the physician suggested that he tell his concerned family. Michael was reluctant to tell them and asked his physician and therapist to tell his family.

Respecting Michael's wishes, Michael, his parents, physician, and family therapist met in the hospital. Michael was silent as the physician explained the pneumonia to the parents. Although well-educated, the parents did not respond when they were told that their son had pneumocystic pneumonia or HIV infection. They did respond to the word *AIDS* and anxiously asked Michael how he had acquired the virus. When he answered, "Sexual contact," his mother became very upset and said that she could not accept homosexuality. The therapist and physician interrupted and helped the family work through the anger so they could plan to provide immediate post-hospital care for their son.

Like most families who have a member with AIDS, Michael's family eventually became less angry. Their initial reaction is not unlike that of many families. The physician and therapist expected that the parents would be upset but not that they would focus exclusively on Michael's homosexuality. They may have found it easier to concentrate on their son's behavior rather than on his terminal illness, yet their negative focus could have created damaging barriers in the family. The therapist and physician played a crucial role in helping the parents acknowledge their disappointment and anger and also elicit support for their son. In this situation, the family was able to provide care for Michael until he became well enough to return to his out-of-state college.

Some of what the family experiences when a member has AIDS or cancer differs according to the culture's acceptance of the disease. Therapists Gillian Walker (1991) and Judith Landau-Stanton and colleagues (1992) have written extensively about these differences, particularly about AIDS and families. Even when families readily accept their family member with AIDS, they worry about how others will respond. They often keep the diagnosis secret and tell others that the person is ill with cancer, suggesting that cancer has now lost its former stigma. The ubiquitous question asked about a person with AIDS is how the disease was contracted. The question most frequently asked about a person with newly diagnosed cancer is whether the person smoked. These questions represent a search for blame or understanding or perhaps a way for others to feel safe from the disease.

Secrecy is often part of the illness context for families of homosexuals and drug users. Families make decisions about who is close enough to be a confidant about the illness. At work, lovers may pretend that "a good friend is sick" and forfeit receiving support from colleagues when a partner is dying. Heterosexual parents sometimes struggle with how to include their son's lover in family rituals during their son's illness and death. Hospitals have revised policies, for example, for visits to patients in intensive care and now recognize various family and friendship networks. Many families need support for negotiating these new relationships among themselves and with others, and the role for informed family therapists throughout this process can be crucial.

UNTIMELY DEATH

The acceptable time in the life cycle for death is old age, but cancer and AIDS can occur in young, previously healthy people, unexpectedly affecting their families during active periods of life. Since death is not supposed to occur during early life stages, untimely deaths often have far-reaching consequences. Monica McGoldrick and Froma Walsh (1991) describe family responses to death for various family developmental stages. Death of a parent, for example, complicates the young adult's move toward independence, as described by the following young man (Freedman, 1984, p. 48):

> And so to become a man I had to hurt and reject the woman who brought me into the world. I realize that most acutely because my mother died when I was 19 years old, on the cusp of manhood, in the midst of leaving home. Her illness tied me to home, yet I lived a thousand miles away. Duty and love called me home, yet I chose independence and distance.
>
> Had my mother lived longer, there would have been time for discussion, explanation, reconciliation. . . . as it is, we are frozen in a moment without resolution and I am stuck with choices that I see now as both necessary and shameful. . . . The 28-year-old I am would celebrate this amazing woman, his mother, show her off to friends; the 19-year-old I was tried to hide her as a vestige of childhood and

239

dependence. And because she died soon after, there was never a time to change, or at least to apologize.

When parents outlive their children, extended periods of mourning for the family may occur as well as distancing in the marital relationship. The death of children, even adult children, represents a loss of hopes and dreams. Relationships with surviving children may become strained and pressured, and the dead person can become idealized. Therapists can help families discuss their intense feelings about these losses, assisting them to consider one another as resources rather than as persons on whom to project their anger.

Strategies for Helping Families with Terminal Illness

Just as there is no one correct way to grieve and cope with loss, so there is no single correct clinical strategy to use with families experiencing terminal illnesses. The medical family therapist can help families identify their concerns, share honest discussion, make decisions, and support each another. Clinical issues to be considered include facing the inevitability of death, providing care for the dying family member, dealing with unfinished emotional concerns, facilitating agency around medical management, utilizing rituals, and saying good-bye.

FACING THE INEVITABILITY OF DEATH

Throughout a terminal illness, family members often covertly agree to avoid discussing death. This can be helpful for maintaining hope and optimism but prevents planning and open communication. Acknowledging the closeness of death frees family members to honestly share their feelings, fears, and plans with one another. When a family member is being treated for cancer, acknowledging that death is near helps patient, family, and physicians stop intrusive and sometimes painful treatments like chemotherapy. In cancer treatment, it can be tempting to hope that additional treatments will slow disease progression. Determining when to stop treatment is a family decision taken in consultation with the medical team and can allow family members to directly help their dying family member be more comfortable. Acknowledgment of the inevitability of death also allows families to share their concerns and plans, as in the following case:

Ella Vasquez, a twenty-two-year-old married woman with two young children, knew that she had AIDS, but she took her medication (AZT) and believed that she would not die from this disease. Her family also remained positive and lived an active life together. Periodically throughout the illness, Ella and other family members met with a family therapist and described how they remained positive in the face of the illness.

When Ella was hospitalized during the terminal stage of her illness, she told the therapist that she now knew that she was going to die and was willing to talk about it with her husband, siblings, and parents. Agreeing to Ella's request, the therapist told the husband and mother that Ella wanted to talk about her death, and the family met without the therapist. The conversations allowed the family to discuss how the children would be cared for and what hopes Ella had for them.

The family did not have to change their general way of interacting. They did not fixate on death and often were quite irreverent with one another, teasing one another with affection. However, Ella and her family separately confided to the physicians that their discussions had made them all feel better about the future. Ella had spoken about her hopes for the children and felt assured that they would be cared for. The family felt that they knew more about what Ella wanted and were comforted that they could carry out her wishes.

PROVIDING CARE FOR THE DYING FAMILY MEMBER

It is important that the patient, family members, and medical team discuss what kinds of care are needed, who provides each form of care, and how decisions about care are made. When possible, families should arrange caregiving responsibilities so that all family members and friends who wish to be involved in direct care have that opportunity. This requires a commitment to negotiate and communicate about caregiving concerns and responsibilities. Past history within families can make this negotiation difficult, as the following case demonstrates:

> Mrs. Larkman, an eighty-four-year-old widow, was diagnosed with pancreatic cancer. In the previous year, she had begun to experience symptoms of forgetfulness and confusion but had maintained her goal of independent living. Five children and many grandchildren lived within a one-hour drive and visited frequently. As Mrs. Larkman aged, the oldest daughter, Emily, took primary responsibility for her mother's shopping, light cleaning, and daily help. Eventually, however, Emily complained to the physician about the difficulties of managing both her mother's life and her own life. When asked if care could be shared, Emily told the physician that her siblings were not responsible enough to provide care consistently. It took the physician a few visits to convince Emily to meet with her siblings, the physician, and the medical family therapist.
>
> Three visits were held with the five adult siblings. Mrs. Larkman attended the first session but was quite disoriented and did not attend subsequent sessions. During the brief therapy, all siblings expressed interest in participating in care but stated that they felt that Emily did things on her own without including them. Instead of blaming Emily for acting like a martyr and not including her siblings in care, the therapist and physician focused on how effective Emily had been and helped the others to express their respect for her leadership. By feeling support for her efforts, Emily was able to allow others to take more active roles in the care of their mother. The siblings easily organized schedules for assistance and chores and arranged ways to communicate with one another.
>
> One and a half years later, Mrs. Larkman entered the hospital and died from her illness. While visiting their mother in the hospital, the siblings again met with the therapist and physician and stated how pleased they had been to provide care for their mother during her terminal illness. Certainly they mourned her death, but their joint care had enabled each of them to say good-bye throughout the year. They were also able to turn to each other for support during their loss.

This case demonstrates two points useful for involving family members in discussions about care and decisions: the family is viewed from a nonpathological perspective, and the focus is on meeting the family's immediate needs. If the therapy of the Larkman siblings had addressed how they had abdicated responsibility to one sister or how the sister controlled access to care, the family would have resisted change. By focusing on the immediate goal of involving all in care and by minimizing history, the siblings were able to meet their mother's needs quickly. Moreover, the joint care of the mother throughout the year changed the family dynamics as the siblings became more involved in care and felt equal to each other. The care of their mother during her terminal illness allowed them to work through some previously unresolved issues, defused any unresolved grief reactions after her death, and positively affected the future relationships of these family members.

Family conflicts are often exacerbated by the intense stress of terminal illness and are not always alleviated as neatly as in this case. When families can be brought together, it is sometimes possible to help them use the immediacy of the crisis to work cooperatively and thus eventually modify family patterns.

This case illustrates the importance of providing support for the primary caregivers of patients with terminal illnesses (see also McDaniel, Campbell, and Seaburn, 1990). In medical family therapy with dying patients, the therapist must consider how the family can care for the dying member and still care for the caregivers. Terminal phases are shorter than chronic phases of illness but still are extraordinarily exhausting and draining for caregivers, who lose sleep, income, and often physical health. They also tend to lose some supports. In M. Vachon and colleagues' (1977) study, widows described a "social death" as friends drifted away throughout the lengthy terminal phase of their husbands' cancer. Throughout and following the terminal phase, medical family therapists can help caregivers describe their losses, anger, disappointment and help identify possible sources of support. This process can continue after the death, even on an occasional basis.

DEALING WITH UNFINISHED EMOTIONAL CONCERNS

Acknowledging the inevitability of death allows families to "balance their emotional ledgers" (Boszormenyi-Nagy and Spark, 1973).

Even dying patients who have experienced extended estrangements from family may feel an urgency to reconnect (Landau-Stanton et al., 1992; Walker, 1991). This reconnection does not require that family members share all their past resentments with each another, but it does permit members to consider what is important to say and what is important to let go:

> When Ella Vasquez knew that she would die from AIDS, she talked with the therapist about some of the conflicts she had experienced with her mother. Discussing what she wanted to leave with her mother allowed Ella to tell her mother that it had not always been perfect but that she knew she had always been loved. She decided that although her mother's perceived favoritism toward a sister still angered her, she did not need to tell her mother how hurt she had been by the slights. Ella was pleased that she expressed her concerns to her mother in ways that helped them feel more for-giveness and closeness.

Family members manage losses according to family experiences and myths. Family therapist John Byng-Hall (1991) reports that during bereavement families tend to engage in replicative scripts that repeat past family patterns and may inadvertently lose the opportunity to be truly intimate with one another. Byng-Hall suggests that the intensity of emotions generated during grieving can be used to help family members alter their structure. They may elect corrective scripts that change previous painful patterns and identify treasured memories that allow them to change the family legacy about loss (Bowen, 1991). The dying person has the singular opportunity to pass on hopes for the future and ways in which he or she would like to be remembered.

FACILITATING AGENCY FOR PATIENTS AND FAMILIES

Medical family therapists can assist patients and families to make choices about medical care and communicate their needs to medical providers. Many families have little experience negotiating care with medical providers and may not have thought about how they would like to share care. When families raise questions or dissatisfactions about care, the therapist can help them to identify their preferences and approach their provider.

Physicians may believe that discussions about care decisions are important but may not initiate such discussions. In a study of 157 doctors involved with patients who had undergone cardiopulmonary resuscitation (Bedell and Delbanco, 1984), 151 believed that patients and families should participate in important medical decisions, such as resuscitation. However, only 10 percent of these physicians had actually discussed CPR with the patient before the event, and only 21 percent had discussed it with the family. Conjoint meetings among family, physician, and therapist to discuss these important concerns should be encouraged.

Although often awkward and painful, open discussions about living wills and specific limits about technological care are useful for families. The federal government and many states have enacted living will legislation (described in chapter 11) that permits patients to state the kind of medical technology that they desire during a terminal illness and the person who is authorized to make necessary medical decisions. Families facing the death of a member have the opportunity to make their desires explicit and therefore elect satisfactory care during this stressful period. With advance discussion, families may avoid the pain experienced by the following family (Hepworth and Harris, 1986, p. 14):

> Ms. Bellum's 24-year-old brother was on life support equipment after his liver cancer had quickly metastasized to his brain, causing large masses and a stroke. His EEG indicated no brain activity and the family and physicians had agreed to remove the life-sustaining system. However, Ms. Bellum felt that hospital personnel had forced her to be more involved with his death than she had desired. In an interview following her brother's death, Ms. Bellum stated:
>
> "(The nurse) kept saying 'well, look at him. It is part of accepting it.' And I will never forget these things. . . . It was like follow the dots to me. This is where you go to do this, and here we go to do this, and there was no human touch to it. I'm sure she (the nurse) is used to doing this—helping families through this, whatever, the dying process—But to me it was like 'well here is our new family and we are going to help you deal with this, and then let's hurry on because we have another family.' "
>
> In this situation, the hospital had implemented a protocol to help

families. Yet Ms. Bellum remembered the situation as one which removed her choice:

"And I think in order to handle death you have to feel that you are part of it. . . . I don't think you should be forced to see someone like that if you want to remember him (differently). . . . I think I was being told what to think and to feel and that you'll accept it better if you see him this way. And I don't think you will. I mean I think you sort of know what you can handle."

Medical family therapists can help families decide what they can handle. In addition to decisions about medical treatment, families often make decisions about how best to provide care. Some families choose to provide full care for a dying family member at home. Others select a form of hospice situation, within or separate from a hospital, in which skilled nursing care is available. Frequently, families choose an intermediate option with skilled nursing care of some kind available in the home. Each of these options results in different kinds of stresses for families— the inability to obtain relief from continuous care, guilt from not always being with the patient, or the stress of travel to visit the ill relative.

Learning how to be involved in medical management and identifying how much one wants to be involved can be a difficult process. It requires family members to consider honestly their values, beliefs, and priorities. Families may choose to be minimally involved with decision making, for example, and to provide emotional support for one another. Medical family therapists can be instrumental in facilitating these significant decisions and providing support after decisions are made. If a family comes to a decision through negotiation and honest sharing of feelings, their sense of agency is increased. Even with great loss, it is possible for families to recognize new strengths and abilities.

UTILIZING RITUALS

One way to enhance agency during terminal illness and bereavement is to help families incorporate their own rituals into their lives. Some families may be unaware that they have special beliefs or practices, and the process of selecting desired rituals helps them consider what could be comforting. Organized religions provide structured practices for mourning and burying the dead. Families are frequently comforted by religious affiliations, but families who have not been actively involved with a formal religion may be reluctant to utilize its formal rituals:

> After an untimely death of an adult daughter in one family, the parents chose to have her funeral in a church ceremony. An elderly relative was initially critical of the parents' decision, since the family had not attended the church for many years. The pastor was very responsive to the parents, however, and agreed that a church service was part of the extended family experience and an appropriate way to respond to their sorrow. The parents received much comfort from the service, which represented their belief that they were connecting their daughter to the family members who had lived before. The elderly relative was surprised by his own appreciation of the church rituals and was grateful that the parents had chosen the church practice.

Rituals should be chosen to simultaneously honor the past, alter the present, and enable the future (Imber-Black, 1991, p. 215). They must be selected carefully to represent what is meaningful for each family. Many families may not want to return to abandoned religious traditions, and some churches might not be accommodating to lapsed members. Families need to carefully consider what would work well for them.

Therapists can ask families to consider how they will change a holiday celebration, for example, to acknowledge a terminal illness as well as the holiday. In one family, a son with a long-term debilitating illness died four months prior to his brother's wedding. Since some wedding guests had not traveled for the funeral, the family wanted to acknowledge their loss at the wedding. At the wedding dinner, the groom gave a special toast to his deceased brother, and another sibling responded by saying that she knew that their brother would have been pleased at the groom's good fortune.*

When therapists help families choose their rituals, the family should guide the creative process. Bagarozzi and Anderson (1989) rec-

---

*This case also provides an example of the frequently observed pattern of family loss occurring prior to the formation of intimate relationships (see Hepworth, Ryder, and Dreyer, 1984).

ommend leaving some details of the proposed rituals undecided. In the this family, the therapist and engaged couple discussed making a toast at the wedding. It was not decided that the sibling would respond. In other families, members may meet to agree about where to scatter ashes, for example, but not to stipulate the details of each member's eulogy at the ceremony. By remaining fully responsible for making their practices their own, families devise rich and meaningful acknowledgments.

SAYING GOOD-BYE

Much of this chapter underscores the importance of creating ways for family members to say good-bye to each other. By caring for the ill person and each other, removing disrupting emotional barriers, and creating meaningful rituals, families have the opportunity to say good-bye.

Family members also have the opportunity to release some of their feelings about how well they or others have cared. It is an unfortunately common experience for surviving family members to use perceived inequities in bequests or caregiving as excuses for turning against each other. The conflicts often are repeated family patterns but also may reflect projected anger about having to say good-bye. For some families, it is easier to show rage than to show sadness.

Even by meeting only a few times with families anticipating or experiencing bereavement, medical family therapists can help limit later family discord. Therapists can facilitate discussion of mourning, describe the kinds of unacceptable feelings that may exist, and discuss the consequences of not acknowledging sadness. Families can help each other feel good about the roles they accepted and the ways they supported one another during the illness. For illnesses like cancer and AIDS, families may work together to limit the stress of the illness but may feel discouraged when they cannot "beat the illness" and the family member dies. Family therapists and physicians can remind families about the biological realities of the illnesses and help them limit blame toward each other.

Around the time of death, medical family therapists should be flexible about ways in which they can be available to families. Therapists may be most helpful if they are willing to meet families in different settings, such as home or hospital, are available for telephone support, and allow the family to decide about future meetings. Families should have the opportunity to meet with the therapist and physician after the death.

Medical family therapists can support grieving medical team members. Although the medical family therapist is part of the treatment team, the therapist can be the catalyst for encouraging team members to discuss their responses to a particular family and loss. Our physician colleagues have stated that medical family therapists have been very helpful to them at these times.

Sharing the Family's Loss

Just as families find it difficult to say good-bye, therapists may have difficulty saying good-bye to a dying client and then to the family. Therapists working with terminally ill patients and families should have professional peer support to discuss their feelings of sadness, loss, and helplessness. Therapists can also discuss these feelings briefly with the families. Therapists and physicians may choose, in consultation with the family, to attend funerals or memorial services, which may be healing for both families and providers.

Working with families experiencing loss changes the therapeutic relationship. Therapists and families share some of the intense emotions surrounding loss, and usually develop deep respect for one another. As families can use the experience of loss to grow closer, more honest, and more appreciative of life, so can therapists respond to these extraordinary challenges.

CHAPTER 11

Practice Issues in Medical Family Therapy

"**I**F YOU BUILD IT, they will come." This message from the 1989 film *Field of Dreams* can be applied to medical family therapy: if we are available for families facing medical problems, we will be sought out. Therapists who work with medical problems readily build referral networks from physicians and families referred by former patients. Building a practice of medical family therapy, however, requires more than just being available.

In chapter 3, we identified some of the collaborative skills of joining, networking, consultation, and larger systems assessment and intervention required for effective medical family therapy. We suggested that family therapists could facilitate collaborative work by initiating meetings with physician colleagues. Yet it is not enough to invite a physician to lunch and essentially "sell our wares." We must recognize the economic context for health care providers, be responsible about how we work together, and monitor our personal reactions to medical issues. In this final chapter, we address three significant areas for practicing medical family therapists, which we label health care economics, ethics, and personal development issues.

250

The Economics of the Health Care System

American students of family therapy generally receive no systematic education about the history of the health care system in the United States. In many family therapy education courses, history starts in the mid-1950s, and family therapy and mental health care are removed from the context of general health care trends in the country. In this section, we outline some of the main trends in the health care system in the United States. For a more detailed discussion of this important area, see Paul Starr's *The Social Transformation of American Medicine*, (1982), William C. Cockerham's *Medical Sociology* (1986), and David Mechanic's *Handbook of Health, Health Care, and the Health Professions* (1983).

A HISTORICAL OVERVIEW

In the eighteenth and nineteenth centuries, American health care was delivered by family members, general practice physicians, general surgeons, nurses, and eventually a few specialists. The training model in American medicine developed in a disorganized fashion and centered around proprietary medical schools and loose apprenticeships. Until the late nineteenth century, American medicine lacked much of a scientific basis for diagnosis and treatment, and medicine struggled for professional prestige (Cockerham, 1986).

In the first two decades of the twentieth century, American medicine consolidated its training programs in a university-based, science-oriented curriculum and established itself with state governments and with the public as the quintessential profession in the country. All other treatment professions have oriented their identity formation and their claims to uniqueness around the power and presence of the medical profession (Cockerham, 1986; Starr, 1982).

In this century, the clinical treatment model that emerged was based on a biomedical paradigm and a fee-for-service private sector providing health care delivery. Physicians and nonprofit hospitals controlled most health care decisions. In 1941, a major shift began when government-mandated wage controls during the war years led enterprising companies to seek and receive permission to increase their

251

employees' compensation by granting health care benefits. From this unplanned start, employer-sponsored health insurance programs proliferated—a fateful course in light of successful contemporary efforts of European countries to establish publicly sponsored health benefits.

Specialization and Private Insurance

From the late 1940s until the mid-1960s, American health care was characterized by a rapid increase in specialization and was dominated by powerful insurance carriers such as Blue Cross/Blue Shield, which was created in 1929 as a private insurer contracting with individuals. These insurance carriers, which themselves were dominated by physicians, set fees according to "usual and customary" standards and dictated the kinds of policies purchased by companies (Starr, 1982). During this period, there was a movement away from primary care and general practice and an increase in the use of technology in medicine.

Psychiatry was the only major player in mental health care during the first five decades of this century and controlled the activities of social workers, nurses, and the handful of psychologists working in medical settings. Psychiatry was dominated by biological models until the post–World War II period, when psychoanalytic therapy became popular. After later flirtations with social psychiatry and community-based (rather than institutional) treatment, psychiatry again returned to an emphasis on biology in the 1970s and 1980s (Grob, 1991). During the period when psychiatry emphasized psychological and community-based therapies, however, psychiatry's boundaries with other mental health professions began to blur. Clinical psychologists first achieved new status as independent mental health professionals in the 1950s, and their advances were followed by growing efforts by social workers, psychiatric nurses, and marriage and family therapists. The blurred boundaries among mental health professionals continue to create conflict, particularly between psychiatry and the newer mental health professions (Grob, 1991).

Government Programs, HMOs, and PPOs

Government became closely involved with health care in the 1960s with the creation of the Medicare and Medicaid programs. Medicare was developed for the elderly and is paid for by the federal government and contributions from the elderly. Medicaid is a program for people with low incomes and is supported by states and the federal government. These programs began a period of increased government activity in health care and were the forerunners of a movement toward a national comprehensive program for health care for Americans (Rosenthal, 1983).

The major development in the 1970s was the expansion, and federal encouragement of, health maintenance organizations (HMOs), which marked a striking departure from the conventional U.S. health care system's emphasis on third-party insurance and fee-for-service providers (Luft, 1983). HMOs, which have expanded rapidly since the 1960s, involve an enrolled, defined population for which the HMO assumes contractual responsibility to provide health care for prearranged costs. The HMO assumes part of the risk if costs exceed predictions and part of the gain if costs are less. Since HMO providers are not paid according to the level of services generated, they have few incentives to provide questionably necessary services and more incentives to keep the population healthy. HMOs have been supported by government regulators as a means to reduce health care costs, but the HMO and other prepaid plans also may have an incentive to restrict needed services and to enroll only a healthy population (Luft, 1983).

The 1970s and 1980s also witnessed a proliferation of kinds of health insurance and health care delivery systems. Preferred provider organizations (PPOs) were generated by hospitals and private practice physician groups to try to compete with HMOs. PPOs are groups of providers who promise to charge reduced fees in order to be members of a network to which subscribers must turn for their health care. Employers, buffeted by extraordinary increases in health insurance costs during this period, began turning to self-insurance that used employee assistance programs and managed care groups to channel employees to the most cost-efficient sources of health care.

The 1970s and 1980s were a trial period for many experiments in health care plans. As the corporate for-profit sector invested in health care in a major way, they swept aside a number of public and nonprofit hospitals and established HMOs (Starr, 1982). Mergers and bankruptcies were rampant and continued into the 1990s. Meanwhile, health care costs escalated from 8 percent of gross national product in 1975 to 12 percent in 1990 to an estimated 15 percent in the year 2000 (Aaron and

Schwartz, 1990). Many citizens speculate about whether rationing may be necessary in U.S. health care.

MENTAL HEALTH COSTS

Because mental health costs have increased faster than overall health care costs since the early 1980s, they have attracted the attention of health care cost-containers. The biggest increases have been with inpatient hospitalizations, particularly for adolescents. Third-party payers and HMOs are increasingly limiting hospitalizations, length of stays, and number of outpatient visits. Prior authorizations and limited numbers of sessions have become routine for mental health professionals. Mental health professionals have joined physicians in feeling increasingly frustrated by the limitations placed on their professional autonomy and judgment by third parties.

In addition to rapidly increasing costs, the country also has high numbers of citizens without health care insurance at all—generally part-time workers, workers between jobs, and the working poor who do not qualify for Medicaid. In the early 1990s, approximately 31 to 37 million Americans lack access to health care because they are uninsured (Aukerman, 1991)—the casualties of a nonplanned policy of basing U.S. health care insurance on a voluntary employment-based model. These high numbers of uninsured and the increasing costs of health care paid by companies, the government, and individuals have fueled a national impetus toward some kind of universal health care plan.

This analysis provides the context for medical family therapy practice and reimbursement. Many family therapists in private practice include medical family therapy as one of the services they provide. Some in private practice join PPOs and managed care services, from which they receive referrals. Payment is based on the therapist's usual payment arrangements, which differ according to state regulations and professional licensure. Some private practice therapists may find it easier to receive prior authorization for service from insurance companies when diagnosis includes therapy that augments treatment for a medical condition with physician referral.

Other medical family therapists work within a structured health care delivery system, including HMOs, private physician offices, or hospital units. In hospital settings, medical family therapists can be specialists assigned to particular units, like dialysis or cardiac care services. Medical family therapists also provide services to many hospital units, as do consult-liaison psychiatrists, and to families with acute or chronic medical problems. Reimbursement can be similar to private practice fee-for-service arrangements or can be based on salaried positions negotiated with the hospital or medical service.

It is a complex and unstable health care system in which medical family therapists work in the 1990s. Being a competent therapist in this arena requires careful attention to developments in the larger health care system. And being a socially responsible therapist requires that we add our voices as citizens and professionals to the public debate about equitable, effective, and affordable health care in the United States.

•

Ethics in Medical Family Therapy

Some traditional ethical concerns in family therapy are particularly significant for medical family therapists—especially the relationships between the therapist and other health care providers as well as the relationships between the therapist and family members. Negotiating the potentially competing agendas of the participants in this complex treatment system requires that therapists be vigilant about their roles in representing themselves accurately, encouraging informed consent, maintaining respect for the family's autonomy, and clarifying issues of confidentiality.

ROLE CLARITY

Medical family therapists are responsible for being informed about their areas of expertise and acknowledging their limitations. As described in chapter 2, medical family therapists should learn about medical problems through readings and discussions with physicians and families. They should ask medical colleagues about medical and psychosocial complications for individual illnesses. Physicians and families may wrongly assume that the therapist already has pertinent information, and the therapist needs to identify areas of experience and limitations. Medical family therapists, for example, should not advertise themselves as health behavior experts or as stress-reduction experts if they have not trained in behavioral medicine techniques.

Although some experienced medical family therapists have joked that they could "practice medicine without a license," role distinctions are essential. Medical family therapists should resist *any* temptation to give medical advice. (Medical family therapists who also are primary care physicians usually do not provide therapy for their own medical patients to avoid blurring these roles.) Families who ask their therapists to validate their treatment or medication regimens should be referred back to their medical provider. During case discussions with medical colleagues, therapists should question new terms and procedures. Far from indicating ignorance, such questions can clarify roles, show respect for the medical provider, as well as demonstrate confidence in the therapist's own skills.

INFORMED CONSENT

Medical family therapists are responsible for helping families and the referring medical providers negotiate the contract for therapy. Informed consent has two principal components—information and consent (Lipp, 1986). Confused and overwhelmed families may accept a physician's referral to a therapist, without understanding the purpose of treatment. Therapists and physicians should provide the information that patients need to make intelligent decisions. If a physician believes that a child's recurrent asthma attacks are related to stressful parental interactions and has not communicated this belief to the family, the therapist may be tempted to engage the family by giving a vague purpose for the therapy, such as "helping the parents treat their child's asthma." Ideally, physicians and therapists should together consider suggestions for framing treatment, appealing to the family's concerns, explaining how underlying physical disease can be exacerbated when family stress increases and how the illness might also increase family stress. If the initial contract is not accurately clarified by the physician, the therapist needs to negotiate an informed contract with family members. The therapeutic contract raises no false hopes that the therapist will cure the asthma and allows the family to enter treatment with a realistic expectation of treatment goals.

RESPECT FOR AUTONOMY

Often called the patient's right to self-determination, respect for patient autonomy is a legal right derived from U.S. constitutional provisions. Therapists and physicians are expected to help families make informed decisions about care without imposing provider values. Patients and families have the right to participate with or refuse medical care throughout all phases of treatment, including establishing living wills and advance directives for the care of the terminally ill and permanently legally incompetent.

Effective December 1, 1991, a national law, the Patient Self-Determination Act (Public Law 101-508), requires that all persons admitted to nursing homes and hospitals receive information about advance directives—including forms of medical and comfort treatments desired and do-not-resuscitate (DNR)* orders. States have latitude about how to implement this legislation, but all patients entering hospitals are required to begin to face these issues. Family therapists can help families discuss their desires by becoming informed about their state's interpretation of the law. Many hospitals and most medical schools have medical ethicists who can provide information for therapists. A useful questionnaire resource, *The Values History* (Doukas and McCullough, 1991), provides information and suggestions for guiding decision making in this area.

It is relatively easy to help families make treatment decisions when family members agree about desired outcomes. Even when the therapist would make a different decision, family consensus usually allows the therapist to support the family in their decision. More complicated processes arise when family members disagree or when the therapist believes that the interests of the family conflict with the interest of the patient (McDaniel, Campbell, and Seaburn, 1990). In such cases, as in any family disagreement, the therapist needs to articulate the competing positions, create space for the less powerful coalition to be heard if necessary, and facilitate joint discussion and decision making. Because

*In most states, any patient who has not consented to a DNR order will receive cardiopulmonary resuscitation (CPR) if his or her heart stops. Many medical ethicists urge that the term *DNR* be replaced with *DNAR* (do not *attempt* resuscitation) to provide a more accurate description for patients and families about the low likelihood of resuscitation.

medical decisions often involve emotion-laden or "life and death" topics, the therapist needs to monitor self responses. Depending on their therapeutic point of view, therapists differ about how overtly they make suggestions or state when a patient appears to have been treated unfairly. It is particularly helpful for therapists to use peer support or consulting groups as a way of checking partiality and ensuring family autonomy (McDaniel et al., 1986).

CONFIDENTIALITY

When family therapists and medical providers work together, whether in the same office or with limited contact, they share some patient and family information. Each set of providers determines what information is useful, but all providers and family members need to know what information is shared. A number of arrangements for information exchange are possible, including therapists' notes entered in medical charts, formal written case summaries, and verbal discussion.

Satisfactory management of confidentiality requires that families know how therapists and medical providers share care. This sharing circumvents the ever-present potential for triangulation among family, physician, and therapist (Doherty and Baird, 1983). Therapists and physicians also have the responsibility to respect family requests about confidentiality, recognizing that these requests may be similar to attempts to maintain any family secret. Each therapist works with this issue according to his or her understanding of its meaning for the family. These challenging issues can stimulate personal issues for the medical family therapist to identify and address.

Personal Development Issues for Medical Family Therapists

Family therapy students generally obtain experience in family of origin and personal awareness work. It is our belief, however, that this traditional training typically is insufficient to prepare therapists to cope with the unique issues that medical family therapists face every day.

TOLERANCE FOR UNCERTAINTY AND LOSS

The most important issue facing therapists is their tolerance for dealing with uncertainty, loss, and death, which permeate the experience of families facing an illness in one of its members. Families and physicians wrestle with the uncertainty that so often is a major part of illness diagnosis and treatment. Much of medical education emphasizes what is known rather than what is unknown. Most patients and families want their medical providers to cure their ills and not apologize for what science does not yet know. The medical family therapist who remains relatively nonanxious while facing these difficult issues of uncertainty can provide useful consultation for medical colleagues and modeling for patients and families who struggle with prognosis, treatment, and questions about "why me" and "why now." (For an excellent discussion of the importance of uncertainty in medicine, see Bursztajn et al., 1981.)

In working with illness, loss, and death, a spiritual dimension to medical family therapy becomes unavoidably poignant and rewarding. Medical family therapy deals directly with death anxiety in reality, not just in the abstract. Therapists face their personal mortality as well as that of their patients. As Donald Williamson has said, "Any person who is dying is simply dying a little bit ahead of the observer" (1991, p. 234). Facing these issues allows therapists and families to reflect on the meaning of their lives—what it means to be human, to live, to love, and to die. Even illnesses that are not terminal often serve as a "call to consciousness" (Williamson, 1991, p. 229) for the patient and sometimes for the family as well. As with a midlife crisis (which also deals with issues of mortality), the medical family therapist may help the patient and family to evaluate their priorities and whether they are living their lives in the most meaningful ways.

Just as the therapist provides a safe, supportive environment for the patient and family to explore these issues, so the therapist can benefit from a safe, supportive environment in which to share and consult with colleagues about the stresses and strains, as well as the rewards, of working with families with a sick member. McDaniel and colleagues (1986) reported on a group of physicians and family therapists who provide this kind of environment for each other.

FAMILY OF ORIGIN ISSUES

Dealing with uncertainty, loss, and death in the course of medical family therapy stimulates medical family of origin issues for the therapist. Broadly speaking, these issues relate to the therapist's family experience of illnesses, loss, health behaviors, health beliefs, and interactions with physicians and other health professionals. In an obvious example, the therapist whose father or mother is a physician will have a clear connection between medical and generic family of origin issues, but every family has a health history that is loaded with feeling and meaning. Our assumption is that it is important for medical family therapists to sort out and come to peace with these issues. A useful training technique is to have trainees do a "health and illness" genogram focusing on how their families responded to medical problems and crises. The case of Dr. P illustrates some of these concepts:

Dr. P was a medical family therapist who grew up with an obstetrician father. Her father was a sensitive man who rarely expressed his feelings. He was an excellent surgeon with little psychosocial training who said he chose obstetrics so as not to have to deal with dying people on a daily basis. Dr. P dedicated her career to training physicians to be skillful in dealing with the psychosocial issues of their patients. The link between family and professional focus was not subtle, and early in her career, Dr. P made several mistakes by trying to push this psychosocial approach too hard. While presenting her "health and illness" genogram to colleagues, she recognized that she was trying to convert the medical profession as a way of trying to resolve issues with her father. Recognizing this dynamic allowed her to relate her concerns directly to her father and move more slowly in teaching physicians who were struggling with psychosocial concepts or skills. She also recognized her father's concerns about avoiding death and worked to desensitize herself to become less anxious around dying patients and issues of her own and others' mortality.

PERSONAL HEALTH ISSUES

A third area for personal development work is the therapist's personal history with illness, health behavior, and health care professionals. A therapist who is ashamed of his or her own stress-related physical problems will not work effectively with patients who have similar problems. A therapist who survives cancer will have both special empathy and possible bias when dealing with cancer patients and their families. A therapist who struggles with a sense of being overweight or who smokes cigarettes must sort through the meaning of these issues when working with health behavior problems. Similarly, as discussed later in this chapter, a therapist who has had negative personal experiences with physicians must work through these feelings in order to be able to collaborate with physicians in medical family therapy. (See also chapter 3 for a discussion of successful collaborative strategies.)

ANXIETY ABOUT ILLNESS

Medical family therapists often have anxiety about the physical aspects of illness and treatment—blood, needles, wounds, deformities, smells, body fluids, and an assortment of other assaults on one's sensitivities. This is particularly an issue for therapists who work in acute care and rehabilitation hospitals, but it must be faced by medical family therapists when families discuss how they deal with cleansing wounds, replacing ostomy bags,* and dealing with the public embarrassment of visible symptoms. Some therapists say that they avoided medical school precisely because they don't like "blood and guts." To do medical family therapy well, these therapists will have to become desensitized to the physical processes of disability, illness, and treatment. Some physicians allow therapists to accompany them on rounds or observe them during an afternoon of standard patient care. These experiences can help the desensitization process, as illustrated by Mr. D:

Mr. D found himself working in a medical context as a therapist in spite of his lifelong anxiety about medical procedures, blood,

*Ostomy bags are bags that collect feces or urine after surgical redirection of the gastrointestinal or genitourinary tracts.

and injections. His mother died of cancer when he was an adolescent, and prior to her death, he was never told of the seriousness of her illness or allowed to visit her in the hospital. Her death was a shock that eroded his trust of physicians and procedures. In the first six months of his job, he rounded at the hospital with several medical colleagues and also observed outpatient sessions on a weekly basis. These experiences allowed him to build trust in his medical colleagues as he watched them share information with patients and families. He retained his skittishness about blood, injections, and procedures but no longer turned white when they were described or discussed with colleagues or families.

POTENTIAL ISOLATION FROM COLLEAGUES

Medical family therapists also need to deal with their potential isolation from family therapy colleagues. Because of cultural and training differences between family therapists and physicians (detailed in chapter 3), therapists can feel isolated and unappreciated when among physicians. Medical family therapists, particularly those working in a medical setting, can feel both valued and extraneous to the medical system. Role clarification is essential, as are supportive colleagues who are familiar with medical settings. Medical family therapists may benefit from continued involvement with family therapy colleagues in more traditional positions. Jeri Hepworth and colleagues (1988) describe how training family therapy interns within a medical setting provides the supervisor with a generative role and a means to remain rooted in traditional family therapy.

Isolated therapists can feel overwhelmed by the technical knowledge required in medical family therapy or by the pressure to perform in difficult situations. Cole-Kelly and Hepworth (1991) identify ways in which the severity of problems and time demands in medical situations can lead therapists to neglect their self-care strategies and respond in defensive or inappropriately authoritarian ways. When unconsciously reacting to pressure to prove oneself to colleagues, therapists compromise their strengths as contributors to the medical system.

POWER AND STATUS

Medical family therapists need to monitor power and status issues in their relations with physicians. It is not uncommon to hear therapists express resentment and even hostility toward physicians as a group. Working with physicians triggers whatever personal ambivalence therapists have about their own status and power as professionals and as persons. The twin temptations are to treat physicians as authority figures instead of collaborators or as figures of contempt or avoidance. Differences in cultural prestige, associated power, and salary are difficult to acknowledge and discuss. Without open acknowledgment, however, these differences remain barriers to effective collaboration and more cooperative care for families.

A piece of the therapist's personal work may have to do with what Donald Williamson (1991, p. 238) labels "intergenerational intimidation." By this he means that professionals who have not resolved issues with parents may have difficulty claiming personal authority in interactions with colleagues perceived to be powerful. Williamson applied this problem to young primary care physicians who must interact with subspecialists, but it also applies to therapists who interact with physicians. To paraphrase Williamson, as medical family therapists resolve intergenerational intimidation within their personal families of origin, they are increasingly better prepared psychologically to handle issues of professional intimidation as well.

Negative attitudes toward physicians compromise the therapist's ability to do medical family therapy. Dealing with complex family of origin issues can help medical family therapists revise negative attitudes, and increased contact and interest in medical colleagues and their work can help them overcome feelings of intimidation. Close collaboration that allows for sharing the rewards and frustrations of caring for patients makes clear all that medical family therapists and medical colleagues have to offer one another.

The Future of Medical Family Therapy

Many exciting trails are being blazed by innovative medical family therapists throughout the United States and abroad. Their insights and breakthroughs should be included in family therapy training programs and continuing education opportunities. We envision that some day most degree programs will include medical family therapy in survey courses and offer it as an elective. Already, some programs—like the Marriage and Family Therapy Program at Nova University in Florida— make medical family therapy training a prominent part of the curriculum. More family therapy internships will specialize in medical family therapy, and more postgraduate training programs will offer advanced training in medical family therapy, such as that offered by the University of Rochester fellowship program in family systems medicine, which trains both physicians and therapists. Therapists in practice will form supervision and case consultation groups for medical family therapy issues.

The cases presented throughout this book represent families who have benefitted from physicians and family therapists working together, but working with these families has resulted in great benefits for the providers. We have learned much about the culture of medicine, our colleagues in health care, and families' experiences with illness. We also have learned more about our professional strengths, our professional weaknesses, and our ability to find comfort and satisfaction with our roles as family therapists.

Medical family therapy provides needed services to families, physicians, and other health providers. It also challenges family therapists to grow in new directions and to contribute to humane, comprehensive, and socially responsible health care services. It provides support for our colleagues in health care who share similar family-centered visions. And who knows? If we continue to build it, others in the medical system may also come along to continue the collaboration and add to the vision.

References

AARON, H., AND SCHWARTZ, W. (1990). Rationing health care: The choice before us. *Science, 247,* 418–442.

AMERICAN ACADEMY OF FAMILY PHYSICIANS. (1989). *The 1989–90 compendium of AAFP positions on selected health issues.* Kansas City, MO: AAFP.

AMERICAN CANCER SOCIETY. (1987). *Cancer facts and figures.* New York: ACS.

AMERICAN COLLEGE OF OBSTETRICIANS AND GYNECOLOGISTS. (1989) *Infertility.* ACOG Technical Bulletin 125. Washington, DC: ACOG.

ANDERSEN, T. (1984). Consultation: Would you like co-evolution instead of referral? *Family Systems Medicine, 2,* 370–379.

ANGELL, M. (1990). New ways to get pregnant. *New England Journal of Medicine, 323,* 1200–1202.

ANTONOVSKY, A. (1979). *Health, stress, and coping.* San Francisco: Jossey-Bass.

ASHTON, J. (1980). The psychosocial outcome of induced abortion. *British Journal of Obstetrics and Gynaecology, 87,* 1115–1122.

AUERSWALD, E. (1968). Interdisciplinary versus ecological approach. *Family Process, 7,* 202–215.

AUERSWALD, E. (1985). Thinking about thinking in family therapy. *Family Process, 24,* 1–2.

AUKERMAN, G. (1991). Access to health care for the uninsured: Perspective of the American Academy of Family Physicians. *Journal of the American Medical Association, 265,* 2856–2858.

BAGAROZZI, D., AND ANDERSON, S. (1989). *Personal, marital and family myths: Theoretical formulations and clinical strategies.* New York: Norton.

BAIRD, M. A., AND DOHERTY, W. J. (1990). Risks and benefits of a family systems approach to health care. *Family Medicine, 18,* 5–17.

BAKER, L. (1987). Families and illness. In M. Crouch and L. Roberts (eds.), *The family in medical practice.* New York: Springer-Verlag.

BARSKY, A. (1970). Patients who amplify bodily sensations. *Annals of Internal Medicine, 91,* 63–70.

BEDELL, S., AND DELBANCO, T. (1984). Choices about cardiopulmonary resuscitation in the hospital: When do physicians talk with patients? *New England Journal of Medicine, 310,* 1089–1093.

BENTS, H. (1985). Psychology of male infertility: A literature survey. *International Journal of Andrology, 8,* 325–336.

BERGER, D. (1980). Couples' reactions to male infertility and donor insemination. *American Journal of Psychiatry, 137,* 1047–1049.

BEWLEY, B. R., AND BLAND, J. M. (1977). Academic performance and social factors related to cigarette smoking by school children. *British Journal of Preventive and Social Medicine, 31,* 18–24.

BHATT, A., TOMENSON, B., AND BENJAMIN, S. (1989). Transcultural patterns of somatization in primary care: A preliminary report. *Journal of Psychosomatic Research, 33,* 671–680.

BIEGEL, D., SALES, E., AND SCHULZ, R. (1991). *Family caregiving in chronic illness.* Newbury Park, CA: Sage.

BLECHMAN, E., AND BROWNELL, K. D. (EDS.) (1988). *Handbook of behavioral medicine for women.* New York: Pergamon Press.

BLOCH, D. (1983). Family systems medicine: The field and the journal. *Family Systems Medicine, 1,* 3–11.

BORG, S., AND LASKER, J. (1981). *When pregnancy fails: Families coping with miscarriage, stillbirth, and infant death.* Boston: Beacon Press.

BOSS, P., CARRON, W., AND HORBAL, J. (1988). Alzheimer's disease and ambiguous loss. In C. Chilman, E. Nunnally, and F. Cox (eds.), *Chronic illness and disability.* Newbury Park, CA: Sage.

BOSZORMENYI-NAGY, I., AND SPARK, G. (1973). *Invisible loyalties: Reciprocity in intergenerational family therapy.* New York: Harper & Row.

BOWEN, M. (1976). Theory in the practice of psychotherapy. In P. J. Guerin (ed.), *Family therapy: Theory and practice.* New York: Gardner Press.

BOWEN, M. (1991). Family reactions to death. In F. Walsh and M. McGoldrick (eds.), *Living beyond loss: Death in the family*. New York: Norton Press.

BROWNELL, K. D., KELMAN, J. H., AND STUNKARD, A. J. (1983). Treatment of obese children with and without their mothers: Changes in weight and blood pressure. *Pediatrics, 71,* 515–523.

BRUCH, H., AND TOURAINE, A. B. (1940). Obesity in childhood: V. The family frame of obese children. *Psychosomatic Medicine, 2,* 141–146.

BURNS, L. (1987). Infertility as boundary ambiguity. *Family Process, 6,* 359–372.

BURNS, L. (1990). An exploratory study of perceptions of parenting after infertility. *Family Systems Medicine, 8,* 177–189.

BURSZTAJN, H., FEINBLOOM, R., HAMM, R., AND BRODSKY, A. (1981). *Medical choices, medical chances: How patients, families, and physicians can cope with uncertainty*. New York: Dell.

BYNG-HALL, J. (1991). Family scripts and loss. In F. Walsh and M. McGoldrick (eds.), *Living beyond loss: Death in the family*. New York: Norton.

CA: A cancer journal for clinicians (1991). *41,* 24–25.

CAIN, A., AND CAIN, B. (1964). On replacing a child. *Journal of the American Academy of Child Psychiatry, 3,* 443–455.

CALLAHAN, D. (1991). Caring and curing: Striking the right balance. Plenary address at the Annual Meeting of the Society of Teachers of Family Medicine, Philadelphia, May 7.

CAMPBELL, T. (1986). *Family's impact on health: A critical review and annotated bibliography*. National Institute of Mental Health Series DN No. 6, DHHS Pub. No. (ADM)86-1461. Washington, DC: U.S. Government Printing Office. (Also available in *Family Systems Medicine, 4,* 135–328.)

CAMPBELL, T., AND McDANIEL, S. (1987). Applying a systems approach to common medical problems. In M. Crouch and L. Roberts (eds.), *The family in medical practice: A family system primer*. New York: Springer-Verlag.

CAMPBELL, T., AND WILLIAMSON, D. (1990). Presentation at a meeting of the AAMFT-STFM Task Force for Family Therapy and Family Medicine. Washington, DC, October 4.

CARMICHAEL, L. (1976). The family in medicine, process or entity? *Journal of Family Practice, 3,* 562–563.

CARMICHAEL, L., AND CARMICHAEL, J. (1981). The relational model in family practice. *Marriage and Family Review, 4,* 123–134.

CELLA, D., AND NAJAVITS, L. (1986). Denial of infertility in patients with Hodgkin's disease. *Psychosomatics, 27,* 71.

CENTERS FOR DISEASE CONTROL. (1988). Prevalence of overweight in selected states. *Journal of the American Medical Association, 259,* 797.

CENTERS FOR DISEASE CONTROL. (1991a). Cigarette smoking among adults. *Morbidity and Morality Weekly Report, 40,* 757–765.

CENTERS FOR DISEASE CONTROL. (1991b). *HIV/AIDS surveillance report.* U.S. Department of Health and Human Services.

CENTERS FOR DISEASE CONTROL. (1991c). Smoking-attributable mortality and years of potential life lost: United States, 1988. *Morbidity and Mortality Weekly Report, 40,* 62–63, 69–71.

CHABOT, J. (1989). Treating the somatizing patient: countertransference, hate, and the elusive cure. *Psychotherapy in Private Practice, 7,* 125–136.

CHRISTIE-SEELY, J. (ED). (1984). *Working with the family in primary care.* New York: Praeger.

COCKERHAM, W. (1986). *Medical sociology.* 3d ed. Englewood Cliffs, NJ: Prentice-Hall.

COGSWELL, B. (1981). Family physician: A new role in process of development. *Marriage and Family Review, 4,* 1–30.

COHEN, L., ZILKHA, S., MIDDLETON, J., AND O'DONNOHUE, N. (1978). Perinatal mortality: assessing parental affirmation. *American Journal of Orthopsychiatry, 48,* 727–731.

COLE-KELLY, K., AND HEPWORTH, J. (1991). Pressures for omnipotence: Saner responses for family therapists in medicine. *Family Systems Medicine. 9,* 159–164.

COMBRINCK-GRAHAM, L. (1985). A developmental model for family systems. *Family Process, 24,* 39–150.

COOK, C. (1990). The gynecologic perspective. In N. Stotland (ed.), *Psychiatric aspects of reproductive technology.* Washington, DC: American Psychiatric Press.

COREA, G. (1985a). *The hidden malpractice: How American medicine mistreats women.* 2d ed. New York: Harper & Row.

COREA, G. (1985b). *The mother machine: Reproductive technologies from artificial insemination to artificial wombs.* New York: Harper & Row.

CORYELL, W. (1981). Diagnosis-specific mortality: Primary unipolar depression and Briquet's syndrome (somatization disorder). *Archives of General Psychiatry, 38,* 939–942.

COUSINS, N. (1979). *Anatomy of an illness.* New York: Norton.

COYNE, J. C., AND ANDERSON, B. J. (1988). The "psychosomatic family" reconsidered: Diabetes in context. *Journal of Marital and Family Therapy, 14,* 113–123.

CRANE, D. (1986). The family therapist, the primary care physician, and the health maintenance organization: Pitfalls and possibilities. *Family Systems Medicine, 4,* 22–30.

CROUCH, M. A. (1987). Working with one's own family issues: A path for professional development. In M. A. Crouch and L. Roberts (eds.), *The family in medical practice: A family systems primer.* New York: Springer-Verlag.

CROUCH, M., AND ROBERTS, L. (EDS). (1987). *The family in medical practice: A family systems primer.* New York: Springer-Verlag.

CUMMINGS, N., AND VANDENBOS, G. (1981). The twenty-year Kaiser-Permanente experience with psychotherapy and medical utilization: Implications for national health policy and national health insurance. *Health Policy Quarterly, 1,* 159–175.

CZYBA, J., AND CHEVRET, M. (1979). Psychological reactions of couples to artificial insemination with donor sperm. *International Journal of Fertility, 24,* 240–245.

DAHL, N. (1981). Encounter with evolution. *Perspectives in Biology and Medicine, 25,* 497–498.

DAKOF, G., AND LIDDLE, H. (1990). Communication between cancer patients and their spouses: Is it an essential aspect of adjustment? Paper given at the American Psychological Association Annual Meeting, Boston, August 12.

DeFRAIN, J. (1991). Learning about grief from normal families: SIDS, stillbirth, and miscarriage. *Journal of Marital and Family Therapy, 17,* 215–232.

DeGRUY, F., COLUMBIA, L., AND DICKINSON, P. (1987). Somatization disorder in a family practice. *Journal of Family Practice, 25,* 45–51.

DeVRIES, K., DEGANI, S., AND EIBSCHITA, I. (1984). The influence of the post-coital test on the sexual function of infertile women. *Journal of Psychosomatic Obstetrics and Gynaecology, 3,* 101–106.

DICKSTEIN, L. (1990). Effects of the new reproductive technologies on individuals and relationships. In N. Stotland (ed.), *Psychiatric aspects of reproductive technology.* Washington, DC: American Psychiatric Press.

DOHERTY, W. J. (1988). Implications of chronic illness for family treatment. In C. Chilman, E. Nunnally, and F. Cox (eds.), *Chronic illness and disability.* Newbury Park, CA: Sage.

DOHERTY, W. J., AND BAIRD, M. (1983). *Family therapy and family medicine: Towards the primary care of families.* New York: Guilford.

DOHERTY, W. J., AND BAIRD, M. (EDS.). (1987). *Family-centered medical care: A clinical casebook.* New York: Guilford.

DOHERTY, W. J., BAIRD, M., AND BECKER, L. (1987). Family medicine and the biopsychosocial model: The road toward integration. *Marriage and Family Review, 10,* 51–70.

DOHERTY, W. J., AND CAMPBELL, T. (1988). *Families and health.* Newbury Park, CA: Sage.

DOHERTY, W. J., AND COLANGELO, N. (1984). The Family FIRO Model: A modest proposal for organizing family treatment. *Journal of Marital and Family Therapy, 10,* 19–29.

DOHERTY, W. J., COLANGELO, N., AND HOVANDER, D. (1991). Priority setting in family change and clinical practice: The Family FIRO Model. *Family Process, 30,* 227–240.

DOHERTY, W. J., AND HARKAWAY, J. E. (1990). Obesity and family systems: A Family FIRO approach to assessment and treatment planning. *Journal of Marital and Family Therapy, 16,* 287–298.

DOHERTY, W. J., AND PESKAY, R. E. (in press). Family systems and the school. In S. L. Christianson and J. C. Connolly (eds.), *Home-school collaboration.* Washington, DC: National Association of School Psychologists.

DOHERTY, W. J., AND WHITEHEAD, D. (1986). The social dynamics of cigarette smoking: A Family FIRO analysis. *Family Process, 25,* 453–459.

DOUKAS, D., AND McCULLOUGH, L. (1991). The values history: The evaluation of the patient's values and advance directives. *Journal of Family Practice, 32,* 145–153.

DOWNEY, J., AND McKINNEY, M. (1990). Psychiatric research and the new reproductive technologies. In N. Stotland (ed.), *Psychiatric aspects of reproductive technology.* Washington, DC: American Psychiatric Press.

DROEGEMUELLER, W., HERBST, A., MISHELL D., AND STENCHEVER, M. (1987). *Comprehensive gynecology.* St. Louis: Mosby.

DYM, B., AND BERMAN, S. (1986). The primary health care team: Family physician and family therapist in joint practice. *Family Systems Medicine, 4,* 9–21.

EISENBERG, L. (1979). Interfaces between medicine and psychiatry. *Comprehensive Psychiatry, 20,* 1–14.

EISINGER, S. (1991). First trimester bleeding. In J. Beasley and J. Damos (eds.), *ALSO: Advanced life support in obstetrics.* Madison: University of Wisconsin Department of Family Medicine and Practice.

ELKIN, E. (1990). When a patient miscarries: Implications for treatment. *Psychotherapy. 27,* 600–606.

ENGEL, G. L. (1977). The need for a new medical model: A challenge for biomedicine. *Science, 196,* 129–136.

ENGEL, G. L. (1980). The clinical application of the biopsychosocial model. *American Journal of Psychiatry, 137,* 535–544.

EPSTEIN, L. H., VALOSKI, A., WING, R. R., AND McCURLEY, J. (1990). Ten-year follow-up of behavioral, family-based treatment for obese children. *Journal of the American Medical Association, 264,* 2519–2523.

FARICY, L. G. (1990). The role of obesity in marital relationships. Unpublished doctoral dissertation. University of Minnesota, St. Paul.

FIELDING, J. E. (1985). Smoking: Health effects and control. *New England Journal of Medicine, 313,* 491–498, 555–561.

FISKE, V., COYNE, J., AND SMITH, D. (1991). Couples coping with myocardial infarction. *Journal of Family Psychology, 5,* 4–20.

FREEDMAN, S. (1984). A mother's presence. *New York Times Magazine,* February 24, p. 48.

FREY, J., AND WENDORF, R. (1984). Family therapist and pediatrician: Teaming-up on four common behavioral pediatric problems. *Family Systems Medicine, 2,* 290–297.

FRIEDMAN, E. (1991). Managing crisis: Bowen theory incarnate. Audiotape of a presentation at a *Family Systems Theory* seminar, Bethesda, MD, June.

GANLEY, R. M. (1986). Epistemology, family patterns, and psychosomatics: The case of obesity. *Family Process, 25,* 437–451.

GENTRY, W. DOYLE. (ED.) (1984). *Handbook of behavioral medicine.* New York: Guilford.

GEYMAN J. (1981). Education for the practice of family medicine. *Marriage and Family Review, 4,* 103–112.

GILLISS, C. (1984). Reducing family stress during and after coronary artery bypass surgery. *Nursing Clinics of North America, 19,* 1103–1111.

GILLISS, C. L., HIGHLEY, B. L., ROBERTS, B. M., AND MARTINSON, I. M. (1989). *Toward a science of family nursing.* Menlo Park, CA: Addison-Wesley.

GLAZIER, W. (1973). The task of medicine. *Scientific American, 228,* 13–17.

GLENN, M. (1984). *On diagnosis: A systemic approach.* New York: Brunner/Mazel.

GLENN, M. (1985). Toward collaborative family-oriented health care. *Family Systems Medicine, 3,* 466–475.

GLENN, M. (1987). *Collaborative health care: A family-oriented model.* New York: Praeger.

GLENN, M., ATKINS, L., AND SINGER, R. (1984). Integrating a family therapist into a family medicine practice. *Family Systems Medicine, 2,* 137–146.

GONZALEZ, S., STEINGLASS, P., AND REISS, D. (1987). *Family-centered interventions for people with chronic disabilities: The eight-session multiple family discussion group program.* Washington, DC: Center for Family Research, Department of Psychiatry and Behavioral Science, George Washington University Medical Center.

GONZALEZ, S., STEINGLASS, P., AND REISS, D. (1989). Putting the illness in its place: Discussion groups for families with chronic medical illnesses. *Family Process, 28,* 69–87.

GOOLISHIAN, H., AND ANDERSON, H. (1987). Language systems and therapy: An evolving idea, *Psychotherapy, 24,* 529–538.

GOTTMAN, J. M., AND KATZ, L. F. (1989). Effects of marital discord on young children's peer interaction and health. *Developmental Psychology, 25,* 373–381.

GREENSON, R. (1967). The working alliance and the transference neuroses. *Psychoanalysis Quarterly, 34,* 155–181.

GREIL, A., LEITKO, T., AND PORTER, K. (1988). Infertility: His and hers. *Gender and Society, 2,* 172–199.

GROB, G. (1991). *From asylum to community: Mental health policy in America.* Princeton, NJ: Princeton University Press.

HARKAWAY, J. E. (1983). Obesity: Reducing the larger system. *Journal of Strategic and Systemic Therapy, 2,* 2–16.

HARKAWAY, J. E. (1986). Structural assessment of families with obese adolescent girls. *Journal of Marital and Family Therapy, 12,* 199–201.

HARP, J. (1989). Physicians' expectations from therapists. Presentation to the Division of Family Programs, Department of Psychiatry, University of Rochester School of Medicine and Dentistry, April 19.

HECKER, L., MARTIN, D., AND MARTIN, M. (1986). Family factors in childhood obesity. *American Journal of Family Therapy, 14,* 247–253.

HENAO, S., AND GROSE, N. (EDS.). (1985). *Principles of family systems in family medicine.* New York: Brunner/Mazel.

HEPWORTH, J., GAVAZZI, S., ADLIN, M., AND MILLER, W. (1988). Training for collaboration: Internships for family-therapy students in a medical setting. *Family Systems Medicine, 6,* 69–79.

HEPWORTH, J., AND HARRIS, L. (1986). Changing metaphors for the health care process: A model of coordinated care. Paper presented at the annual meeting of the National Council on Family Relations, Dearborn, MI, November 4.

HEPWORTH, J., AND JACKSON, M. (1985). Health care for families: Models of collaboration between family therapists and family physicians. *Family Relations, 34,* 123–127.

HEPWORTH, J., RYDER, R., AND DREYER, A. (1984). The effects of parental loss on the formation of intimate relationships. *Journal of Marriage and Family Therapy, 10,* 73–82.

HERTZ, D. (1982). Infertility and the physician-patient relationship: A bio-psychosocial challenge. *General Hospital Psychiatry, 4,* 95–101.

HOBBS, N., PERRIN, J., AND IREYS, H. (1985). *Chronically ill children and their families.* San Francisco: Jossey-Bass.

HOEPER, E., NYCZ, G., AND CLEARY, P. (1979). Estimated prevalence of RDC mental disorder in primary medical care. *International Journal of Mental Health, 6,* 6–15.

HOLMES, T. H., AND RAHE, R. H. (1967). The social readjustment scale. *Journal of Psychosomatic Research, 39,* 413–431.

HOUSE, J. S., LANDIS, K. R., AND UMBERSON, D. (1988). Social relationships and health. *Science, 241,* 540–544.

HUDGENS, A. (1979). Family-oriented treatment of chronic pain. *Journal of Marriage and Family Therapy, 5,* 67–78.

HUYGEN, F. J. A. (1982). *Family medicine: The medical life history of families.* New York: Brunner/Mazel.

IMBER-BLACK, E. (1988a). *Families and larger systems.* New York: Guilford.

IMBER-BLACK, E. (1988b). The family system and the health care system: Making the invisible visible. In F. Walsh and C. Anderson (eds.), *Chronic disorders and the family.* New York: Haworth.

IMBER-BLACK, E. (1989). Creating rituals in therapy. In E. Imber-Black, J. Roberts, and R. Whiting (eds.), *Rituals in families and family therapy.* New York: Norton.

IMBER-BLACK, E. (1991). Rituals and the healing process. In F. Walsh and M. McGoldrick (eds.), *Living beyond loss: Death in the family.* New York: Norton.

JAROW, J., AND LIPSHULTZ, L. (1987). Urologic evaluation of male infertility. *Contemporary OB/GYN,* Special Issue on Fertility, 85–96.

KAPLAN, C., LIPKIN, M., AND GORDON, G. (1988). Somatization in primary care: Patients with unexplained and vexing medical complaints. *Journal of General Internal Medicine, 3,* 177–190.

KATON, W. (1985). Somatization in primary care. *Journal of Family Practice, 21,* 257–258.

KATON, W., AND RUSSO, J. (1989) Somatic symptoms and depression. *Journal of Family Practice, 29,* 65–69.

KELLNER, R. (1986). *Somatization and hypochondriasis.* New York: Praeger-Greenwood.

KELLNER, R. (1990). Somatization: Theories and research. *Journal of Nervous and Mental Disease, 78,* 150–159.

KELLNER, R., AND SHEFFIELD, B. (1973). The one-week prevalence of symptoms in neurotic patients and normals. *American Journal of Psychiatry,* *130,* 102–105.

KEYE, W. (1984). Psychosexual responses to infertility. *Clinical Obstetrics and Gynecology, 27,* 760–766.

KIELCOTT-GLASER, J. K., FISHER, L. D., OGROCK, P., STOUT, J. C., SPEICHER, C. E., AND GLASER, R. C. (1987). Marital quality, marital disruption, and immune function. *Psychosomatic Medicine, 49,* 13–34.

KIRK, E. (1984). Psychological effects and management of perinatal loss. *American Journal of Obstetrics and Gynecology, 149,* 46–51.

KIRKLEY-BEST, E., AND KELLNER, K. (1982). The forgotten grief: A review of the psychology of stillbirth. *American Journal of Orthopsychiatry, 52,* 420–429.

KLEINMAN, A. (1986). *Social origins of distress and disease.* New Haven: Yale University Press.

KLEINMAN, A. (1988). *The illness narratives: Suffering, healing, and the human condition.* New York: Basic Books.

KLEINMAN, A., EISENBERG, M., AND GOOD, B. (1978). Culture, illness, and care: Clinical lessons from anthropological and cross-cultural research. *Annals of Internal Medicine, 88,* 251–258.

KOSS, J. (1990). Somatization and somatic complaint syndromes among Hispanics: Overview and ethnopsychological perspectives. *Transcultural Psychiatric Research Review, 27,* 5–29.

KRAFT, A., PALOMBO, J., MITCHELL, D., DEAN, C., MEYERS, S., AND SCHMIDT, A. W. (1980). The psychological dimensions of infertility. *American Journal of Orthopsychiatry, 50,* 618–628.

KÜBLER-ROSS, E. (1969). *On death and dying.* New York: Macmillan.

KÜBLER-ROSS, E. (ED.). (1975). *Death: The final stage of growth.* Englewood Cliffs, NJ: Prentice-Hall.

LALOS, A., LALOS, O., AND JACOBSSON, L. (1985). The psychosocial impact of infertility two years after completed surgical treatment. *Acta Obstetrics and Gynecology in Scandanavia, 64,* 599–604.

LAM, S-Y., BAKER, G., AND PEPPERELL, R. (1988). Treatment-independent pregnancies after cessation of gonadotropin ovulation induction in women with oligomenorrhea and anovulatory menses. *Fertility and Sterility, 50,* 26–30.

LANDAU-STANTON, J., CLEMENTS, C., AND ASSOCIATES. (1992). *AIDS, health, and mental health: A primary sourcebook.* New York: Brunner/Mazel.

LAZARUS, A., AND STERN, R. (1986). Psychiatric aspects of pregnancy termination. *Clinics in Obstetrics and Gynaecology, 13,* 125–134.

LEFF, J., AND VAUGHN, C. (1985). *Expressed emotion in families.* New York: Guilford.

LEFF, P. (1987). Here I am, Ma: The emotional impact of pregnancy loss on parents and health-care professionals. *Family Systems Medicine, 5,* 105–114.

LEIBLUM, S., KEMMANN, E., AND COLBURN, D. (1987). Unsuccessful in vitro fertilization: A follow-up study. *Journal of In Vitro Fertilization and Embryo Transfer, 4,* 46–50.

LEPPERT, P., AND PAHLKA, B. (1984). Grieving characteristics after spontaneous abortion: A management approach. *Obstetrics and Gynecology, 64,* 119–122.

LEVIE, L. (1967). An inquiry into the psychological effects on parents of artificial insemination with donor sperm. *Eugenic Review, 59,* 97–107.

LICHTENSTEIN, E. (1982). The smoking problem: A behavioral perspective. *Journal of Consulting and Clinical Psychology, 50,* 465–466.

LIPP, M. (1986). *Respectful treatment: A practical handbook of patient care.* New York: Elsevier Science.

LITMAN, T. J. (1974). The family as a basic unit in health and medical care: A sociobehavioral overview. *Social Science and Medicine, 8,* 495–519.

LORBER, J. (1985). Gender politics and in vitro fertilization use. Paper presented at the Emergency Conference and of Feminist International Network on the New Reproductive Technologies, Sweden.

LOVELL, A. (1983). Some questions of identity: Late miscarriage, stillbirth, and perinatal loss. *Social Science and Medicine, 17,* 755–761.

LUFT, H. (1983). Health-maintenance organizations. In D. Mechanic (ed.), *Handbook of health, health care, and the health professions.* New York: Free Press.

McCALL, C., AND STORM, C. (1985). Family therapists and family therapy programs in hospital settings: A survey. *Family Systems Medicine, 3,* 143–150.

McCARTNEY, C., AND WADA, C. (1990). Gender differences in counseling needs during infertility treatment. In N. Stotland (ed.), *Psychiatric aspects of reproductive technology.* Washington, DC: American Psychiatric Press.

McCUBBIN, H. I., AND PATTERSON, J. M. (1982). Family adaptation to crises. In H. I. McCubbin, A. Cauble, and J. Patterson (eds.), *Family stress, coping and social support.* Springfield, IL: Thomas.

McDANIEL, S., BANK, J., CAMPBELL, T., MANCINI, J., AND SHORE, B. (1986). Using a group as a consultant. In L. Wynne, S. McDaniel, and T.

Weber (eds.), *Systems consultation: A new perspective for family therapy*, 181–198. New York: Guilford.

McDANIEL, S., AND CAMPBELL, T. (1986). Physicians and family therapists: The risks of collaboration. *Family Systems Medicine, 4*, 4–8.

McDANIEL, S., CAMPBELL, T., AND SEABURN, D. (1989). Somatic fixation in patients and physicians: A biopsychosocial approach. *Family Systems Medicine, 7*, 5–16.

McDANIEL, S., CAMPBELL, T., AND SEABURN, D. (1990). *Family-oriented primary care: A manual for medical providers.* New York: Springer-Verlag.

McDANIEL, S., CAMPBELL, T., WYNNE, L., AND WEBER, T. (1988). Family systems consultation: Opportunities for teaching in family medicine. *Family Systems Medicine, 6*, 391–403.

McEWAN, K., COSTELLO, C., AND TAYLOR, P. (1987). Adjustment to infertility. *Journal of Abnormal Psychology, 96*, 108–116.

McGOLDRICK, M., AND WALSH, F. (1991). A time to mourn: Death and the family life cycle. In F. Walsh and M. McGoldrick (eds.). *Living beyond loss: Death in the family.* New York: Norton.

MADANES, C. (1980). Marital therapy when a symptom is presented by a spouse. *International Journal of Family Therapy, 2*, 120–136.

MADANES, C. (1981). *Strategic family therapy.* San Francisco: Jossey-Bass.

MANSON, J. E., STAMPFER, M. J., HENNEKENS, C. H., AND WILLETT, W. C. (1987). Body weight and longevity: A reassessment. *Journal of the American Medical Association, 257*, 353–358.

MATARAZZO, J. D. (1984). Behavioral health: A 1990 challenge for the health sciences professions. In J. D. Matarazzo, J. A. Herd, N. E. Miller, and S. M. Weiss (eds.), *Behavioral health: A handbook of health enhancement and disease prevention.* New York: Wiley.

MATTHEWS, R., AND MATTHEWS, A. (1986). Infertility and involuntary childlessness: The transition to nonparenthood. *Journal of Marriage and the Family, 48*, 641–649.

MATTHEWS, R., AND MATTHEWS, A. (1989). *Infertility treatment: The definition of a health problem and the pursuit of a cure.* Paper presented at the Annual Meeting of the National Council on Family Relations, New Orleans, LA, November.

MAURER, J., AND STRASBERG, P. (1989). *Building a new dream: A family guide to coping with chronic illness and disability.* Reading, MA: Addison-Wesley.

MAUSNER, B. (1973). An ecological view of cigarette smoking. *Journal of Abnormal Psychology, 81*, 115–126.

MAZZOLA, P., AND STANGEL, J. (1984). Artificial insemination performed by husband. *Fertility and Sterility, 41,* 654.

MECHANIC, D. (ED.) (1983). *Handbook of health, health care, and the health professions.* New York: Free Press.

MEDALIE, J. (1978). *Family medicine: Principles and application.* Baltimore: Williams & Wilkens.

MENNING, B. (1977). *Infertility: A guide for the childless couple.* Englewood Cliffs, NJ: Prentice-Hall.

MIALL, C. (1985). Perceptions of informal sanctioning and the stigma of involuntary childlessness. *Deviant Behavior, 6,* 383–403.

MINUCHIN, S., BAKER, L., ROSMAN, B., LIEBMAN, R., MILMAN, L., AND TODD, T. (1975). A conceptual model of psychosomatic illness in children: Family organization and family therapy. *Archives of General Psychiatry, 32,* 1031–1038.

MINUCHIN, S., ROSMAN, B., AND BAKER, L. (1978). *Psychosomatic families: Anorexia nervosa in context.* Cambridge, MA: Harvard University Press.

MULLINS, L., AND OLSON, R. (1990). Familial factors in the etiology, maintenance, and treatment of somatoform disorders in children. *Family Systems Medicine, 8,* 159–175.

MYERS, M. (1990). Male gender-related issues in reproduction and technology. In N. Stotland (ed.), *Psychiatric aspects of reproductive technology.* Washington, DC: American Psychiatric Press.

NATIONAL HEALTH INTERVIEW SURVEY. (1987). U.S. Department of Health and Human Services, National Center for Health Statistics, Series 10, No. 164.

NATIONAL HEART, LUNG, AND BLOOD INSTITUTE. (1982). Management of patient compliance in the treatment of hypertension. *Hypertension, 4,* 415–423.

NAVOT, D., MUASHER, S., AND OEHNINGER, S. (1988). The value of in vitro fertilization for the treatment of unexplained infertility. *Fertility and Sterility, 49,* 854–857.

NOBLE, E. (1987). *Having your baby by donor insemination.* Boston: Houghton Mifflin.

NOTMAN, M. (1990). Reproduction and pregnancy: A psychodynamic developmental perspective. In N. Stotland (ed.), *Psychiatric aspects of reproductive technology.* Washington, DC: American Psychiatric Press.

NOYES, R., AND CHAPNICK, E. (1964). Literature on psychology and infertility. *Fertility and Sterility, 15,* 543–558.

OCKENE, J. K., NUTTALL, R. L., AND BENFARI, R. S. (1981). A psychosocial model of smoking cessation and maintenance of cessation. *Preventive Medicine, 10,* 623–638.

OLSON, D., SPRENKLE, D., AND RUSSELL, C. (1979). Circumplex model of marital and family systems: I. Cohesion and adaptability dimensions, family types, and clinical applications. *Family Process, 18,* 3–28.

OMNIBUS BUDGET RECONCILIATION ACT OF 1990. Public Law 101–508, Section 4751.

PATTERSON, J. M. (1988). Chronic illness in children and the impact on families. In C. S. Chilman, E. W. Nunnally, and F. M. Cox (eds.), *Chronic illness and disability.* Families in Trouble Series, Vol. 2. Newbury Park, CA: Sage.

PATTERSON, J. M. (1989). A family stress model: The Family Adjustment and Adaptation Response. In C. N. Ramsey (ed.), *Family systems in medicine.* New York: Guilford.

PATTERSON, J. (1990). *Systems therapy for infertile couples.* Paper presented at the annual meeting of the American Association for Marriage and Family Therapy, Washington, DC, October 7.

PAUL, N. (1967). The use of empathy in the resolution of grief. *Perspectives in biology and medicine, 10,* 153–169.

PAULSON, R., AND SAUER, M. (1991). Counseling the infertile couple: When enough is enough. *Obstetrics and Gynecology, 78,* 462–463.

PENN, P. (1983). Coalitions and binding interactions in families with chronic illness. *Family Systems Medicine, 1,* 16–25.

PEPPERS, L., AND KNAPP, R. (1980). *Motherhood and mourning.* New York: Praeger.

PILOWSKY, I. (1978). A general classification of abnormal illness behaviors. *British Journal of Medical Psychiatry, 51,* 131–137.

PLESS, I., AND PERRIN, J. (1985). Issues common to a variety of illnesses. In N. Hobbs and J. Perrin (eds.), *Issues in the care of children with chronic illness.* San Francisco: Jossey-Bass.

PRICE, R. A., CHEN, K. H., AND CAVALLI, S. L. (1981). Models of spouse influence and their applications to smoking behavior. *Social Biology, 28,* 14–29.

QUILL, T. (1985). Somatization: One of medicine's blind spots. *Journal of the American Medical Association, 254,* 3075–3079.

RANSOM, D. (1981). The rise of family medicine: New roles for behavioral science. *Marriage and Family Review, 4,* 31–72.

RANSOM, D. (1983a). Random notes: On building bridges between family practice and family therapy. *Family Systems Medicine, 1,* 91–96.

RANSOM, D. (1983b). Random notes: The legacy of the Peckham experiment. *Family Systems Medicine, 1,* 104–108.

RANSOM, D. (1984). Random notes: Patients have families. *Family Systems Medicine, 2,* 109–113.

REISS, D. (1981). *The family's construction of reality.* Cambridge, MA: Harvard University Press.

REISS, D., GONZALEZ, S., AND KRAMER, N. (1986). Family process, chronic illness, and death: On the weakness of strong bonds. *Archives of General Psychiatry, 43,* 795–804.

REISS, D., AND KAPLAN DE-NOUR, A. (1989). The family and medical team in chronic illness: A transactional and developmental perspective. In C. Ramsey, Jr. (ed.), *Family systems in medicine.* New York: Guilford.

RICHARDSON, H. B. (1945). *Patients have families.* New York: Commonwealth Fund.

ROLLAND, J. (1984). Toward a psychosocial typology of chronic and life-threatening illness. *Family Systems Medicine, 2,* 245–262.

ROLLAND, J. (1987). Chronic illness and the life cycle: A conceptual framework. *Family Process, 26,* 203–221.

ROLLAND, J. (1988). Family systems and chronic illness: A typological model. In F. Walsh and C. Anderson (eds.), *Chronic disorders and the family.* New York: Haworth Press.

ROSENTHAL, G. (1983). The federal health structure. In D. Mechanic (ed.), *Handbook of health, health care, and the health professions.* New York: Free Press.

ROSMAN, B., AND BAKER, L. (1988). The "psychosomatic family" reconsidered: Diabetes in context—A reply. *Journal of Marital and Family Therapy, 14,* 125–132.

ROWE, J., CLYMAN, R., AND GREEN, C. (1978). Follow-up of families who experience a perinatal death. *Pediatrics, 62,* 166–170.

SABATELLI, R., METH, R., AND GAVAZZI, S. (1988). Factors mediating the adjustment to involuntary childlessness. *Family Relations, 37,* 338–343.

SADLER, A., AND SYROP, C. (1987). The stress of infertility: Recommendations for assessment and intervention. *Family stress.* Rockville, MD: Aspen.

SARGENT, J. (1985). Physician-family therapist collaboration: Children with medical problems. *Family Systems Medicine, 3,* 454–465.

SAWA, R. (1985). *Family dynamics for physicians: Guidelines to assessment and treatment.* New York: Mellen.

SCHMIDT, D. (1978). The family as the unit of medical care. *Journal of Family Practice, 7,* 303–308.

SCHUTZ, W. C. (1958). *FIRO: A three-dimensional theory of interpersonal behavior.* New York: Holt, Rinehart & Winston.

SCHWARTZ, H. (1986). *Never satisfied: A cultural history of diets, fantasies and fat.* New York: Free Press.

SCHWARTZ, L. (1991). *Alternatives to infertility.* New York: Brunner/Mazel.

SEABURN, D., GAWINSKI, B., HARP, J., McDANIEL, S., SHIELDS, C., AND WAXMAN, D. (in press). Family systems therapy in a primary care medical setting: The Rochester experience. *Journal of Marital and Family Therapy.*

SEABURN, D., LORENZ, A., AND KAPLAN, D. (in press). The trangenerational development of chronic illness meanings. *Family Systems Medicine.*

SELIGMAN, M. (1988). Psychotherapy with siblings of disabled children. In M. D. Kahn and K. G. Lewis (eds.), *Siblings in therapy.* New York: Norton.

SELIGMAN, M., AND DARLING, R. (1989). *Ordinary families, special children: A systems approach to childhood disability.* New York: Guilford.

SELVINI PALAZZOLI, M., BOSCOLO, L., CECCHIN, G., AND PRATA, G. (1980). The problem of the referring person. *Journal of Marital and Family Therapy, 6,* 3–9.

SEWARD, G., WAGNER, P., HEINRICH, J., BLOCH, S., AND MYERHOFF, L. (1965). The question of psychophysiologic infertility: Some negative answers. *Psychosomatic Medicine, 27,* 533–545.

SHAPIRO, S. (1988). Psychological consequences of infertility in critical psychophysical passages in the life of a woman. In J. Offerman-Zuckerberg (ed.), *A Psychodynamic Perspective.* New York: Plenum Medical.

SHERMAN, R., ORESKY, P., AND ROUNTREE, Y. (1991). Hogging center stage: The chronically ill family member. *Solving problems in couples and family therapy.* New York: Brunner/Mazel.

SHIELDS, C., WYNNE, L., AND SIRKIN, M. (1992). Illness, family theory, and family therapy: I. Conceptual issues. II. The perception of physical illness in the family system. *Family Process, 31,* 3–18.

SHORTER, E. (1987). *The health century.* New York: Doubleday.

SMITH, G., MONSON, R., AND RAY, D. (1986). Psychiatric consultation in somatization disorder. *New England Journal of Medicine, 314,* 1407–1413.

SOBOL, J., AND MUNCIE, H. L. (1990). Obesity. In R. E. Rakel (ed.), *Textbook of family practice.* Philadelphia: Saunders.

SOLOMON, G., TEMOSHOK, L., AND ZICH, J. (1987). An intensive psycho-immunologic study of long-surviving persons with AIDS. *Annals of the New York Academy of Sciences, 496,* 647–655.

SONTAG, S. (1978). *Illness as Metaphor.* New York: McGraw-Hill.

SPECK, R., AND ATTNEAVE, C. (1972). Network therapy. In A. Ferber, M. Mendelsohn, and A. Napier (eds.), *The book of family therapy.* New York: Science House.

STARR, P. (1982). *The social transformation of American medicine.* New York: Basic Books.

STEIN, H. (1985). Ethanol and its discontents: Paradoxes of inebriation and sobriety in American culture. In H. F. Stein and M. Apprey, *Context and dynamics in clinical knowledge.* Charlottesville: University of Virginia Press.

STEINGLASS, P., BENNETT, L. A., WOLIN, S. J., AND REISS, D. (1987). *The alcoholic family.* New York. Basic Books.

STEINGLASS, P., AND HORAN, M. (1988). Families and chronic medical illness. In F. Walsh and C. Anderson (eds.), *Chronic disorders and the family.* New York: Haworth Press.

STEINGLASS, P., TEMPLE, S., LISMAN, S., AND REISS, D. (1982). Coping with spinal cord injury: The family perspective. *General Hospital Psychiatry, 4,* 259–264.

STOTLAND, N. (1990). Introduction and overview. *Psychiatric aspects of reproductive technology.* Washington, DC: American Psychiatric Press.

STUART, R. B., AND JACOBSON, B. (1987). *Weight, sex, and marriage.* New York: Norton.

STUNKARD, A., AND PENICK, S. (1979). Behavior modification in the treatment of obesity: The problem of maintaining weight loss. *Archives of General Psychiatry, 36,* 801–806.

SUTTON, G. (1980). Assortive mating for smoking habits. *Annals of Human Biology, 7,* 449–456.

TAPLIN, S., MCDANIEL, S., AND NAUMBURG, E. (1987). A case of pain. In W. Doherty and M. Baird (eds.), *Family-centered medical care: A clinical casebook.* New York: Guilford.

TILLEY, K. (1990). Family medicine—family therapy joint task force established. *Family Therapy News, 21,* 1.

TOTMAN, R. (1979). *Social causes of illness.* New York: Pantheon Books.

ULBRICH, P., COYLE, A., AND LLABRE, M. (1990). Involuntary childlessness and marital adjustment: His and hers. *Journal of Sex and Marital Therapy, 16,* 147–158.

U.S. BUREAU OF THE CENSUS. (1986). *Current Population Survey, No. 406.* Washington, DC: U.S. Government Printing Office.

U.S. BUREAU OF THE CENSUS. (1990). *Statistical Abstract of the United States: 1990.* 110th ed. Washington, DC: U.S. Government Printing Office.

U.S. DEPARTMENT OF HEALTH, EDUCATION AND WELFARE. (1976). *Teenage Smoking: National patterns of cigarette smoking, ages 12–18.* DHEW Publication No. (NIH) 76-931. Bethesda, MD: National Institutes of Health.

U.S. DEPARTMENT OF HEALTH, EDUCATION AND WELFARE. (1979). *Healthy people: The Surgeon General's report on health promotion and disease prevention.* DHEW (PHS) Publication No. 79-55071. Public Health Service. Washington, DC: U.S. Government Printing Office.

U.S. NATIONAL CENTER FOR HEALTH STATISTICS. (1982). Reproductive impairments among married couples: United States. *National Survey of Family Growth.* Series 23, No. 11. Hyattsville, MD: U.S. Department of Health and Human Services.

U.S. OFFICE OF TECHNOLOGY ASSESSMENT. (1988). *Infertility: Medical and Social Choices.* Washington, DC: U.S. Government Printing Office.

VACHON, M., FREEDMAN, A., FORMO, A., ROGERS, J., LYALL, W., AND FREEMAN, S. (1977). The final illness in cancer: The widow's perspective. *Canadian Medical Association Journal, 117,* 1151–1154.

VALENTINE, D. P. (1986). Psychological impact of infertility: Identifying issues and needs, *Social Work in Health Care, 11,* 61–66.

VAN EIJK, J., GROP, R., HUYGEN, F., ET AL. (1983). The family doctor and the prevention of somatic fixation. *Family Systems Medicine, 1,* 5–15.

VENTERS, M. H., JACOBS, D. R., LUEPKER, R. V., MAIMAN, L. A., AND GILLUM, R. F. (1984). Spouse concordance for smoking patterns: The Minnesota Heart Survey. *American Journal of Epidemiology, 120,* 608–616.

VITAL STATISTICS OF THE UNITED STATES. (1991). Mortality, 10 leading causes of death by age group and sex, United States. *CA: A Cancer Journal for Clinicians, 41,* 24–25.

WADDEN, T. A., AND STUNKARD, A. J. (1985). Social and psychological consequences of obesity. *Annals of Internal Medicine, 103,* 1062–1067.

WALKER, G. (1991). *Systemic therapy with families, couples, and individuals with AIDS infection.* New York: Norton.

WALSH, F., AND MCGOLDRICK, M. (1991). Loss and the family: A systemic perspective. In F. Walsh and M. McGoldrick (eds.). *Living beyond loss: Death in the family.* New York: Norton.

WALTZER, H. (1982). Psychological and legal aspects of artificial insemination (AID): An overview. *American Journal of Psychotherapy, 36,* 91–102.

WEAKLAND, J. (1977). "Family somatics": A neglected edge. *Family Process, 16,* 263–272.

WEINSHEL, M. (1990). Treating an infertile couple. *Family Systems Medicine, 8,* 303–312.

WHITAKER, C. AND MALONE, T. (1953). *The roots of psychotherapy.* New York: Blakiston.

WHITE D. (1990). Letter to *USA Weekend.* November 16–18, 9.

WHITE, L. (1969). The self-image of the physician and the care of dying patients. *Annals of the New York Academy of Sciences, 164,* 822–837.

WHITE, M. (1988). The externalizing of the problem. *Dulwich Centre Newsletter.* Summer.

WHITEHEAD, D., AND DOHERTY, J. W. (1989). Systems dynamics in cigarette smoking: An exploratory study. *Family Systems Medicine, 7,* 264–273.

WILLIAMSON, D. (1991). *The intimacy paradox.* New York: Guilford.

WINTER, R. (1989). The family physician as family therapist: The inherent conflicts. Paper presented at the annual conference of the Family in Family Medicine, Amelia Island, FL, March 6.

WOOD, B. (1991). *Beyond the "psychosomatic family": Pediatric biopsychosocial care.* Unpublished manuscript, Bryn Mawr, PA.

WOOD, B., WATKINS, J., BOYLE, J. NOGUEIRA, J., ZIMAND, E., AND CARROLL, L. (1989). The "psychosomatic family" model: An empirical and theoretical analysis. *Family Process, 28,* 399–417.

WRIGHT, L. M., AND LEAHEY, M. (1987). *Families and chronic illness.* Springhouse, PA: Springhouse Corporation.

WYNNE, L. C. (1989). Family systems and schizophrenia: Implications for family medicine. In C. N. Ramsey (ed.), *Family systems in medicine.* New York: Guilford.

WYNNE, L., CROMWELL, R., AND MATTHYSSE, S. (1978). *The nature of schizophrenia: New approaches to research and treatment.* New York: Wiley.

WYNNE, L., McDANIEL, S., AND WEBER, T. (1986). *Systems consultation: A new perspective for family therapy.* New York: Guilford.

WYNNE, L., SHIELDS, C., AND SIRKIN, M. I. (1992). Illness, family theory, and family therapy: I. Conceptual issues. *Family Process, 31,* 3–18.

WYNNE, L., SIRKIN, M., AND SHIELDS, C. (in press). Illness, family theory, and family therapy: II. Clinical issues. *Family Process.*

ZABIN, L. S., HIRSCH, M. B., AND EMERSON, M. R. (1989). When urban adolescents choose abortion: Effects on education, psychological status, and subsequent pregnancy. *Family Planning Perspectives, 21,* 248–255.

ZOCCOLILLO, M., AND CLONINGER, C. (1986) Somatization disorder: Psychologic symptoms, social disability and diagnosis. *Comprehensive Psychiatry, 27,* 65–73.

Index

Abdominal illnesses, 217–18
Abortion, 153, 161–63; spontaneous, 154, 155–57
Abuse, 129, 139
Ackerman, Nathan, 102
Acupuncture, 17, 56
Adolescence, 30, 153
Adoption, 152, 153, 173, 174, 175, 182
Agency, 9–10, 61, 62, 86–89, 93, 121; and bracketing patients' unhealthy decisions, 87–88; and chronic illness, 206–9; and emphasizing the patient's input, 86–87; and facilitating rather than advising, 88–89; and infertility, 172; and smoking, 108, 109, 110
Aging. *See* Geriatrics
AID (artificial insemination by a donor), 174, 176–78, 179–80, 181
AIDS, *xiii*, 45, 94, 214, 232, 234–40, 248; and approaches to terminal illness, 232, 234, 235–49; and chronic illness, treatment of, 190,

214; and confidentiality, 45; statistics, 236; stigma of, 237–39. *See also* Sexually transmitted diseases
AIH (artificial insemination with the husband's sperm), 174, 181
Alcoholism, *xi*, 33, 64, 94, 190; and gender issues, 30; and somatization disorder, 129, 130
Alcoholics Anonymous, 119
Alzheimer's disease, 9, 70, 75, 189, 192; care for individuals with, and gender differences, 196; and tolerance for ambiguity, 195
American Academy of Family Physicians, 19
American Association for Marriage and Family Therapy, 48, 52
American Board of Family Practice, 19
American Medical Association, 19
American Psychiatric Association, 15
Anatomy of an Illness (Cousins), 86
Andersen, Tom, 50, 247–48
Anger, 78–79, 158, 176, 197, 238;